THE INVISIBLE HAND IN THE WILDERNESS

D1738159

WITHDRAWN
AVON PUBLIC LIBRARY
BOX 977 / 200 BENCHMARK RD.
AVON, COLORADO 81620

MERCER
UNIVERSITY PRESS

Endowed by
TOM WATSON BROWN
and
THE WATSON-BROWN FOUNDATION, INC.

THE INVISIBLE HAND IN THE WILDERNESS

Economics, Ecology, and God

Malcolm Clemens Young

MERCER UNIVERSITY PRESS
MACON, GEORGIA

MUP/ P489

© 2014 Mercer University Press
1400 Coleman Avenue
Macon, Georgia 31207
All rights reserved

First Edition

Books published by Mercer University Press are printed on acid-free paper that meets the requirements of the American National Standard for Information Sciences—Permanence of Paper for Printed Library Materials.

Mercer University Press is a member of Green Press Initiative (greenpressinitiative.org), a nonprofit organization working to help publishers and printers increase their use of recycled paper and decrease their use of fiber derived from endangered forests. This book is printed on recycled paper.

Library of Congress Cataloging-in-Publication Data

Young, Malcolm Clemens.
  The invisible hand in the wilderness : economics, ecology, and God / Malcolm Clemens Young. -- First Edition
       pages cm
  Includes bibliographical references and index.
  ISBN 978-0-88146-487-0 (pbk. : alk. paper) -- ISBN 0-88146-487-2 (pbk. : alk. paper)
  1. Human ecology--Religious aspects--Christianity. 2. Ecotheology. 3. Economics--Religious aspects--Christianity. 4. Values. 5. Symbolism. I. Title.
  BT695.5.Y675 2014
  261.8'8--dc23
                                                    2014000364

For Heidi

CONTENTS

And no [one's] belief is in any case a private matter which concerns [oneself] alone. Our lives are guided by that general conception of...things which has been created for social purposes. Our words, our phrases, our...modes of thought, are common property, fashioned and perfected from age to age; an heirloom which every succeeding generation inherits as a precious deposit and a sacred trust to be handed on to the next one...—William Kingdon Clifford, *The Ethics of Belief and Other Essays*

Every individual endeavors to employ his capital so that its produce may be of greatest value. He generally neither intends to promote the public interest, nor knows how much he is promoting it. He intends only his own security, only his own gain. And he is in this led by an invisible hand to promote an end which was no part of his intention. By pursuing his own interest he frequently promotes that of society more effectually than when he really intends to promote it. —Adam Smith, *The Wealth of Nations*

Take up weeping and wailing for the mountains, and a lamentation for the pastures of the wilderness, because they are laid waste so that no one passes through, and the lowing of cattle is not heard; both the birds of the air and the animals have fled and are gone. — Jeremiah 9:10

ACKNOWLEDGMENTS

I have worked on this project for twenty years and it is impossible to mention all the people who have helped me along the way. This work first came into being through conversations in the economics department at the University of California, Berkeley, and at Harvard Divinity School. I am also grateful for the financial help and encouragement of Harvard University and the Episcopal Church Foundation. Marc Jolley has been the ideal editor for me.

The former president of Kamehameha Schools Michael Chun and his wife, Bina Chun, out of their seemingly infinite aloha provided me with a place to live while I wrote much of this manuscript. The people of St. Clement's Episcopal Church in Berkeley, California, and Christ Episcopal Church in Los Altos, California, were kind to encourage me in this work.

Mario L. Barnes, Scott Sherman, Nick Haan, and James Denzil Suite have been wonderful friends and conversation partners over the years. Cliff Frasier, Jamie Shkolnik, Greg Kimura, Margaret Izutsu, Hal Obayashi, Nancy Levene, Bette Manter, Alan Revering, Sally Matless, David Kim, Kimerer LaMothe, Elizabeth Pritchard, Phil Stoltzfus, and Kathleen Skerrett were fellow students who helped me along the way.

I am especially thankful for teachers in the faculties of economics, sociology, philosophy, religion, etc. who have helped me. I wrote my first paper on this subject in Harvey Cox's Contemporary Theology seminar. Gordon D. Kaufman was kind enough to serve as my advisor during the period of time when I worked most intensely on this project. Richard R. Niebuhr also has hugely influenced my thought, especially with regard to symbol and the religious imagination. David Lamberth helped me while he was a doctoral candidate and later as a faculty member. I have learned a great deal from other generous teachers, especially Francis Fiorenza, Cornel West, Sarah Coakley, Ron Thiemann, George Akerlof, Amartya Sen, Jim Pierce, Pat Tiller, Larry Buell, and Ted Heibert. Sallie McFague and John Cobb each read partial drafts of this work and were very generous in supporting me. I cannot adequately express my gratitude to Margaret Ruth Miles, Owen Thomas, Richard Vallantasis, and Jennifer Philips, or to my California colleagues Rick Fabian, Donald Schell, Kitty Lehman, Bruce Smith, and Chris Rankin-Williams. John and Lucy Robinson have done a great deal to inspire this project over the years.

My brother and parents have always encouraged critical thinking, a sense of mystery in spiritual matters, and in thousands of ways have helped me to see nature more clearly. Our children, Micah and Melia, are wonderful companions with great insights and questions. I hope God continues to inspire them to take seriously the needs of the earth and all its creatures.

Finally, thank you to my wife. When we first met, we would walk along the edge of the continent and share our dreams. Now we are realizing those dreams and I cannot imagine a better partner for this journey.

INTRODUCTION

For to what purpose is all the toil and bustle of this world? What is the end of avarice and ambition, of the pursuit of wealth, of power, and pre-eminence? —Adam Smith[1]

Adam Smith, the father of modern economics, was notorious in his day for eccentricity and absentmindedness. One day while walking and talking animatedly to a friend, he tumbled into a pit. Dazzled by his sense of an all-pervading orderliness in the natural and social worlds, he had little attention left for more mundane things. Smith described the miraculous order that seems to govern social systems as the manifestation of God's immediate power and influence in the world.

Smith invented the image of the "invisible hand," which took "private interests and passions" and rearranged them, bringing into being that "which is most agreeable to the interests of the whole society." Since that time, this image of the invisible hand has persevered as one of the most popular secular appropriations of a religious symbol. It is a symbol in a beautiful story about how private interests are counterintuitively transformed into public prosperity as markets reach equilibrium by promoting a balance between supply and demand, and goods are allocated in a way that maximizes overall human well-being. In the modern world, our admiration for this miraculous harmony has been intensified and become entirely detached from any notion of God. The deism and the theological assumptions familiar to many of Smith's first readers have been mostly forgotten in the bustle of the modern age. However, faith in the principle that markets with freely adjusting prices will work out the best outcome for society as a whole has become an

---

[1] Adam Smith, *An Inquiry into the Nature and Causes of the Wealth of Nations*, vol. 2 (Indianapolis: Liberty Classics, 1981) 456.

unquestioned gospel and represents a central foundation of our contemporary understanding of civilization. Over two centuries our faith in markets has become inextricably linked to democratic values, the possibility of technological and humanitarian progress, and our whole notion of political freedom.

In opposition to this model of social order, wilderness over the ages has exemplified the chaos existing beyond the boundaries of human society. In the Bible, wilderness represents a place of refuge and trial for Moses and the people of Israel. It is a sanctuary, the setting of inspiration and struggle for the prophets. It is the context for the baptism and temptation of Jesus. The biblical "voice crying in the wilderness" calls from beyond the periphery, which separates the realm of orderly civilization from the fierce worlds where human beings must accept restraints rather than impose them. Wilderness has historically referred to those places that through brute force subdue even the wisest human efforts to exert ourselves. Only with the technological and social developments of the modern era has our conception of wilderness as unalterable and impermeable begun changing to reflect a concern for its preservation. The massive changes that human beings are now capable of effecting on the world suggest the necessity for a fundamental reorientation of our understanding both of social processes and of our place on the planet. These new conditions necessitate a fundamental change in the habits that govern our thoughts and actions. The system of values suited to a world that carried only a small, less technologically advanced human population may no longer be appropriate or useful in this radically new situation.

This is not a book about hands (invisible or otherwise), nor is it strictly about the wilderness. Instead, it arises out of the effort to understand the human capacity to generate symbols. These embody and direct our sense of meaning and value; they form and influence our deepest desires. Symbols and the stories they support are both the answer to and the means of conveying Adam Smith's question ("For to what purpose is all the toil and bustle of this world? What is the end of avarice and ambition, of the pursuit of wealth, of power, and pre-eminence?"). Economic ideas ultimately cannot be separated from the greater concerns of human meaning.

In Christianity the idea of a sacrament has long been central to questions of faith. Saint Augustine of Hippo (354–430) called a sacrament the visible form of invisible grace. Others since then have called it "an outward and visible sign of an inward and spiritual grace."[2] The sacrament is not the spiritual thing in itself but, rather, presents an embodiment of it. The relation between a sacrament and the holy parallels the relation between specific fields of knowledge and culture. Economics, ecology, and theology work as disciplines, each offering us a glimpse into truths of the human condition. However, they are systems of symbols that both enable understanding, and also limit it. They necessarily make possible and at the same time distort our experience of reality by directing our attention. These disciplines shape our awareness and determine whether we notice busy English shopkeepers or the cathedral's lofty spires or the first spring blossoms or the yawning pit in front of us.

In the twenty years after the fall of communism in Europe, our collective faith in markets has vastly expanded. In the United States we have become used to selling naming rights for public stadiums, giving gift cards instead of actual gifts, seeing advertisements in schools and on airport televisions, local school districts that pay their students for good grades and test scores, concierge medical doctors for the wealthy, human sterilization incentive payments for the poor, a campaign-financing system that disenfranchises ordinary citizens, even to the point of outsourcing pregnancy to third-world surrogate mothers. Market values have expanded into realms of life where we used to believe they did not belong and are being used to make an increasing range of decisions. We are outsourcing police and military actions to private security firms and making similar policy decisions with regard to schools, hospitals,

---

[2] "...if he is a bad man, God performs the visible action of the sacrament through him, but Himself gives the invisible grace." Augustine, *Writings of Saint Augustine* (New York: Cima Pub. Co., 1948) 205. *The Book of Common Prayer* (New York: Church Hymnal Corp., 1979) 857.

government, and prisons. In the past, wealthy people had better access to luxuries like fine jewelry, expensive dresses, European vacations, private jets, large mansions, etc. Increasing inequality means that today, in many situations, money is the only way to have access to the political system, medical care, education, and even general safety. When everything is bought and sold, poor and middle-class people cease to fully participate in society and our relation to the natural world is necessarily distorted.

With this encroachment of economic values into every sphere of modern life has come an increasing faith in the ability of markets to solve virtually every kind of human problem. After the 2008 mortgage crisis in the United States and the unscrupulous banking and investment practices that led to it nearly resulted in a global financial meltdown, Americans by a 2 to 1 margin regarded this as the fault not of finance executives but of the federal government.[3] George Akerlof and Robert J. Shiller make the case that macroeconomic explanations of the last forty years have depended too much on unrealistic accounts of human rationality and not enough on the way that our stories affect the aggregation of human behavior. They write, "Finally, our sense of reality, of who we are and what we are doing, is intertwined with the story of our lives and of the lives of others. The aggregate of such *stories* is a national or international story, which itself plays an important role in the economy."[4] Economics does not just identify stories as an input into understanding the economy; it is itself a story about human flourishing and the world that members of society, to some degree or other, tacitly agree to abide by. We have stories about nature, too. These include an old story about how nothing we did could ever change it and

---

[3] Frank Newport, "Americans Blame Government More than Wall Street for Economy," Gallup Poll, 19 October 2011, www.gallup.com/poll/150191/Americans-Blame-Gov-Wall-Street-Economy.aspx (accessed 10/1/13). Cited in Michael J. Sandel, *What Money Can't Buy: The Moral Limits of Markets* (New York: Farrar, Straus, and Giroux, 2012) 12.

[4] These italics are in the original. George A. Akerlof and Robert J. Shiller, *Animal Spirits: How Human Psychology Drives the Economy, and Why It Matters for Global Capitalism* (Princeton: Princeton University Press, 2009) 6.

a new one about how human-generated changes in the atmosphere are fundamentally altering climate on a global scale. We have personal stories about the religious and artistic meaning of our environment, ethical stories about our responsibility to other forms of life. In many respects, theology consciously sifts through ancient stories and proposes new ones about the place and role of human beings. It entertains questions about the meaning of our lives and how we should spend our time and energy within the various communities around us. This book seeks to find points of connections between economic, ecological, and theological stories. What are the characteristics of these kinds of stories, and what do they have to say to each other?

Although theological approaches to the environment usually seek to inspire a special regard and care for the natural world, they often do little to address the social causes of environmentally destructive behavior. In de-emphasizing mediating institutions and values (formed over history in a social environment), and in attending too little to the various influences on the modern Western sense of the individual, the religious world may be missing valuable means of contributing to this effort. A great deal of contemporary theological reflection obscures the impact of social systems on our world. On the other hand, a brashly materialist view of these matters neglects the sense of the heart, which influences how we decide to commit our boundless desires, talents, and energies. Religious interpretations have lacked savvy in their simplistic call to love nature without regard for the subtleties of our shared social life. Social scientific outlooks traditionally have underestimated the complexity of human systems of meaning in their stark utilitarian vision and their simplifying assumptions.

The source of environmental degradation is not a blind rage against nature. But rather it arises from the complicated essence of our symbolic lives—the complex of powerful stories that we tell about ourselves. The objective tone of scientific and historical method itself obscures the tremendous power of these myths. As human beings, we tell stories about ourselves. We weave tales about the independent, self-made entrepreneur; the stylish, fashionable consumer; the headline-seeking, provocative, environmental radical; the clear-reasoning, syllogism-generating, post-Enlightenment scholar. We find meaning in these stories. They make our attention possible. And yet in our discussions of the environment we forget that these are myths that we created. The compelling power of stories like these makes their mythic quality invisible to us.

This application of economic and theological ideas to the problem of environmental degradation does not attempt to fully integrate all the central concepts within these disciplines. Neither, however, does it argue that these fields of study represent entirely discrete and distinct enterprises. Instead, it seeks to benefit from the intentional calculations and pragmatic approach that characterizes economic decision-making, from the holistic perspective of ecology and from the insights of theology into our understanding of human meaning. The complexity of our environmental problems requires this triangulation of perspective in order to compensate for the oversights of each method of analysis, for the particular blindness inherent in each of these languages that describe our experience.

Chapter 1 includes a short summary of the more obvious results of our environmentally destructive activities. It clarifies the connection between the acquisitiveness that characterizes our consumer culture and the breadth of the changes we are making to this world. The chapter concludes with a very brief summary of the connections that bring together economics, ecology, and theology. Chapter 2 concerns the primary theological (and popular philosophical) approaches to environmental degradation. It asserts that anyone interested in the relationship between faith (formed in community and out of tradition) and the material world must take seriously those social institutions that mediate this relationship. Economics as the primary formalization of the relation between the material world and society in modern times is the subject of the middle chapters. Chapter 6 introduces the language of symbol and symbolization that makes it possible to relate the dominant concepts in discussions regarding the environment, our economic systems, and our theological concerns. An analysis of property in chapter 7 provides an example of economic thinking and its impact on our understanding of the world. Finally, chapters 8 and 9 engage more explicitly theological principles to understand the relation between economics and the environment, ourselves and our world. This final section discusses the role of theology in expressing human commitment and in directing and explaining the powerful forces of ethics and desire. The unifying theme that lies immediately behind this essay's concern with environmental ethics, social scientific thought, and the religious life is this question of commitment. By understanding our environmental troubles as a crisis of faith, we take an important step toward unraveling the knotty complexity of this pressing problem.

1

ENVIRONMENT AND ACTION

The Angels

Wilderness is the element in which we live encased in civilization, as a mollusk lives in his shell in the sea. It is wilderness that is beautiful, dangerous, abundant, oblivious of us, mysterious, never to be conquered or controlled or second-guessed, or known more than a little. It is wilderness that for most of us most of the time is kept out of sight, camouflaged, by the effects and the busyness and the bothers of human society. —Wendell Berry[1]

High above the multimillion-dollar beaches of Malibu, and covered with scrubby chaparral, odd cactus and dust, the tallest peaks of the Santa Monica Mountains provide one of the best vantage points for surveying the California Southland. Standing on the inland ranges in winter, surrounded on three sides by an endless expanse of suburbs, one could never forget the orange sun's beauty as it descends far beyond Catalina Island and the hazy air hovering over the Santa Monica Bay. The dazzling sun reflects off an ocean filled with the silent sails of boats from the largest manmade marina in the world and other points along the coast. Long afternoon walks along the many trails through these mountains offer a magnificent study in contrasts.

The misty ridges of mountains and hills to the far north toward the desert Tehachapis disappear in the limits of our vision on a clear afternoon and lend a gentler perspective on the seamless suburbia of San Fernando Valley that grew ranch houses and streets by the thousands from orange orchards in less than fifty years. Further east, the regal San

---

[1] Wendell Berry, *The Unforeseen Wilderness: An Essay on Kentucky's Red River Gorge* (Lexington: University Press of Kentucky, 1971) 111.

Bernardino and San Fernando Mountains reflect the mixed hues of the setting sun and the bright sky in their snowy palettes. They tower over the many clusters of skyscrapers whose metal and glass walls also shine but with much more intense clarity. Like the stalagmites that grow on the bottom of caves, these recently constructed business and financial centers (including downtown Los Angeles, Burbank, Century City, Westwood, Long Beach, Encino, Woodland Hills, Hollywood, Santa Monica, etc.) seem shocking to an eye accustomed to the familiar smoothness that characterized the landscape only forty years ago. Toward the south, even on the clearest of days, the eye can only rarely penetrate the smog to see beyond the expanse of concrete that now covers most of the Los Angeles basin to recognize Saddleback Mountain on its far rim. The massive traffic jams on the freeways below and in the flight corridors over Los Angeles International Airport seem strangely silent in the strong winds and serenity of these quiet mountain passes and empty dirt fire roads. The desert conditions and nearly treeless landscape in the immediate foreground of the picture I am painting seem remarkably incongruous with the almost infinite number of green lawns and gardens that stretch out into what could be the greatest concentration of single-family homes ever constructed. As the colors of the sky darken, millions and millions of lights from cars, houses, streets, sewage treatment plants, airplanes, office buildings, parking lots, oil refineries, and hundreds of other sources will illuminate the sky in that peculiar color of orange so typical of a modern metropolis. Even over the lonely Santa Monica Mountains, the stars shine only faintly in their constellations as the light of the city erases all competition.

In only a little over a hundred years, Los Angeles has grown from a dusty and unimportant frontier town of 1,610 people (in 1850) to its status as the second largest city in America (and fourteenth largest city in the world). The thirteen million people who today call this city their home depend on a complex infrastructure of reservoirs, dams, canals, pumping stations, and power plants merely to provide the water that they need to keep the desert at bay and to survive. The phenomenon called Los Angeles is probably the parched West's best example of its guiding creed: "Water flows uphill toward money."[2] The acquisition of the Owens River 250 miles away (through questionable methods) during the early part of this century allowed the population of the city to grow such that no river within six hundred miles is safe from its insatiable thirst.[3] Giant siphons bring water over the 3,000-foot high Tehachapi Mountains in five stages. (The last stage, at 1,926 feet, is a height equivalent to the Eiffel Tower stacked on top of the Empire State Building! The electricity required to accomplish this amounts to six billion kilowatt-hours every year, which is equivalent to the total output of a power plant.)[4] Complex networks of canals bring water from the Feather River (which at one time flowed out through the San Francisco Bay) 444 miles along the concrete California aqueduct (the distance from Boston to Washington). Among the lakes and rivers that have fallen victim to Los Angeles's thirst is Mono Lake (the second largest lake in California), once beautiful and then endangered, as the streams that fed it were redirected into canals bound south. In Southern California, water from these massive projects allows hundreds of acres of land per day to be chaotically developed into parking lots, subdivisions, and shopping malls.

---

[2] Although a significant population living in and farming Owen's Valley naturally opposed the appropriation of their water by thirsty Los Angeles, the power (and the illegal tactics) of investors who had bought the San Fernando Valley (at the other end of the pipeline) proved to be too much for them. From chapter 2 of Marc Reisner, *Cadillac Desert: The American West and Its Disappearing Water* (New York: Viking, 1986).

[3] Six hundred miles represents the distance traveled by the water the city currently uses (from the Colorado, which drains the Rocky Mountains). The North America Water and Power Alliance (NAWAPA, proposed in the 1950s) represents an ambitious plan to move water from British Columbia to the parched American Southwest and other destinations. The Klamath River in California near the Oregon border was a far more likely intermediate target for Los Angeles, however. Ibid., 506–14.

[4] California consumes more electricity moving water than several states use for all purposes. Ibid., 369–70.

The City of Angels came of age after the consummation of the country's love affair with the automobile. Virtually unchecked by history here, the centrifugal forces currently contributing to urban sprawl in every major American city have flung the outer edges of L.A. beyond the imagination, and a hundred miles out into the desert. The desire for independence and land of one's own has been the impetus behind the construction of the tightly packed constellations of cities filled with thousands upon thousands of single-family residences. The fulfillment of the American dream, a single-family home far from the tensions of the city, and instant automobile transportation, has made Los Angeles a trendsetter among cities around the world. Decentralized shopping centers, the mini-mall, drive-throughs, and hundreds of other icons of the modern age first became popular here before permanently altering the lives and landscapes of other North Americans. As the setting for many of the world's modern stories, Hollywood and the people who live and work here mesmerize the rest of the world through the power of the global entertainment media.

World famous for shopping malls such as Beverly Glen or the Galleria, and fashion meccas like Rodeo Drive and Beverly Hills, conspicuous consumption reigns uncontended in this modern metropolis. Los Angeles exercises an impact on its region and the world that far exceeds its city limits as it consumes extraordinary quantities of goods and generates legendary levels of waste. The air residents breathe and the ocean water off her beaches from Malibu to Newport are notoriously polluted.[5] Urban neglect accompanying the city's segregation on the basis of race and class, enabled by the transportation revolution, has attracted the world's attention to the brutal gang violence here and the L.A. riots. Los Angeles and its problems differ from those

---

[5] Although the strictest air quality laws in the nation have led to a decline in air pollution, increasing numbers of vehicles on the streets of Los Angeles mean that regulators have not met with the success for which they had hoped. Ocean water pollution in L.A. County has meanwhile reached serious levels. Storm sewers dump tons of untreated waste directly into the ocean during heavy storms.

in other American cities only in their extremity. The city's manic growth (almost entirely without design), the development of its agricultural lands into industrial parks, the massive extent of pollution accompanying urbanization, and its reputation for extravagant consumption make it particularly representative of our world's most serious ecological problems. Although individually we may have difficulty seeing the full extent of the environmental degradation that is so fundamentally altering our atmosphere, oceans, and land, the view from the mountains surrounding Los Angeles can provide us with a less abstract insight into the greater effects of humanity on Earth. From here we see a glimpse of the world through the eyes of angels.

A Changing World

> Crossing a bare common, in snow puddles, at twilight, under a clouded sky without having in my thoughts any occurrence of special good fortune, I have enjoyed a perfect exhilaration. I am glad to the brink of fear. In the woods, too, a man casts off his years. In the woods is perpetual youth. Within these plantations of God, a decorum and sanctity reign, a perennial festival is dressed, and the guest sees not how he should tire of them in a thousand years. In the woods, we return to reason and faith. In the wilderness, I find something more dear and connate than in streets or villages. —Ralph Waldo Emerson[6]

The environmental disruption that has characterized the last hundred years of development in Southern California was not the result of an evil mastermind. Los Angeles does not represent the culmination of an inner circle's dastardly business scheming so much as the fulfillment of some of our society's most broadly accepted goals. The value of autonomy, broad access to industrial products, individualism, efficiency, consumer

---

[6] Ralph Waldo Emerson, *The Collected Works of Ralph Waldo Emerson: Nature, Addresses, and Lectures*, ed. R.E. Spiller et al., vol. 1 (Cambridge MA: Belknap Press, 1971) 10.

choice, affluence, and privacy, which we regard so highly in North America, have been etched into the landscape in our efforts to create a modern utopia. We defile our environment not through the failure of our dominant values but in their success. We build our world on foundations that embody our peculiarly human shortcomings. In the fulfillment of our very dreams lurk unanticipated possibilities for disaster. But this begins to move us too quickly ahead of ourselves.

A remarkable thing happened in the 1990s. More than 1,600 top scientists, including 102 Nobel Laureates (a majority of the living Nobel Laureates of the sciences), came together in agreement and published an urgent press release issued in 1992.[7] They wrote that "human beings and the natural world are on a collision course that may so alter the living world that it will be unable to sustain life in the manner that we know." Perhaps even more alarming was their prediction that "no more than one or a few decades remain before the chance to avert the threats we now confront will be lost and the prospects for humanity immeasurably diminished." These brilliant scientists called for a "new ethic" that would emphasize caring for ourselves and our world.

Concluding this press release, they sound more like ancient Hebrew prophets than like technological elites: "We the undersigned senior members of the world's scientific community hereby warn all of humanity of what lies ahead. A great change in our stewardship of Earth

---

[7] Union of Concerned Scientists, "World's Leading Scientists Issue Urgent Warning to Humanity," Washington DC Press Release, 18 November 1992. Although this statement may seem like it was issued a long time ago, scientists continue to offer even more dire warnings about the effects of global climate change: "If we continue with business as usual, the projected rise in Earth's temperature of 1.1–6.4 degrees Celsius (2–11 degrees Fahrenheit) during this century seems all too possible. These projections are the latest from the Intergovernmental Panel on Climate Change (IPCC); the world body of more than 2,500 leading climate scientists in 2007 released a consensus report affirming humanity's role in climate change. Unfortunately, during the several years since the study was completed, both global CO2 emissions and atmospheric CO2 concentrations have exceeded those in the IPCC's worst-case scenario." Lester Russell Brown, *Plan B 4.0: Mobilizing to Save Civilization* (New York: W.W. Norton, 2009) 58.

and the life that is on it is required if vast human misery is to be avoided and our global home on this planet is not to be irretrievably destroyed."

This unprecedented level of concern indicates the beginning of a massive change in perspective. Our culture has begun to react to the evidence that we have fundamentally transformed the planet.

Despite the definitive tone of this statement, it is notoriously difficult to accurately predict the results of the huge changes we are making to the world. Measures of economic progress themselves are a relatively recent product of the modern age. Adequately noting the condition of the natural environment through statistics and broadly accepted standards for comparison has not yet become a reality. Despite our very recent and genuine concern for the effects of human activity on the physical world, understanding the magnitude and nature of the changes resulting from the industrial activity of the last century remains elusive.

Global climate change is already happening quickly and with unpredictable effects. The twenty-five warmest years on record have all come since 1980. The ten warmest years since records began to be kept in 1880 have all happened since 1996. Earth's temperature has gone up .6 degrees Celsius (1 degree Fahrenheit) since 1970, and is projected to rise by up to 6 degrees Celsius (11 degrees Fahrenheit) by the end of this century. This will not affect all areas uniformly. The change will be much greater at the higher latitudes than around the equator. The sea level rose by 7 inches in the entire twentieth century. Current projections expect sea level to rise 7 inches each *decade* in the years leading to 2100.[8] This will have massive effects on food production and species habitats, and will displace millions of people.

With huge increases in both population and consumption, resource depletion has become a central problem for humanity. According to the World Resources Institute, more than 80 percent of the Earth's natural forests have already been destroyed. Up to 90 percent of West Africa's

---

[8] Ibid., 55–56.

coastal rainforests have disappeared since 1990.[9] Deserts continue to expand around the world. This has been causing massive amounts of human suffering. In the last twenty years severe droughts, such as the one that put ten million people in East Africa at risk in 2011, have become more common.[10] The degradation of topsoil means that the land we have dedicated to farming is growing increasingly less productive. According to the United Nations Population fund, between 1999 and 2011 the world's population increased by 1 billion (that was the world's total population in 1800).

Scientists draw our attention to substantial changes in the atmosphere, which have affected global temperatures. Levels of atmospheric carbon dioxide, which have increased by 26 percent since the Industrial Era began, continue to increase by .04 percent every year.[11] Scientists attribute recent record temperatures to this change in the composition of our atmosphere. Our ability to significantly alter the composition of the atmosphere in a relatively short time is demonstrated by the depletion of the atmospheric ozone layer over various sections of the world. Spring ozone levels over Antarctica are 50 percent thinner than thirty years ago. Despite many predictions and estimates regarding the effects of these monumental changes (ranging from projections of crop loss in dollar terms, to changes in climate, to forecasts of land-loss levels resulting

---

[9] *National Geographic*, "Deforestation and Desertification." http://www.nationalgeographic.com/eye/deforestation/effect.html (accessed 1 October 2013.)

[10] Carine Richard-Van Maele, World Meteorological Organization Press Release, "Ten Million People at Risk as East Africa Faces Worst Drought in 60 years," 1 August 2011. www.wmo.int/pages/mediacentre/press_releases/pr_WMO_UNCCD.html. United Nations Convention to Combat Desertification Press Release, "Ten Million People at Risk as East Africa Faces Worst Drought in 60 Years," 1 August 2011, (accessed 1 October 2013).

[11] In the 1960s, the annual mean growth rate of carbon dioxide measured at Mauna Loa, Hawaii, was less than 1.0 parts per million per year. The growth rate for carbon dioxide is now twice as high (2.0). Pieter Trans, NOAA Earth System Research Library, "Trends in Atmospheric Carbon Dioxide, Manna Loa, Hawaii," http://www.esrl.noaa.gov/gmd/ccgg/trends/ (accessed 1 October 2013).

from global warming), scientists do not understand precisely how these massive environmental changes will affect human life.

Environmentalists predicting doom in the 1970s from the total depletion of non-renewable resources have been proven wrong countless times as the technology for resource discovery and exploitation has improved. Our supply of minerals has almost kept pace with demand as the market encourages substitutes for those materials that become scarce. Since these early predictions, however, the primary concern of environmentalists has changed. We have stopped worrying so much about what goes into our gas tanks and have begun wondering about what comes out of the exhaust pipe. In the 1990s the central issue became the degree to which humans have transformed Earth and its atmosphere and the extent to which concentrations of chemicals (such as carbon, sulfur, nitrogen, phosphorus, ionizing radiation, trace pollutants, etc. resulting from human activities) exceed Earth's ability to assimilate them.

Indeed it would be better if we were only limited by constrained natural resources like coal, oil, copper, etc. Instead we have begun to realize that the world, which we thought of as boundless, is even more finite than our capacities for destruction. We now recognize that just as we are causing the deterioration of the ozone in the upper levels of the atmosphere, we are rapidly filling up the lower levels with carbon. All of known life depends on a thin film of atmosphere that we are permanently damaging. The troposphere extends only five to seven miles above Earth's surface. If one could walk straight up, it would take less than two hours to leave the sections of the atmosphere that we utterly depend upon to live. We have begun filling up the sky with the exhaust from our internal combustion engines.

Scarcity (of arable land, water, etc.) remains a perennial problem. According to the United Nations, half the world's population will be living in areas of high water stress by 2030. Already 1.2 billion people suffer from the physical scarcity of water. Another 500 million people will soon find themselves in this same situation, and yet another 1.6 billion people live in places that lack the infrastructure to deliver

16

water—this is one quarter of the world's population.[12] Some controversial estimates suggest that the proportion of the world's land surface damaged to the point where it is useless for agriculture constitutes an area the size of Africa.[13]

Today, Canada has 14,000 dead lakes; the Aral Sea (between Uzbekistan and Kazakstan), which yielded 40 million kilograms of fish in 1960, also has become a casualty of industrialism. Stocks of the Atlantic bluefin tuna have been depleted by 94 percent, and Canada's commercial fishing industry has experienced massive decline as a result of overfishing. One-third of our continent's fish are now either rare or imperiled.[14]

Figures like these leave us numb and we react like a deer, motionless on the highway, a confused animal whose eyes reflect back the light from a rapidly approaching truck. Mountains of facts regarding the degradation of soil, atmosphere, oceans, coral reefs, shorelines, freshwater, and air, with staggering data regarding species extinction, the persistency

---

[12] United Nations Convention to Combat Desertification, "Water Scarcity and Desertification," Thematic Fact Sheet Series No. 2, http://www.unccd.int/Lists/SiteDocumentLibrary/Publications/Desertificationa ndwater.pdf. United Nations, "International Decade for Action—Water for Life, 2005–2015," http://www.un.org/waterforlifedecade/scarcity.shtml (accessed 1 October 2013).

[13] Fifteen million square kilometers of land, or 10 percent of global land area (equivalent to Antarctica), are under permanent cultivation, while 20 million square kilometers of formerly productive land has been irreversibly lost (to desert, pavement, etc.). The annual loss of productive land amounts to 60,000–70,000 square kilometers (the area of Sierra Leone), a rate 30 to 35 times the average yearly losses during the last 10,000 years. Boris G. Rozanov, Viktor Targulian, and D.S. Orlov, "Soils," in *The Earth as Transformed by Human Action: Global and Regional Changes in the Biosphere over the Past 300 Years*, ed. B. L. Turner (Cambridge: Cambridge University Press, 1990) 205.

[14] Lester R. Brown, "A New Era Unfolds," in *State of the World 1993: A Worldwatch Institute Report on Progress Toward a Sustainable Society*, ed. Lester R. Brown (New York: Norton, 1993) 7–8. Sandra Postel, "Facing Water Scarcity," in *State of the World 1993: A Worldwatch Institute Report on Progress Toward a Sustainable Society*, ed. Lester R. Brown (New York: Norton, 1993) 6.

of introduced chemicals, and the rapidity of massive population increase, can paralyze even the strongest sense of resolve. The interrelationships between each of these phenomena make accurate analysis even more challenging. Air pollution destroys European forests, ozone depletion limits crop yields, chemical waste decreases species diversity, etc. Despite the difficulties inherent in such an enterprise, there is no shortage of predictions of future doom.

Beauty

> Something will have gone out of us as a people if we ever let the remaining wilderness be destroyed; if we permit the last virgin forests to be turned into comic books and plastic cigarette cases; if we drive the few remaining members of the wild species into zoos or to extinction; if we pollute the last clear air and dirty the last clean streams and push our paved roads through the last of the silence, so that never again will Americans be free in their own country from the noise, the exhaust, the stinks of human and automotive waste.
> —Wallace Stegner[15]

In our time, utility has become the measure of all things, and arguments based on beauty rather than usefulness seem oddly suspect or strangely out of place. This could be one of the reasons we experience such a great gulf between Plato, Aristotle, and the medieval theologians on one side and ourselves on the other. We ask, "How much beauty are people ready to pay for?" and in this way subsume all things under utility. Even beauty becomes yet another sort or category of usefulness to be measured on the imprecise scales of modernity. We read this written into the very fiber of our contemporary institutions. In the methods of cost/benefit analysis (which anchor many of our legal codes), there is no ledger large enough to contain a sense of yearning for the beautiful. We have lost the sensitive touch that *feels* beauty. Today, we concern ourselves only with cold calculations of worth. Perhaps this adoration of utility is one of the major reasons skepticism has so much power in our

---

[15] Wallace E. Stegner, *The Sound of Mountain Water* (New York: Ballantine Books, 1972) 146.

age. Worries about the continuing existence of humanity should not be our only motivation for cultivating sensitivity to the environment.

One example of this concerns the argument that the removal of rainforests destroys Earth's capacity to convert carbon. Some claim that the primary reason for preserving rainforests in developing countries should be their role in cleaning the planet's air. Indeed, rainforest trees do serve as "carbon sinks"; however, new trees perform this service far better than do old forests.[16] The argument that forests have primary value for their contribution to the content of our atmosphere could be a justification for clearing old forests.

Arguments for saving the biological richness of life on our planet often mention the possibility of discovering future pharmaceutical uses for endangered species. They argue for preserving other sensitive species as an environmental early warning system for humanity. Massive numbers of amphibians around the world are dying off. This has increased concern that their sensitivity to environmental changes may predict the future reaction of humans to poorer air and water quality. Beyond these pragmatic reasons for preserving wildlife diversity lie important aesthetic and moral concerns. Is it right for one generation to so substantially and permanently alter our planet? When we were born, we shared the planet with thirty million other species. Is it morally justifiable that there will be only one tenth of this number at our death? What responsibility do we have both to future generations and to the other beings with whom we share our world? Does beauty unrecognized by the calipers and gauges of our economic mechanisms matter? Can the value of all our experiences, all the physical things in the world, be compared in terms of price?

We know the answers to these questions without understanding why. Great novelists and poets teach us to learn about ourselves by listening to our strongest emotional responses. Many of our detached utilitarian arguments break down when we consider our response to decreasing biodiversity. Belief in something greater than the merely human, perhaps even belief in God, is implicit in our alarm. Killing off

---

[16] Oceans also serve as major carbon sinks.

thousands or even millions of other species is not foolish because another natural resource is being depleted. It is not immoral only because future generations will be deprived of a particular experience of Earth's riches. Our concern indicates a deep ethical sense that human beings are not the measure of all value. In his essay "Nature," Ralph Waldo Emerson writes, "Nature never becomes a toy to a wise spirit."[17] Other life is not simply a plaything or a tool. At some level in our consciousness we, too, realize that we are not the center, that value cannot be simply measured as only usefulness to human beings or culture.

The religious or artistic inspiration arising from the complexity and diversity of the natural world cannot be simply measured in dollar terms. Through history the idea of wilderness has shaped what we recognize as human. The value of nature transcends our power of control and manipulation. It can never be reckoned since we can scarcely be aware of the influence wilderness has on our consciousness. Recognizing the impact that any particular scene of beauty has had on us is as difficult as remembering when we first learned the word "sunset" or "oak tree" or "star." These moments and experiences of beauty have shaped our identity. Just as we would be profoundly impoverished had we not learned a relatively complete vocabulary or had no opportunity to speak our native language, so would we be destitute if natural beauty were lacking from our lives. An experience of beauty in the natural world often draws out a part of us that we scarcely even know. It always leaves us changed. Our civilization will never be whole without the periphery, the unbounded wildness necessary for its completeness.

In the diversity of natural life exists a beauty impossible to replicate. Yet, whole ecosystems have been erased from the face of the planet. These include the tall grass prairies of North America, the cedar groves of Lebanon, the old-growth hardwood forests of Europe, and the Sandalwood forests of Maui. The loss of these ecosystems and the creatures dependent upon them, the climate change, and the desertification that

---

[17] Emerson, *The Collected Works of Ralph Waldo Emerson: Nature, Addresses, and Lectures*, 1.

has accompanied these planetary revisions leave us all impoverished. Certainly the transient economic value of environmentally destructive activities has not exceeded their cost to the beauty of our world and the benefit of future generations. Our involvement in the economic world may make it more difficult to receive the gift that can be discovered in nature. We see the world in a new way, through real experiences, through nights watching the meteor showers over the Rockies in August, feeling the benediction of spring clouds that bring rain in the desert, the sense of time passing, experienced concretely during autumn in a Maine forest. No one can know if the massive changes that we have seen in the past fifty years will destroy human civilization. No one can accurately estimate the damage that will result from human activity in the twenty-first century. The possibility of humanity's own extinction is a question that can be debated by experts. All of us have responsibility to nature, however. Understanding the social systems that affect the environment is important for everyone. The next chapters focus on how social policies and conventions determine the context for our relation with the natural world.

The Poor and the Rich

> I never knew how poor I was until I had a little money. —A banker, quoted by Lewis H. Lapham[18]

Between 1950 and 1994, when the world's population doubled, the population of Rwanda more than tripled from 2.5 million to 8.8 million. In this, the most densely populated African country, there were eight children for every mother in 1992. Although grain production increased dramatically with the help of technological improvements, the grain output per person still decreased by nearly half between 1960 and the 1990s. Furthermore, the fresh water supply dipped so precipitously that hydrologists came to classify this nation as one of the twenty-seven water-scarce countries in the world. As is the custom in East Africa,

---

[18] L.H. Lapham, *Money and Class in America: Notes and Observations on the Civil Religion* (New York: Ballantine Books, 1989) 28.

family plots were divided among the surviving sons until average farm size became less than half a hectare. These demographic and environmental facts were not themselves the cause of the explosive civil war in Rwanda. Instead they are indications of the type of pressure that makes ethnic and tribal differences more likely to flare up into devastating violence. In 1994 two million Rwandans were refugees, and more than 800 thousand others had been brutally slaughtered.

The natural world cannot be regarded as anything less than the grand context for all societies. After the Panguna copper mine on Bougainville (an island of Papua New Guinea) dumped 600 million tons (at a rate of 130,000 tons per day) of metal-contaminated tailings into the Kawerong River, the wastes covered 1,800 hectares of the river system, killing all aquatic life in the delta and for 30 kilometers downstream from the mine. This was a precipitating cause in a secessionist revolution. Political unrest on the island of Haiti was certainly heightened by the loss of all but 2 percent of its forests and much of its topsoil through erosion. In nations from Somalia to Mexico, the quality of the environment has come to exercise an important influence on politics.

Although some estimates suggest that greater than one-sixth of the world's population is already very seriously affected by environmental catastrophe, such figures do little to help us grasp the extent of the problem in this world in which 2.5 billion (62% of the world's population) do not have access to improved sanitation, 780 million people do not have access to clean drinking water, and 3.4 million die every year from waterborne diseases. More people have cell phones than access to a toilet.[19] With world population increasing by 88 million people annually (roughly adding the population of Germany each year), the developing world shoulders a disproportionate burden of this increase. This population explosion strains the most basic of Earth's chemical and biological processes.

---

[19] As of 2013, water.org "Millions Lack Safe Water" (accessed 1 October 2013) http://water.org/learn-about-the-water-crisis/facts/.

Those living in industrial societies should not be too quick in their judgment of developing countries and these rapid population increases.[20] Over 1 billion people survive on less than $2 per day in a world that spends $249 per person on military expenditures.[21] In 2013, 870 million people suffered from chronic undernourishment.[22] Some have estimated that the average American will consume thirty-five times as much in his or her lifetime as an average East Indian. Many statistics suggest that our affluence rather than our numbers may be having the greatest impact on the world. Anyone alive since 1950 has witnessed an extraordinary change. In a generation, the world population more than doubled. Perhaps even more remarkable is that in this same period the world's economic output increased by seventeenfold.[23] While this measure of global output includes the production of goods and services (and our production methods today require fewer inputs), this figure implies the creation of extraordinary quantities of waste and depleted raw materials.

The rate of consumption in industrial nations has a staggering impact on our world. Perhaps rather than "consumers," we should be called "wasters." Americans with less than 5 percent of the world's population account for one-third of total soda consumption (in excess of

---

[20] The Western industrial countries have similarly experienced a period of rapid population growth. History seems to suggest that population slows with increases in wealth, affluence, and education, thus creating a catch-22. Both affluence (as defined by economic standards) and population degrade our world.

[21] Jonathan Lash, World Resources Institute "Growing the Wealth of the World's Poor," 7 October 2008. www.wri.org/stories/2008/10/growing-wealth-worlds-poor. Anup Shah, "World Military Spending" updated 30 June 2013, www.globalissues.org/article/75/world-military-spending.

[22] World Hunger Education Service, "2013 World Hunger and Poverty Facts and Statistics," updated 27 July 2013 www.worldhunger.org/articles/Learn/world%hunger%20facts%202002.htm.

[23] Although economic growth is not equivalent to environmental degradation, such a measure can begin to approximate the relative effects of population and production on the environment.

160 quarts per person per year).[24] In the forty years between 1950 and 1990, Americans came to own twice as many cars, drive 2.5 times as far, consume 21 times as much plastic and fly 25 times as far by air.[25] Yet surveys suggest that we are no happier than we were in 1950, when our total output was a tiny fraction of our current level standard.[26] Social scientists are currently producing studies showing that, beyond a baseline level of material well-being, happiness is not correlated with wealth.[27]

Although population increase imposes a massive burden on the ecosphere, the boundless consumption and waste of developed countries should be the focus of attention for the people of the industrial world. While our concerns should remain global, our perspective and influence must by necessity always remain grounded in our own experience. Humility should be our guiding principle as we begin reviewing solutions to these enormous problems. We need to take responsibility for our own excesses and those problems over which we have the most control.

For the whole period of our existence as human beings, the primary limits to our endeavors have usually been external. The Sumerians, Babylonians, Incas, Greeks, Phoenicians, Egyptians, Polynesians, and every civilization and every tribe that has ever existed were limited by the technology that they applied toward their problems. They were limited,

---

[24] Annie Richardson, Food Democracy, "Chew on This—US Soda Consumption," 9 November 2007, http://fooddemocracy.wordpress.com/2007/11/09/chew-on-this-us-soda-consumption/ (1 October 2013).

[25] Alan Durning, "Asking How Much Is Enough," in *State of the World 1991: The Worldwatch Institute*, ed. Lester R. Brown et al., (New York: W.W. Norton & Company, 1991) 154.

[26] Gross Domestic Product in 1960 was less $520 billion. In the third quarter of 2013 it was $16,257 trillion. United States Bureau of Economic Analysis, "Grass."

[27] Carter Christine, *Raising Happiness: 10 Simple Steps for More Joyful Kids and Happier Parents* (New York: Ballantine Books, 2010); Dacher Keltner, *Born to Be Good: The Science of a Meaningful Life* (New York: W.W. Norton & Co., 2009).

for instance, by the number of boats that they could devote to fishing in the world's great rivers and oceans. Today, we are limited only by the number of fish in the ocean. Our technology has ceased to be the constraining factor in the equation. Our culture, which devoted itself to expanding the bounds of our technology, must now begin to face a constraint of a wholly changed nature. We must begin to think and act in the world according to an entirely different system of rules as we come to adjust to this new power, to our increasing numbers and our magnificent desires. Today we need to acknowledge the unique power that we as a species have in forming and re-forming the world. We must recognize the necessity of restraint and limits as we build institutions that allow us to best respond to this new context.

Economics, Ecology, and God

> When I consider your heavens, the work of your fingers, the moon and the stars you have set in their courses, What is man that you should be mindful of him? the son of man that you should seek him out? You have made him but little lower than the angels.
> —Psalm 8[28]

The idea of God does not belong to theologians or even to any particular religious sect. For centuries poets and artists have made use of divine imagery to express truths about the human condition. In the pages that follow, we will consider how monotheistic symbols and theological ideas out of the Western tradition can clarify the effects of economic symbols, which are starting to dominate the social organization of every culture in the world. Perhaps these traditions with ancient roots can help us to understand the effects that human social systems have on nature at this time when technology and economics together have brought about such radical changes in nature and society.

The power of ideas like liberty, equality, democracy, freedom of speech, evolution, unconscious thought, and free markets could not have been stifled within the narrow confines of a compartmentalized

---

[28] *The Book of Common Prayer*, 592.

academic discipline, or viewed as the exclusive property of one nation or religious denomination. As we begin to face up to our environmental challenges, the insights of ecological biologists, natural resource economists, and environmental theologians similarly must be shared, or all will suffer.

The intersection of these three topics represents the focal point of this book. Although a greater divergence in guiding principles, assumptions, philosophies, and methodologies could hardly be imagined, a discussion among these fields is richly worthwhile. In certain sections of the text, a deliberate vagueness with respect to the membranes and boundaries that delimit each subject prevails in the interests of open dialogue. At other points, a clearer definition of the edges and borders contributes to the debate. Four arrangements of these themes and a very brief history of mutual participation among them follow. The remaining chapters of the book try to find a common language for examining consumer culture in light of these topics.

1. Ecology and Theology—During the last four thousand years, human beings have wrestled with the meaning of their existence and recorded their exertions as theology. Countless cultures have contributed in this effort to understand our world and ourselves. From the ancient Chinese, Indians, Egyptians, Babylonians, Assyrians, Hebrews, and Greeks, to the modern liberation theologians, from Anselm and Augustine to Zen Buddhists and Zoroastrians, they have sought to articulate statements concerning a divine reality that cannot be adequately defined by words.

We may be tempted to believe that we have advanced beyond the point where the wisdom of these venerable ancients will be useful to us. Perhaps we think that a society without theology has already come into being or is possible in the future. In any of these cases, we slip into a form of naiveté peculiar to the modern age. It is all too easy for many of us to begin believing that the most profound questions about human life have simple, technical answers easily discoverable by science.[29]

---

[29] Ronald Heifetz draws the distinction between technical problems, for which solutions already exist, and what he calls adaptive challenges, which out of necessity involve groups of people creating new knowledge in order to solve

26

The whole notion of ecology and environmental science came into being within a single generation. Although Henry David Thoreau wrote in his journals about the decline of New England's forests (forests that have since returned) and James Fenimore Cooper wrote about the wanton destruction along America's frontier, the great magnitude of environmental damage of which we are capable has only relatively recently become clear to us. In some senses it is a new problem. Rachel Carson's *Silent Spring*, which raised consciousness about the effects of DDT, was only published in the 1960s.[30] Satellites only confirmed ozone depletion in our atmosphere during the 1980s. The effects on plant and animal life that will accompany the changing composition of our atmosphere, our land, and oceans still remain not entirely known.

At the intersection of theology and ecology, where dusty ancient manuscripts and sensitive atmospheric instruments meet, lies a unique opportunity for creative thought. Although these two interests have been combined prior to the 1960s, since that time this endeavor has been pursued with substantially more vigor. These debates usually revolve around various means of conceptualizing God, the world, individuals, and society. In suggesting new metaphors describing the relationship between humanity and the natural world, such as stewardship or covenant, theologians have sought to transform our understanding of our place, role, and responsibility within the environment. Employing both obscure ancient texts and postmodern philosophy, they attempt to cultivate a greater recognition of humanity's absolute dependence on the natural world. They seek to inspire and nurture a genuine appreciation for its beauty. Divine mandate for more sensitive environmental care represents an important element for many of these theologians. While this may not seem very controversial, the re-appropriation of ancient

---

problems. Ronald A. Heifetz, *Leadership Without Easy Answers* (Cambridge MA: Belknap Press of Harvard University Press, 1994).
[30] Rachel Carson, *Silent Spring* (New York: Fawcett Crest, 1962).

texts and the introduction of perspectives that diverge from tradition have provoked opposition.[31]

2. *Theology and Economics*—Theologian Bernard Lonergan described theology as a discipline that mediates between a culture, and the role that religion plays in that culture.[32] As a central element in our cultural inheritance, economic ideas have long been important to theologians. The basic philosophical superstructure of economic thought includes metaphors and methods, problems and concepts that arose out of the theological tradition. The long history of dialogue between these two fields of knowledge began before the moral philosopher Adam Smith introduced his ubiquitous ideas regarding political economy. The English clergy who initially endorsed Smith's proposals played a central role in the continued popularity of this sort of analysis. Governmental and industrial procedures, ranging from employment policies to development issues, to the distribution of relative tax burdens, to the effects of government transfers, have been subjects of vehement debate as ethical issues of central importance to both theologians and economists.

Since Adam Smith, the primary issues of concern in this dialogue have been questions relating to income differences. People have questioned, for instance, the justice and necessity of poverty in an economically efficient society. Macroeconomists for a great deal of time believed that there was a tradeoff between unemployment (which is largely an issue for poorer people) and inflation (which concerns wealthy people and those on fixed incomes). The very basis of most moral debates over economic questions, from Marxist socialism to Reaganomics and welfare reform, has addressed the fairness of wealth's distribution within society. Indeed the major economic revolutions (which have been one of the most powerful influences on the last century's history) revolved around questions concerning the distribution of wealth and power.

---

[31] Many arguments against these environmental theologies depend on a falsely constructed, monolithic version of tradition. Theological reasoning has always drawn on traditions composed of many conflicting elements.

[32] Bernard J. F. Lonergan, *Method in Theology* (New York: Herder and Herder, 1972).

Whether economics is seen merely as a means of legitimating differences in power and position, or as a profound insight into the mechanism that rewards labor and entrepreneurial initiative, this tool for social analysis has always been subject to ideological conflict. The notion of a tradeoff between equity and productivity continues to be a central interest for both theologians and economists. However, the assumptions that form the basis for economic theorizing should also be of interest to theologians. This philosophical framework includes presuppositions about individuality, the quality and satiability of desire, sources of value, the commensurability of various goods, competition, equilibrium, growth, community, human rights and flourishing, etc. All of these influence the social values that economic models promote. As the dominant means of making social decisions in the modern world, economic assumptions should be interesting to any theologian concerned about contemporary life.

In many respects, two means of viewing the world seem to be at odds: the utilitarian ideal, which recognizes value as measurable and equivalent to material well-being, as contrasted with a romantic/ expressivist ideal, which views worth as inhering and expressed within a thing in itself.[33] One wonders if a system that evolved to maximize human well-being in a world without limits can be easily modified to take into consideration a broader range of values. This level of analysis, as we seek to understand our place in the world, has had less appeal historically than have more concrete policy issues. However, this sort of question must be asked in order to fully comprehend how we make the judgments of worth so important to the environment.

3. Economics and Ecology—Overlap in these two fields has only relatively recently been considered a worthwhile topic of interest. Both environmentalists and public policymakers have adopted the tools of economics in using cost-benefit analysis, creative reallocation of property rights, risk assessment methods, and accounting procedures in an effort to make environmental tradeoffs more explicit. Although in the last

---

[33] Charles Taylor, *Sources of the Self: The Making of the Modern Identity* (Cambridge, MA: Harvard University Press, 1989) 368–390.

thirty years economics has been applied to our ecological efforts (for example, to analyze how a firm's incentive to pollute can be controlled), innovative economists have begun to think of economics in ecological terms. The importance of sustainability, and of production and consumption processes that do not generate waste but rather produce inputs to other processes, has been a very recent interest among economists. As we recognize that there is no "away" where we can throw things away, economists will go further to incorporate environmental degradation into their analytical calculations. With massive increases in populations, trade, and standards of living, we can also expect an explosion in the complexity of our dependence on others and the world.

4. *Economics, Ecology, and Theology*—Addressing these three topics together is, not surprisingly, a fairly new development. Usually the main aim in this sort of study has been to conform economics to ecological principles through the use of the ethical and moral resources of theology. This sort of approach recognizes the importance of economic reasoning in describing the relation between the social and natural worlds. Those who have combined an interest in these three subjects usually know our modern tendency to see virtually everything in terms of prices determined by a market. They understand the influence of economists and the business community and the power of our own acquisitiveness on the environment. They recognize the social pressures on us to succeed and consume. The dominant approach with respect to these three themes usually frames the discussion in economic terms that have been translated to account for ecological concerns. For example, it might reject Gross National Product as environmentally destructive, but instead promote a different quantification of our well-being (such as Measure of Economic Welfare or MEW), which also accounts for national output in numerical terms (although it discounts this number, to adjust for environmental damage).

Any discussion about the relation between society and the environment that fails to mention economic principles is insufficient. Unfortunately, however, virtually all of those who use economic methods rarely question the most fundamental economic assumptions.

The language of economics can eclipse other frameworks of meaning. It, too, easily becomes for us simply the way the world is, rather than our lens for understanding the world.

Perhaps the first successful book about the environment in economics and theology was *For the Common Good* by economist Herman Daly and theologian John Cobb.[34] They advocate specific policy changes, as exemplified in their arguments concerning their Index of Sustainable Economic Welfare (which they propose as a substitute for GNP). They also focus their efforts on educational reform and suggest important changes in how economics is taught. These more specific objectives are evident in their table of contents (for instance, part 1 is titled, "Economics as an Academic Discipline," and part 3 is "Policies for Community in the United States"). In this book, religion enters the picture almost as an afterthought, as a moral mandate for responsible economic practices. Only the last of twenty chapters considers it.

Their important book represents the first significant effort to use the tools of economic and theological analysis to understand and reverse environmental degradation. Their pragmatic approach should certainly be applauded. The pages that follow do not explicitly put forward specific policies, but rather explore the problem of our environment as an indication of a much deeper conflict within our society and our consciousness. Neither economists nor theologians historically have recognized the complexity of motives that guide the behavior revealed in our everyday decisions. The remaining chapters ask deeper questions about human motivation, our institutions, and the various sources of both our values and our methods of determining worth. Religion as the primary lens through which human beings understand meaning and commitment therefore represents a more central part of my thesis.

***

In three of these four perspectives, economics represents the dominant view, the *lingua franca* of the discussion. This essay will highlight the

---

[34] Herman E. Daly, John B. Cobb, and Clifford W. Cobb, *For the Common Good: Redirecting the Economy toward Community, the Environment, and a Sustainable Future* (Boston: Beacon Press, 1989).

power and extent to which we use economic thought to describe the driving impulses motivating (and shaping) many of our personal and social decisions. However, it will also suggest possible limitations in this system of thought, which has become ingrained habit for industrial peoples. Rather than using theology to mold economics according to moral principles, I hope to expose the theological presuppositions underlying economic theory and judgments. I want to reintroduce these distant cousins within the university in the hope of gaining insight from their renewed conversation. Although economics and theology each has exercised a heavy influence on the other, these fields represent very different means of understanding the world. This difference in perspective should not be eradicated but recognized as an excellent means of overcoming the deficits implicit in each field of thinking, the blindness of each worldview. The value of adopting a multiplicity of views regarding the environment should not be underestimated. Taking a step back to consciously recognize the values that our economic system embodies is particularly important as these ideas take hold in China, Eastern Europe, Asia, and what we call the developing world.

These three subjects represent far more than areas of academic interest or measures of political loyalty. Economics, ecology, and theology all act as different languages, different systems of thought that form our understanding of the relation between individuals, societies, and the world. Each has its own creeds, its own concepts and variables proposed as essential for analysis. Each has a different set of criteria describing the good, the true, the beautiful.[35] They have different standards for defining success, acceptable loss, and disaster. Each of these fields has a tendency toward inflexibility, narrowness of thinking, and the manifestation of entirely unique limitations. In this manner, their differences are more extreme than those that exist between languages and cultures. These differences can also at times be more deceptive since communication between economists, ecologists, and theologians on the

---

[35] Economists since Adam Smith have been acutely conscious of beauty as manifested in the mathematical "elegance" of an economic formulation.

surface may seem relatively unhindered.[36] It is my intention to clarify the issues at stake in this dialogue and to benefit from the unique contributions of each of these fields.

The next chapter concerns the issues that have prevailed in most discussions of ecology and theology. This is presented in part to suggest the importance of recognizing both the results of our acquisitiveness and the centrality of economic reasoning in our understanding of the material world. Following this description of typical theological approaches to ecology will be a short introduction to the evolution of economics as a social science. Although all of the chapters address these three languages, the emphasis on each varies throughout the book. Untangling these themes and reconstituting their melodies represent a primary aim of the work that follows.

"What is man that thou art mindful of him?" These silent and imposing words are carved deeply into the brick building housing the philosophy department in Harvard Yard. They call to mind the all-powerful Godhead of the psalms and Ralph Waldo Emerson's famous essay, *Nature*, in which he presents the case for coming to know the Divine firsthand. Most universities across the country have similar quiet messages etched deeply into their very institutions, yet conveniently disregard them in the busyness of daily life. It takes a special kind of attentiveness to discern the questions of meaning that lurk behind the more technical problems that dominate much of our education. It requires a special vision to see behind the ivy of details covering the substance cut deeply into the marble foundations underneath.

Although theological conversation can become mired in arguments over specific dogmatic beliefs, this sort of attention, this discernment as we wrestle with our understanding of those things that have ultimate importance, is crucial. Like Jacob we must exhaust ourselves in wrestling with God and with our own questions. In putting aside partisan

---

[36] The sublanguages of these fields can often make communication difficult, as terms like "consumer choice matrix" or "watershed" or "homousia" provide practitioners of these various fields with jargon that often serves as shorthand for describing complicated topics.

disputes, perhaps we can begin to ask questions about those things that are most central in our lives, those things that we consider most worthwhile, most meaningful. The emphasis in theology on the ultimate concern, on our most closely held values, certainly makes it an excellent starting point in better understanding the dynamics of our environmental problems.

2

NATURE THEOLOGY

Ilkayoni

> In the time when God created all things, he created the sun.
> And the sun is born and dies and comes again.
> He created the moon,
> And the moon is born and dies and comes again.
> He created stars,
> And the stars are born and die and come again.
> He created man.
> And man is born and dies and comes not again.
> —Sudanese Prayer[1]

The Southern Cross shined brightly on the horizon over the terraced hills of the Machakos District in Kenya as we read Hemingway short stories out loud by flashlight and watched the summer meteor showers overhead. My friend and I had traveled fourteen thousand miles to surprise our college buddy and to abate his sense of loneliness at his remote Peace Corps site. After a long night under the unfamiliar constellations of Equatorial Africa, the giggles of local children woke us up just before dawn. As we arose, drenched with dew, we made an embarrassed retreat to my friend Nick's tin-roofed hut down the hill before the adults of Ilkayoni could notice our bizarre behavior. An evening spent watching the stars seems as odd to those Kenyans as a day spent on the high embankments of an American superhighway watching traffic jams would appear to us.

---

[1] George Appleton, *The Oxford Book of Prayer* (New York: Oxford University Press, 1985) 348.

Perhaps the most important thing for us living in industrial societies to recognize is the grand extent of what we take for granted. This includes not just the electricity, roads, or running water that these children lacked, nor any of the other wondrous benefits of living in a consumer society. The villagers of this town have a profoundly different understanding of the world that surrounds them, of their place in it, and of their ability to effect changes on it than do we.[2] Our distinction between the natural universe and the world of human concerns distances us from many societies in the world and from our own ancestors.[3]

There is a connection between the two senses in which we use the word "nature" both as synonymous with the environment and as a description of the intrinsic character or quality of a thing. Although the human power to radically alter and modify the world continues to accelerate, we still see the way that the world resists us. Many authors who share an interest in ecology devote a substantial amount of effort to defining exactly how we use the word "nature." But, the elusiveness of its complex usage makes this task unrewarding. The most common employment of this term today describes the world that encompasses humanity but is still relatively unmodified by us. Given the long, complicated, and often unconscious changes that we have effected on the natural world, the first sense of this term can never refer to an ideal state. Even in the most remote sections of California's San Joaquin Valley, where power lines, factories, water projects, roads, farms, and towns are entirely unseen, 63 percent of the grassland vegetation, 66 percent of the woodland vegetation, and 54 percent of the chaparral were introduced as a result of European settlement during less than two hundred years.[4] We modify the world even in our efforts to "preserve

---

[2] Love, family, respect, dignity, loyalty, and freedom have a different meaning in that culture, too.

[3] The distinction between humanity and the world, self, and other so deeply imbedded and enshrined in our consciousness and language can never be completely transcended. Our most basic conception of ourselves depends fundamentally upon this dualism.

[4] Alfred W. Crosby, *Ecological Imperialism: The Biological Expansion of Europe, 900–1900* (New York: Cambridge University Press, 1986) 154.

nature." The effects of humanity on our planet extend globally such that even wilderness areas like Yosemite or Yellowstone National Park must be managed by a host of scientific professionals to preserve their "natural" condition.

It is strange. The English language does not really have a word for it. "Environment" in some ways suggests that it is something entirely under control, a context defined by our wishes and needs. Environment sounds like the product of a detached scientific consciousness, like an independent variable. The word "nature" implies that it is something set apart from us when really nothing is.[5] The nature or the environment that theologians are concerned about includes both mountain meadows and downtown shopping malls. It applies to something more specific than the world but with more far-reaching effects than any particular ecosystem. In this instance, when no tool of language seems perfect for the task at hand, when humanism breaks down because the subject extends beyond the interest of the merely human, theologians introduce the idea of God.

Theologians and philosophers concerned about the environment expend much of their energy debating this definition and the question of how we should regard nature. Fluctuating like an electrical current between alternating poles, disputants first argue about humanity's distinctiveness from other species in our destructive capabilities and then about our total dependence on the non-human world. Human beings are both part of nature and yet alter it. These arguments ultimately must focus on judging human activity and on the nature of nature. Each of the philosophical and theological positions described in the following pages concentrates our attention on this direct relationship between human beings and the natural world. Each position describes a solution to environmental problems in which humanity as a whole comes to have a greater regard for the natural world. Other chapters will describe a different approach.

---

[5] R. G. Collingwood, *The Idea of Nature* (Oxford: Clarendon Press, 1945). Also Arthur O. Lovejoy, *Essays in the History of Ideas* (New York: Putnam, 1960).

There are no totally value-neutral positions in theology or in economics. Before facing these theological issues in earnest, I should write something about my own theological presuppositions. In the pages that follow, you will be reading a monotheistic theology written from an individual Christian's perspective. The arguments here make use of insights and illustrations from other religious traditions. The aim is to make arguments about meaning, economics, and nature as accessible to all faiths as possible, while still being honest about my own starting point. This text avoids making simple appeals to doctrine rather than reason in deciding among various theological positions. My primary point is that our economic language has begun to function in many ways like an ideology, a dogma that disables us as human beings by overly restricting the terms in which we see the natural world. I do not intend to replace economic ideology with a religious one but to consider ways of expanding the variety of models and language that we use to understand our condition and responsibility.

Over the last thirty years, religious thinkers have employed a variety of strategies in their efforts to articulate an environmental ethic. Biblical scholars have sought out scriptural texts that they believe are a mandate for greater sensitivity toward nature. Ethicists have drawn analogies between human rights and our understanding of the value of nature. Historians have searched the Christian record for exemplary saints and theologians concerned about the ethical treatment of animals and the appreciation of natural phenomena. Constructive theologians have attempted to introduce new metaphors that will result in a more sensitive treatment of the natural world. Other theologians have studied the effect of modern institutions on the environment (like politics or the economy) and have written liturgies intended to expand our awareness of our place within nature.

The next sections do not represent a complete survey of the rich and growing body of theological literature. Although Hindus, Buddhists, Jews, Christians, Muslims, Jains, native peoples, and others have done very important work, much of this must necessarily be passed over in the interest of brevity.[6] The theological models described below are included not to give an overview of the field but to show an important consideration that has been overlooked in this debate.

A change in season can lend an entirely new perspective to an afternoon walk in a Vermont forest, and will fundamentally alter our experience of its beauty. This next section affirms the great contributions made by theological and philosophical environmentalists but also attempts to see them in a different quality of light, in the altered shadows of a new season. We must attend more carefully to economic and political institutions if we intend to make progress with regard to the environment. I hope that this change in the direction of our insights and the focus of our attention will enable us to look at the issues lying behind environmental degradation with a new eye and a renewed vision.

A Secular Challenge

> Nature, the world has no value, no interest for Christians. The Christian thinks only of himself and the salvation of his soul.
> —Ludwig Feuerbach[7]

A history of environmental literature certainly is not appropriate here. Henry David Thoreau, James Fenimore Cooper, Susan Cooper, John Muir, Mary Austin, Aldo Leopold, Annie Dillard, Barry Lopez, and others have changed the meaning of nature for us and said something important about God as they did this. Most of what has been written about religion as an institution and nature, however, has been published since 1960. This growing body of thought originated in a debate about the culpability of Christianity in destroying nature. It has evolved from

---

[6] Harvard University Press with the Center for the Study of World Religions published a series of books based on conferences held at the university on ecology and the world religions (Buddhism, Hinduism, Judaism, Daoism, Christianity, Islam, Confucianism, Jainism). Dieter T. Hessel and Rosemary Radford Ruether, *Christianity and Ecology: Seeking the Well-Being of Earth and Humans* (Cambridge MA: Harvard University Press, 2000).

[7] Ludwig Feuerbach, *The Essence of Christianity*, trans. George Eliot (New York: Harper, 1957) 287.

rough, oversimplified pictures of a monolithic, irrationally destructive Christianity to a more nuanced vision of the historical record.[8] In later chapters, I hope to participate in this evolution by suggesting that mediating institutions like governments and economies need to be more carefully considered by scholars interested in understanding the relation between religious values and environmental well-being. Before attempting this, however, such an approach should be differentiated from work that has already been done.

In 1967, the historian Lynn White published an article that still vexes many theologians. Its contents remain thoroughly lodged in the thick of ecological debate. In his article titled, "The Historical Roots of our Ecologic Crisis," he outlines the moral culpability of Judaism and Christianity in fostering values destructive to the environment.[9] White held Western faith responsible for the exploitation of nature, which he said resulted from a constructed dichotomy that emphasizes the dominion of humanity over the rest of creation. For him, the terrible spirit of environmental destruction can be traced directly to God's command to humanity to "have dominion over the fish of the sea, the

---

[8] Nash argues that Judaism and Christianity are hostile to the very idea of wilderness. Stone and Eisler tell stories about a preliterate shared human past of gentle goddesses that was interrupted by violent monotheists worshipping nature-destroying male deities. Roderick Nash, *Wilderness and the American Mind* (New Haven: Yale University Press, 1967); Riane Tennenhaus Eisler, *The Chalice and the Blade: Our History, Our Future* (Cambridge MA: Harper & Row, 1987). Rosemary Radford Ruether offers a critical interpretation of the literature concerned about an exemplary woman-centered early age along with doubts of its historical validity in her book. Bron Raymond Taylor, *Dark Green Religion: Nature Spirituality and the Planetary Future* (Berkeley: University of California Press, 2010); Rosemary Radford Ruether, *Gaia and God: An Ecofeminist Theology of Earth Healing* (San Francisco: HarperSanFrancisco, 1992).

[9] Lynn White, Jr., "The Historical Roots of Our Ecologic Crisis," *Science* 155 no. 3767 (1967): 1,203–1,207. White taught medieval history and wrote his critique of Christianity's ecological consequences in a way that was deeply informed by his perspective as a faithful Christian.

birds of the air, and over every living thing that moves upon the earth."[10] White believed that our tendency to regard all life as being "at our disposal" arises from the monotheism that desacralizes nature. All theologies incorporating a unique human soul, or suggesting a possibility of human salvation, or representing the world as existing for human benefit, or claiming that humans were created in God's image were suspect according to his analysis.

Since then theologians have only intensified the general interest in this discussion through their voluminous responses and heated debate. While some theologians entirely agree with White's claims and seek to modify Western religion, many others search excitedly for proof texts to exonerate Jewish and Christian thought. Very few authors, however, asked whether this type of question represents the best way to correct for the devastating effects of environmental degradation.

How helpful is it to pinpoint the blame on ancient religious innovators who lived thousands of years ago? Can we hold responsible these ancient Hebrews who thought they were responding to a God who created the world and could not be adequately represented by anything in it? All of our culturally imbedded influences—from the Enlightenment to the US Constitution, from our understanding of history, our popular heroes, and the content of literature to our concepts of justice, rights, the individual, and love—all of these are so thoroughly intermixed with and influenced by each other that raising a finger of condemnation at one source or one group within society seems like a fairly futile undertaking.

The formation of our identity, the cultivation of our sense of self, incorporates an extraordinary variety of influences from tradition and, thus, requires us to admit that the sources of traits destructive to the environment cannot so easily be pinpointed. Furthermore, other elements of our cultural heritage may have a greater influence on our behavior in the modern age. Does religion or commerce, liturgical practices or advertising, sermons or sitcoms influence our treatment of

---

[10] Genesis 1:28. NRSV.

the environment more? Ultimately, the sources for our social behavior include the complex interrelation between each of these.

While Lynn White has certainly advanced our understanding of the cultural dimensions of our environmental problems, today we need more nuanced reflections that explain modern institutions and behavior. It is too easy to hold our ancestors and the biblical authors morally responsible for ecological standards that would have made little sense in their world and to ignore our own failings.[11] Debates over responsibility distract the participants from creatively seeking to adapt to a radically different condition in which a single species has the capability of destroying all others. Although White's contentions were offensive to many and thus deflected the debate, his historical understanding of the origination of our most common ideals can aid in elucidating our current position and in implementing change. Before beginning this discussion, however, we should note what many theologians share in common with White.

Sacred Earth

> Are Gaia, the living and sacred earth, and God, the monotheistic deity of the biblical traditions, on speaking terms with each other? — Rosemary Radford Ruether[12]

Perhaps the most controversial aspect of White's thesis was his criticism of Judaism and Christianity for displacing animism and pantheism, which he believed were more ecologically sound worldviews. His concern that the entire Earth should be considered sacred by humanity has been echoed by others as a panacea for our environmental ailments. By recognizing the divine element in all creatures and the inanimate

---

[11] Environmental change effected by human societies is as old as humanity. The deforestation of Greece and England, the species extinctions of the new world, and the extinction of fauna supporting human life on Easter Island provide only a few of many examples of large changes resulting from human activity. It is difficult to understand the complex cultural forces that led to these disasters.

[12] Ruether, *Gaia and God: An Ecofeminist Theology of Earth Healing*, 1.

matter that provides the foundation for our world, he hopes that individuals will begin to more enthusiastically seek to heal Earth of the ills inflicted by humanity.

Supporters of the Gaia hypothesis include a broad range of adherents who describe the entire Earth as a single self-regulating organism (with a neo-Hegelian cosmic consciousness).[13] Many make passionate arguments that our concept of the sacred should be expanded to embrace our entire planet. Similarly, some Christians have called for a more encompassing notion of the divine and have joined many seeking solutions in New Age, earth-centered religion. They have incorporated these views into tradition-bound Christianity. Pantheism, the notion that everything is God (as opposed to omnipresence, the idea that God is everywhere), has never been more popular. Both Christians and non-Christians have composed beautiful poetry and moving liturgies expressing this concern. They have cultivated a genuine ecological sensibility in their enthusiastic endorsement of the cause.

However, an understanding of Earth as sacred does have certain drawbacks as a general theological proposition. Many commentators today use the word "sacred" in an ambiguous way. Traditionally, God is regarded as divine, holy, as the creator. Parts of the world can be called holy and in a derived sense sacred.[14] Under this view it is hard to imagine what all-encompassing sacredness could mean. Etymologically, an all-inclusive sacrality contradicts the dualism inherent in the word's definition.

---

[13] "Gaia" is the name for the Greek Earth goddess and has been adopted by biologists to describe Earth as a single system, a unified organism. James Lovelock, *Gaia: A New Look at Life on Earth* (New York: Oxford University Press, 1987); ———, *The Ages of Gaia: A Biography of Our Living Earth* (New York: Norton, 1988); Lynn Margulis and Dorion Sagan, *Microcosmos: Four Billion Years of Evolution from our Microbial Ancestors* (New York: Summit Books, 1986); William Irwin Thompson, *Gaia, a Way of Knowing: Political Implications of the New Biology* (Great Barrington MA: Lindisfarne Press, 1987).

[14] Owen C. Thomas, *Introduction to Theology*, rev. ed. (Wilton CT: Morehouse-Barlow, 1983).

The Latin root of the word "sacred," *sacrum*, means belonging to, or in the power of, the gods. It refers to a cult ritual and the specific location of the sacrifice within the temple (*sacer*, or set apart from the surrounding space). *Profanum*, the root for our word "profane," referred to the sections of the temple where sacrificial animals would await the time of sacrifice. For the Romans, the sacred and the profane were each reciprocal parts of one temple. No value judgments were implicit within these terms (i.e., sacred as good, profane as bad). Each word was dependent upon the other for its definition. In order for a term such as "sacred" (or set apart as special) to make any sense, it must be set apart *from* something else. Defining everything as sacred is, thus, fundamentally inconsistent with the word's meaning.

The implications of this contradiction become clearer in concrete examples. In court decisions favoring increased timber "harvesting," attorneys have argued on the behalf of lumber companies that humans and their activities also constitute an element of the natural world. On a planet where everything is sacred, chainsaws and bulldozers could be revered in the same way that we respect burrowing owls and lodge pole pines. Universal sacrality as a theological principle does not necessarily include a means of distinguishing between saving national parks and preserving downtown parking structures. Such a theology leaves unaddressed all the difficulties of discerning the way that humans are part of nature and those qualities and characteristics that make us unique within the natural world.

The self-contradictory nature of an all-inclusive sacrality is only one shortcoming of this family of environmental metaphors. In some senses these views suffer from the same problem that humanism does in its application to environmental problems. When God is everything, the idea of God changes. This naturalizes the idea of God, and God becomes for us yet another object in a world of objects instead of the transcendent presupposition for all of creation. In this model it becomes too easy to make human beings the measure of all things since God is fundamentally no different than silent nature. When God is a physical entity, God becomes subject to human dominion, and we lose the radical sense in which we and our world depend on God.

The idea of an all-sacred world touches on the truth that our universe seems to display evidence of a greater consciousness at work than our own. It reminds us that we do not inhabit a dead mechanism or machine but rather a miraculous garden of life filled with breathtaking beauty. Unfortunately, it does not provide answers about how one should proceed in making environmental decisions, it has contradictory elements, and it comes close to suggesting that God's future is in our hands rather than the other way around.

Other Theologies

> The earth is the Lord's and all that is in it,
> the world and all who dwell therein. —Psalm 24:1[15]

Covenantal theology asserts that God is necessarily distinct from creation. Such a view regards God more as a distant personal agent (capable of entering into legal contracts) than as a planetary system or a creative impersonal power. Thinkers committed to this metaphor believe that human beings and God have already worked out an arrangement for looking after the world. God will provide the conditions for sustaining life. Human beings now have responsibility to care for it. Apocalyptic consequences are implied should humanity fail to live up to this promise. For Christian theologians, the tradition of the Hebrew Scriptures gives voice to this perspective, which they argue is expressed primarily in the creation accounts, the story of Noah, Moses, Second Isaiah, Enoch, Hosea, and Joel.[16] This theological notion of a contract or a legal agreement, however, is more deeply rooted in our social systems

---

[15] *The Book of Common Prayer*, 613.

[16] Bernhard Anderson, "Creation in the Noahic Covenant," in *Cry of the Environment: Rebuilding the Christian Creation Tradition*, ed. Philip N. Joranson and Ken Butigan, (Santa Fe NM: Bear, 1984); Robert Murray, *The Cosmic Covenant: Biblical Themes of Justice, Peace, and the Integrity of Creation* (London: Sheed & Ward, 1992).

than in our explicit understanding of the relation between human beings and nature.

Political philosophy and the law bear this biblical witness in their core system of assertions. For centuries sovereigns justified their right to rule through the notion of covenant, just as modern democracies legitimize government power in a similar manner. Thomas Hobbes (1588–1679), John Locke (1632–1704), and Jean-Jacques Rousseau (1712–1778) use political theories deeply indebted to covenantal notions of justice and fairness. Seventeenth-century philosophers, in particular, loved the idea of a social contract. Hobbes imagined what he called a state of nature without government, which he described as a "war of all against all" in which life was "solitary, poor, nasty, brutish, and short." For this reason, he argued that submitting to tyrants makes sense and is ultimately in our best interest. Locke believed in a milder form of social contract. He thought that we have inalienable rights to life, liberty, and property. We surrender certain rights like that of self-defense in order to have objective judges and punishments, and a generally more orderly society.[17] Although for some this way of thinking seems like an antiquated fantasy, a kind of unrealistic thought experiment, others today would argue that modern governments theoretically do derive their power from the consent of the governed. They might even regard this as having a biblical basis in the claim that God loves all human beings and, in particular, their freedom to decide their future. In American political discourse, we have become accustomed to the familiar promises of individual salvation in a nation set apart by a special covenant with God. Religious values and systems of meaning lie at the very heart of our political and economic organization.

Instead of scrutinizing the historical power of these ideas on our institutions, environmental theologians have sought to extend the metaphor. A few argue that natural entities should be included among those bound by God's covenant. Most, however, see the natural world as

---

[17] Thomas Hobbes, *Leviathan* (Charleston SC: Forgotten Books, 1976) 86. John Locke, *Two Treatises of Government*, ed. Peter Laslett, 2nd ed. (London: Cambridge University Press, 1967).

the *means* by which we show our loyalty to God. For those subscribing to this approach, the natural world represents the arena where God and human beings manifest their mutual and particular responsibilities. In scripture, a covenant binds God to preserving life on the planet and to maintaining order in the universe. Human beings as created in the image of God must then represent God's will on Earth and care for it.[18] The element of theodicy, or divine punishment, for human failures to act as promised represents an important element for many who articulate such a theology. Implicit in many environmental predictions of future doom is the motif of sin and just punishment. That human failures to care for the environment will be subject to retribution as manifested by nature's revolt seems to be suggested in many of these scenarios. Perhaps this metaphor's greatest beauty lies in its reciprocity and its familiarity to all societies that share a common tradition of binding contracts.

Indeed, scriptural religions and societies founded on legal principles could find this sort of theology especially appealing. Some Christian denominations have relied on this metaphor more than others. One important shortcoming of this way of understanding the relationship between human beings and the world is the historical bias that this view seems to imply. I doubt that many covenantal theologians believe that God created the world and then left it on its own until human beings arrived on the scene and took over its management. However, this view, familiar to us from deism and the "watchmaker" God of the natural theologians of past centuries, is just the sort of idea an ancient covenant

---

[18] The covenant decision as outlined in the Bible is a free decision in the sense that it is repeatedly offered, but there are more deterministic aspects to this theology also. God acts on the basis of covenants established earlier; these primordial contracts do not permit the current generation any real choice. They only affirm earlier decisions rather than originating free decisions. One may indeed rightfully wonder whether any contract between an individual and God (or a government for that matter) can be described as a choice. Human covenants made under duress are usually considered invalid. The possibility of reciprocal agreements with God or governments can certainly be questioned.

suggests.[19] Despite the use of this image in New Testament parables, I am not sure how many people of faith would subscribe to an idea of God as an absentee landlord who almost never acts on the world after it was finished on the sixth day. The stewardship model in part corrects for this implication and represents a third alternative to Earth as sacred and covenantal theologies.

The stewardship and the covenantal theological metaphors, despite quoting different texts of the Bible and their at times differing views of God, share many similarities. Long before ecology made front-page news, Walter C. Lowdermilk (1888–1974) described ecological stewardship as part of his eleventh commandment, which he attempted to popularize in the 1930s and 1940s.[20] Since then many theologians have advocated stewardship as a means of describing an ideal relationship between humanity and the surrounding world. They have cited Matthew 20:8, Luke 8:3, and John 2:8 as examples of human accountability to God for the environment.[21] This metaphor represents

---

[19] Deists (like John Toland [1670–1722], Matthew Tindal [1655–1733], and Voltaire [1694–1778]) hoped to entirely reconcile religious revelation with the demands of reason. This often led to a view of creation in which God set up natural and moral laws at the beginning and then left the system to run on its own. Although William Paley (1743–1805) himself did not invent the idea of God as the cosmic watchmaker (Voltaire himself used this illustration), he did much to popularize it. It articulates his argument for God's existence on the basis of the design of the world. If one found a watch on the heath, we would assume that someone made it. It did not just come into being through natural processes. Paley goes on at length to show that the "contrivances" we see in anatomy and nature are proof of the God who caused them to come into being. This static view that everything has already been designed also implies a relatively uninvolved God. William Paley, *Natural Theology; or Evidences of the Existence and Attributes of the Deity, Collected from the Appearances of Nature* (London: F. C. and J. Rivington, 1822).

[20] Roderick Nash, *The Rights of Nature: A History of Environmental Ethics* (Madison WI: University of Wisconsin Press, 1989).

[21] Matthew 20:8 is from the parable of the landowner hiring workers for the vineyard. Luke 8:3 is an obscure reference to followers of Jesus ("and Joanna, the wife of Herod's steward Chuza, and Susanna, and many others, who

God as the rightful master of the world. Humanity, as God's lieutenant or valet, must care for it. Jesus' parables about absent owners and loyal overseers are interpreted as reminders to modern Christians of their proper place and of the humility appropriate for a servant.

Douglas John Hall, in his book *The Steward: A Biblical Symbol Come of Age,* describes the primary characteristics of the steward:

> One pole—the positive one, if you like—is the close identification of the steward with his master. The steward can be regarded almost as the representative or vicar of the one who has employed him— though he is only a servant, perhaps even technically a slave or (like Joseph) virtually a prisoner. The other (negative) pole is the insistence that the steward is not, after all, the owner or master. He is strictly accountable to his lord, and he will certainly be deprived of his authority unless he upholds, in his actions and attitude, the true character and wishes of this other one whom he is allowed to represent.[22]

Stewardship and covenant share these themes of accountability and the special responsibility that humans have as creatures set apart by God from the world. Advocates of stewardship as an environmental ideal point out that human beings have already acquired such a dominant role in every ecosystem on the planet and that the metaphor of management, for good or ill, is unavoidable.

However, many people in the environmental movement see this last understanding of humanity as destructive arrogance and manifest concern with any vision describing the natural world only as a means of incurring divine favor and not as important for its own sake.[23] Ruth

---

provided for them out of their resources"). John 2:8 is from the story of the wedding in Cana, when the newly made wine is brought to the steward.

[22] Douglas John Hall, *The Steward: A Biblical Symbol Come of Age* (Grand Rapids MI: W.B. Eerdmans, 1990) 34.

[23] Theologians may want to be more careful about which biblical accounts they use to express their concerns. Biblical scholar Theodore Hiebert writes that the Genesis 1 creation account cannot be interpreted as a healthy example of stewardship. Instead this text should be read as a projection of the priestly writer's own view of his class as uniquely representing God's authority on Earth.

Page argues that while "steward" might be a better image than "exploiter" or "consumer," ultimately this leaves human beings in a dominating position with respect to the rest of creation. A view whose loftiest ideal is this kind of environmental management ultimately perpetuates what she calls "a culture of control."[24]

Although the poetic beauty of theologies that call for tending God's garden is often striking, the faith in human ability to understand and control the mysterious and complex forces of the environment may be an unhealthy exaggeration. Care and control are frequently confused. The intricacies and subtle relationships among ocean currents and atmosphere, soil and sunlight, electrons, seagulls, desert, snow, chaparral, mountains, mites, magnesium, and all of those entities composing our rich world are not adequately accounted for through comparison with a garden or household. Although human beings produce chemicals with the persistency of DDT (which is found in virtually every habitat, as measured in tissue samples from Arctic penguins to creatures inhabiting our most desolate deserts), we will never be able to fully understand or to mediate for the effects of its introduction. The illusions of human control in a world of decreasing biological and cultural diversity are particularly dangerous as new technologies rapidly homogenize human lifestyles globally.[25] This

---

Hiebert recommends that ecotheologians should instead consult the Genesis 2–3 tradition, which represents human beings as farmers in solidarity with creation. Theodore Hiebert, "The Human Vocation: Origins and Transformations in Christian Traditions," in *Christianity and Ecology: Seeking the Well-Being of Earth and Humans*, ed. Dieter T. Hessel and Rosemary Radford Ruether, 135–154 (Cambridge MA: Harvard University Center for the Study of World Religions, 2000) 135.

[24] Ruth Page, *God and the Web of Creation* (London: SCM Press, 1996). She quotes Nigel Cooper in her discussion of a "culture of control" on p. xiii.

[25] The broadcast media certainly decrease the regional differences within the United States as individuals have a higher level of exposure to characters on the screen and associate less with the people who live near them. American films, with all of the consumer products typical in an upper-middle-class North American household, are shown globally in theaters from Nairobi to New Delhi promoting a specific concept of the good life. Jet travel, communications

increases the demand for specific products, and quickly disseminates the effects of their use. Mass production has new meaning in a world of seven billion consumers, many of whom are anxious to keep abreast of the latest changes in style and gadgetry.

This new reality in which human cultural changes have global effects requires a fundamental reorientation in how we understand the relation between the world and us. Even the changes that environmentalists have fought hardest for have had completely unpredictable effects. The reforestation of the northeastern United States in this last century and the suburbanization of its population have brought human beings closer to nature, but they have also brought about an unforeseen resurgence of tick-borne diseases like Rocky Mountain Spotted Fever and Lyme disease. Ecological systems and human behavior are sufficiently complex that we can never control nature.[26] Larry Rasmussen describes the planet as more like a room that needs to be made safe for infants than it is like a spaceship with a competent pilot at the controls.[27]

Emil Brunner's comment that "the worst state of man is that in which he has complete confidence in himself" may be particularly appropriate in our embrace of scientific technology as the only solution to our problems.[28] We expect that even environmental ills caused by advanced technology will be abated through future discoveries. Although this indeed is the case for some problems, such an optimism will have devastating effects on the generations that follow. We have created millions of tons of radioactively unstable compounds with half-lives of thousands of years for weapons and our insatiable energy production needs without knowing how to dispose of them. In nature we still are discovering industrial pollutants with terrible potency but whose source still eludes us. Researchers discovered a greenhouse gas that is 18,000

---

technology, and greater mobility within the population also serve to homogenize global demand for industrially produced goods.

[26] Arno Karlen, *Biography of a Germ* (New York: Pantheon Books, 2000).

[27] Larry L. Rasmussen, *Earth Community Earth Ethics* (Maryknoll NY: Orbis Books, 1996).

[28] Emil Brunner, *The Divine Imperative*, trans. Olive Wyon (Philadelphia: The Westminster Press, 1947) 71.

times as powerful in its heat retaining capacity as carbon dioxide and which is increasing in its concentration by 6 percent each year. Theologies of the future will need to correct for our overconfidence and better account for our limitations.[29]

Ecofeminist theologians have probably done more than any others to expose the role of power in our consideration of nature. They are the first to point out that words like "covenant," "stewardship," or "management" obscure the hubris that takes lightly human decisions on behalf of all creation. Their distrust of metaphors that legitimate and domesticate even a responsible vision of domination has enhanced the discussion. Rosemary Radford Ruether describes ecofeminism as the examination of interconnections between the domination of women and the domination of nature. She bluntly states that "[s]tewardship is not a primal command, but an ex post facto effort of dominant males to correct overabuse and become better managers of what they have presumed to be their patrimony…the world."[30] Although many other ecofeminists might disagree with her, she is sharply critical of any idea of paradise in the past or future, up above or here below. For her, this kind of idealism inevitably leads to a desire to transcend our finite limitations through the domination and exploitation of others.

While some might find this an exceptionally liberating vision, other orthodox believers of different faiths will have difficulty accepting her connection between paradise and oppression. Regardless of this point, however, the ecofeminist ideal lacks specificity in proposing an alternative way to make decisions about nature. Certainly relationships characterized by some subtle degree of power and domination will persist. How much of this can we live with? What political plan would

---

[29] Andrew L. Revkin, "Potent New Greenhouse Gas Is Found, But It's Quite Rare," *The New York Times*, 28 July 2000. Although terms such as "sin" and "fallenness" may best describe this aspect of the human experience, perhaps their usage is not as inspiring as these other metaphors.

[30] Rosemary Radford Ruether, "Ecofeminism: The Challenge to Theology," in *Christianity and Ecology: Seeking the Well-Being of Earth and Humans,* ed. Dieter T. Hessel and Rosemary Radford Ruether (Cambridge MA: Harvard University Press, 2000) 104.

move us closer to this nurturing model? Presumably sinfulness cannot simply be reformed out of us, so how should sin be addressed by society?

Ecofeminists continue to work on just these sorts of questions. Despite this, there might be a larger issue that environmentalists have failed to consider adequately. Global sacrality, stewardship, covenant, and ecofeminism all share a common assumption. They all presume that the evils of environmental destruction can be mitigated by re-appropriating symbols in order to suggest a more perfect relationship between humanity and the natural world. In this, they tend to associate our most deadly environmental atrocities with God's commandment in Genesis to have dominion over the Earth (Genesis 1:28). This direct approach, which associates environmental destruction with human attitudes about the natural world, characterizes the majority of efforts to reverse trends that could prove so devastating to our environment. Other theologians, such as H. Paul Santmire, use different metaphors but with the same intention.[31] While these searches for an eco-metaphor occupy theologians, several popular philosophers use a similar strategy. They assume that if human beings care more *about* the natural world, then they will necessarily take better care *of* it. Before proceeding to describe a different means of understanding the problem, these other popular approaches to environmentalism should be mentioned briefly.

Deep Ecology

> Why, here is Walden... It is the work of a brave man surely, in whom there was no guile! He rounded this water with his hand, deepened and clarified it in his thought, and in his will bequeathed it to Concord. I see by its face that it is visited by the same reflection; and I can almost say, Walden, is it you? —Henry David Thoreau[32]

---

[31] H. Paul Santmire, *The Travail of Nature: The Ambiguous Ecological Promise of Christian Theology* (Philadelphia: Fortress Press, 1985). In his book, Santmire describes two ecological biblical motifs (fecundity and migration to good land) and one anti-ecological motif (ascent).

[32] Henry David Thoreau, *The Illustrated Walden*, ed. J. Lyndon Shanley (Princeton NJ: Princeton University Press, 1973) 193.

As this chapter's first example illustrates, the language of environmentalism reveals much about the motivation of its various proponents. Just as our use of the word "nature" reveals a firmly engrained dichotomy concerning human intervention in the world, other terms similarly disclose much about our basic assumptions. Perhaps the most enduring class of these includes the words that describe various ecosystems as "resources" that need to be preserved. The proliferation of both academic and governmental departments of natural resources and arguments that refer to environmental "goods" provides an important insight into our primary understanding of the environment's role with respect to human society. The rhetorical richness of this language as used by the Department of Forestry and proponents of preservation introduces the primary point of contention that many popular eco-philosophers have raised in the last thirty years.

They argue that nature has intrinsic value. Rivers should not remain undammed, because they are scenic, or provide good fishing, or because they are an important source of water for those far downstream, or because people will lose the use of valuable land to flooding. Rivers and other natural features and species relatively unmodified and unmolested by humans should be saved because they have value in themselves. These environmentalists oppose unrestrained exploitation, resource conservation, resource development, resource preservation, and use of language that suggests that natural entities exist primarily for human use. Deep ecologists, bio-centricists, eco-centricists, and anti-humanists all emphasize that the world surrounding us has value apart from human experience of it. Since neither the specific points of difference between these schools of thought, nor a more careful examination of their voluminous publications, will be helpful here, we will consider only the general thrust of these ideas.

Arne Naess (1912–2009), a distinguished mountaineer and Norwegian philosopher, first coined the term "deep ecology" in 1972 in an effort to differentiate the human centeredness of "resource" conservation ecological motivations (shallow ecology) from ecological models that understood the environment as intrinsically valuable (deep ecology).

Deep ecologists continue to argue that justifying environmental efforts on the basis of human interest represents an intolerable arrogance. They assert that human beings have no philosophically viable claim to privilege over other biological beings or other physical entities. George Sessions and Arne Naess (who both looked to Gandhi and Spinoza for inspiration) suggested the following eight-plank platform as representative of the basic principles of deep ecology:

1. The well-being and flourishing of human and nonhuman life on Earth have value in themselves. These values are independent of the usefulness of the nonhuman world for human purposes.

2. Richness and diversity of life forms contribute to the realization of these values and are also values in themselves.

3. Humans have no right to reduce this richness and diversity except to satisfy vital needs.

4. The flourishing of human life and culture is compatible with a substantial decrease of the human population. The flourishing of nonhuman life requires such a decrease.

5. Present human interference with the nonhuman world is excessive, and the situation is rapidly worsening.

6. Policies must therefore be changed. These policies affect basic economic, technological, and ideological structures. The resulting state of affairs will be deeply different from the present.

7. The ideological change is mainly that of appreciating life quality (dwelling in situations of inherent value) rather than adhering to an increasingly higher standard of living. There will be a profound awareness of the difference between big and great.

8. Those who subscribe to the foregoing points have an obligation directly or indirectly to try to implement the necessary changes.[33]

---

[33] Bill Devall and George Sessions, *Deep Ecology: Living As If Nature Mattered* (Salt Lake City: Gibbs Smith, 1985).

Other deep ecologists summarize these by arguing that the movement can be spiritually conceptualized as the striving for an expanded sense of self, beyond the isolated ego, to include all things.[34] This gets us back to Earth as sacred notion. It argues for dissolving the conceptual boundaries between self, God, and the world. For these authors, ecology can be understood almost as a religious pilgrimage, a journey in which the devotee works toward transcending the very boundaries of her soul. They hope that when our relationship with the natural world is at the center of our identity, the environment will be holy, not just a material "resource" that has a particular use. These activists employ language that many would use to describe the human desire for salvation, the pilgrim's quest for enlightenment. The ideal person for them, thus, has an expanded sense of caring. These arguments against anthropocentrism generally advocate a broader field of human concern that extends beyond humanity, beyond all animals and plants to include rivers, mountains, deserts, and our atmosphere. They combat a faith in material progress with their own doctrines, their own conceptions of human well-being.

Just as it was not necessary for the purpose of this essay to further explore the specific details of ecophilosophy, in fairness the arguments against it will be only briefly summarized here. Philosopher Warwick Fox lists objections to intrinsic value approaches to the environment (such as deep ecology).[35] He classifies these in four categories, including arguments relating to the possibility, the necessity, the logic, and the practical consequences of deep ecology. Although each of these represents an important category for criticizing intrinsic value theories,

---

[34] Warwick Fox, *Toward a Transpersonal Ecology: Developing New Foundations for Environmentalism* (Boston: Shambhala, 1990). The bibliography of this book is a particularly useful source for texts relating to deep ecology.

[35] Fox, *Toward a Transpersonal Ecology: Developing New Foundations for Environmentalism*, 114.

perhaps the most significant of these is the first. In what sense is it possible to transcend anthropocentrism?[36]

As limited creatures, human beings lack the ability to conceive of nonhuman systems of meaning. Intrinsic meaning thus depends in some manner upon a human observer or judgment, since meaning is a particularly human conception. We must therefore be careful to recognize that our concern for our descendants or for species extinction must always find its basis within our own constructions of meaning, just as does our desire for a higher standard of living. Differentiating between a rainforest's intrinsic value and that of a canning plant similarly depends on human systems of meaning—other such systems simply are not available to us. To distinguish the difference in the intrinsic value of a toxic chemical factory and the frigid waters of an alpine lake requires a human observer and her moral imagination. Human beings' identity and capacity for ethical judgment arise out of our role in communities.

This argument against the possibility of the intrinsic value ideal (as held by deep ecologists) has been sorely criticized. These critics charge that just because only human beings have developed meaning systems, this does not mean that nature can have no intrinsic value. We can understand better what it means for nature to have or not to have intrinsic value from the following thought experiment. Suppose I said, "I'm going to stop thinking like a human being right now." This would be true in the sense that I can try to imagine the inner life of a squirrel, for instance. I could try to picture what the world looks like from above on a slender oak tree branch, or I could imagine the gnawing hunger it might feel after a long winter, or its pain after being caught in a trap. It would be false, however, if I were to mistake my imaginative efforts for the way in which a squirrel really experiences the world.

---

[36] The most popular arguments against deep ecology are those concerned with perceived misanthropic tendencies (as especially implied by philosophies such as anti-humanism). Many disputants argue that these ecophilosophies are intrinsically misanthropic.

In short, things can have intrinsic value in the sense that they do not need to have human worth in order to be valuable. However, as a question, intrinsic value for whom or what cannot be avoided. We are not able to transcend the limits of our own humanity. We cannot simply choose to cease seeing the world from our own point of view. We can imagine the inherent worth of a thing but we can only do this as human beings. Our conclusions will always be subject to debate because we simply do not have access to an independent God's-eye view. The ethical importance of trying to imagine the needs of other beings and entities is part of the reason why the idea of God or "Nature" is so important to the environmental debate. It is the reason scientific data about climate change or species extinction is not enough. The idea of God or Nature or Gaia helps to connect our understanding of value to the environment and to the institutions that structure our treatment of it. A theological vocabulary may help to clarify questions of value in a world in which economic judgments of it seem to be overwhelming us.

Many strains of ecophilosophy represent secular versions of Earth as sacred theology and are subject both to the same limitations and the same benefits. All intrinsic value approaches ultimately must include careful criteria for making judgments in order to be practically useful. A tendency toward the absurd has always marred the debate over deep ecology. If we truly value all things equally and a flower has as much worth as a human being, how do we decide what we can eat? Should Picasso have left the organic compounds in his paints undisturbed in nature? Furthermore, despite frequent criticisms of Western individualism, it is interesting that even the most anti-individualist philosophers express themselves in primarily individual terms. The deep ecologists' concern with self-actualization and individual rights cannot be extracted so easily from the complicated web of thought that they seek to criticize.

Deep ecologists seem fascinated with arguments based on endowing natural phenomena with the rights that we typically reserve only for human beings. Claiming that a wild river or a section of redwood forest has an intrinsic right to continue undamaged by human activity is one way of expressing how something can have non-instrumental value. John

Locke's social contract that emphasizes individual self-sufficiency and the primacy of the independent ego therefore seems like an unusual source for these modern arguments against atomism. The environmentalist's goal of eliminating (in a philosophical sense) the boundary separating self from other seems to be quite naturally at odds with any sort of approach that uses natural rights. The tension between these two suggests how deeply atomistic and individualistic thinking permeate our society.

Environmentalists may take for granted the individualistic presuppositions that they believe distort our everyday economic thinking. However, even in our attempts to transcend our own ego, we have difficulty considering value or worth in any other terms than those that presume a particularly lonely individualism. Ultimately, any analysis that depends on "the rights of nature" also must reflect the individualistic nature of our society. When we feel compelled to translate concepts like respect, worth, and dignity into the legal language of individual rights, it is time to recognize the extent to which we ourselves are limited by our own narrowly atomized view.

Despite its controversial claims, ecophilosophical discussion both has brought attention to the environmental crisis and has pointed out many of the flaws inherent in resource conservation environmentalism. The idea that all things are valuable in their self-expression counterbalances the pervasive utilitarian values of our age that make usefulness to industrial society the only criterion of worth. The contribution of deep ecology to a broader understanding of the value that natural features and species have apart from human use certainly represents a timely argument in a world in which biological diversity is rapidly decreasing and our atmosphere, forests, soil, rivers, etc. are being depleted quickly.

Crisis and Criticism

> As history has gradually replaced theology, so science has replaced philosophy. —Carl Becker[37]

When we hear about the environmental crisis, we should remember that the ancient Greeks used the word *krisis* to mean judgment. Difficult times require us to make shrewd decisions, to overcome both our tender-minded and tough-minded tendencies. In these moments, we are judges and judged. While some of the theological and ecophilosophical responses listed above may initially seem to be both radically different from each other and even at times mutually antagonistic, they all share several methodological assumptions. Implicit in each of these approaches is the hope that a new way of considering humanity's relationship with the natural world will lead us to exercise better care for it. This focus on the direct regard that humanity has for the environment represents the most popular means of diagramming solutions for ecological problems. Although the importance of "pulling" humanity toward greater care for the world is often recognized, very few approaches as explicitly address the push of social forces.

The way human beings act in social situations ironically may be more important to the environment than their genuine sense of care for it. Pollution and other forms of environmental degradation do not occur because a majority of our population supports such practices, but because many of our socially formed goals and aspirations remain fundamentally incompatible with a clean environment. Social values relating to status, concepts of success, material acquisition, birth control, economic growth, personal entitlement, and our ideal of the good life represent the fundamental barriers to a healthily functioning world. Although cultivating a greater sense of care for the environment may be one way to redirect human activity, closer attention to social forces and the power of historically formed values could be a more effective means

---

[37] Carl Becker, *The Heavenly City of the Eighteenth-Century Philosophers* (New Haven: Yale University Press, 1932).

of bringing about significant change than looking beyond our social lives in an attempt to redeploy metaphors or philosophical ideals.

Theological and philosophical theories that posit special human antagonism toward the environment or deep historical drives to dominate or enslave nature (whether originating in anthropocentric thinking or in our biblical heritage) do not seem true to actual experience.[38] George H. W. Bush, in four years changed from calling himself the environmental president to acting as the environmental legislation moratorium president and was thus considered by many environmentalists to be the archenemy of the natural world. [39] After failing to be re-elected, he announced plans to spend his retirement fishing and enjoying the outdoors. North Americans do not need theology or philosophy to aid them in appreciating the environment as much as they need a system of meaning that enables them to find value in activities that do not damage the natural world. We need a politics that better expresses our passion for the outdoors. We need to recognize that values we learn in the social world lead to the degradation of our environment.

H. Paul Santmire and many others, including Lynn White, deplore "spiritual" biblical interpretations and theologies because they do not value the natural world highly enough.[40] Ironically, promoting devotion

---

[38] Although environmental consciousness has been increasing along with our awareness of the extraordinary changes that humans have been making globally, these assumptions also overestimate the extent to which we recognize the effects of our behavior. While the marginal damage of individual wastefulness is shared, we receive the benefits of the activities that generated the waste in total.

[39] President H.W. Bush, during the last months of his presidency, both refused to be a part of the first global assembly of nations addressing the environmental crisis (the Earth Summit in Brazil, during 1992) and promised to veto any environmental legislation, saying, "I don't want to be part of a bad deal. I want to protect the environment and the growth of this country." This environmental legislation moratorium included opposition to goals limiting the emission of ozone depleting chemicals that had been ratified by every other major industrialized country.

[40] Santmire, *The Travail of Nature: The Ambiguous Ecological Promise of Christian Theology.*

over consumerism may actually represent a more successful strategy in certain cases than attempting to incorporate an explicit love for nature within our theologies. The Disneyland near Tokyo attracts as many visitors each year as Mecca or the Vatican.[41] If the North American public could be convinced to spend forty hours in prayer and two hours on the job, rather than our current arrangement, the environment would most likely be better off than if they continued to work for forty hours a week with a more appreciative concern for the natural world. Although this is an absurd example, it does illustrate the relative importance of our opinions regarding the natural world to other values we hold that do not explicitly relate to the environment, but that actually may have a greater influence on its well-being.

Americans on average spend six hours per week shopping. They go to shopping centers, on average, once per week. This is more often than they visit churches, temples, or synagogues. In a survey, 93 percent of American teenage girls cited shopping as their favorite pastime. This may be appropriate to our social goals since the number of shopping centers exceeds the number of high schools.[42] Perhaps egocentricism rather than anthropocentricism, our regard for our place in social systems rather than our disregard for ecosystems, represents more likely sources of our environmental woes. The media does not receive billions of dollars per week to promote an explicit hatred of nature, but to fan the flames of desires cultivated and nurtured by our experiences within society. Ironically perhaps, promoting the public's interest in the natural world may be less helpful for the environment than dampening our ambitions to earn and produce more.

Another common oversight of prevailing ecophilosophies and ecotheologies is an often exclusive concern with all of humanity rather than a recognition that responsibility for our environmental problems is not evenly distributed. Although individualism probably represents one of many sources for environmental disaster, we must also recognize that

---

[41] Alan Thein Durning, *How Much Is Enough: The Consumer Society and the Future of the Earth* (London: Earthscan, 1992).

[42] Alan Durning, "Asking How Much Is Enough.".

not all people are equally responsible for the crisis. Anthropocentrism, by definition, does not differentiate between humans but rather aggregates them into one whole. Behind this characterization of the problem is the implicit assumption that human beings work for the benefit of each other, that the battle lines are drawn simply between human and nonhuman species. However, according to some estimates, North Americans consume on an individual basis thirty-five times the amount of citizens in developing nations.[43] Human beings are not as anxious to help other members of their species in a way that the word "anthropocentricism" may suggest. Furthermore, not all of humanity suffers the effects of environmental degradation equally. In the United States, three-fifths of all African Americans and people of Hispanic descent live in communities with uncontrolled toxic waste sites.[44] In grouping all of Earth's inhabitants together (as anthropos), we miss the extent to which people suffer differently in kind and degree from Uzbekistan to Namibia, New York City to Love Canal, Death Valley to the Sahel.

Too narrowly focusing on the direct relationship between human beings and the natural world (rather than on the importance of mediating institutions) leads us into absurd arguments. Rather than recognizing the impact of measuring a country's well-being in terms of its economic growth, for example, we frame the argument around whether or not burrowing owls or snail darters are as important as people. A radical response in this debate does nothing to educate people that such an opposition is false (in reality, it most often is a contest between a few people's economic benefit and the habitat of the owls). By stating that certain animals, insects, etc. should have an equal right to exist, we deflect debate from the excesses of our own extravagant

---

[43] Language relating to the environment is not the only example of economic classifications implied in our most common language. We divide the world up on the basis of economic success in our use of words such as "developing" or "less-developed" nations.

[44] Carol Robb and Carl J. Casebolt, eds., *Covenant for a New Creation: Ethics, Religion, and Public Policy* (Mary Knoll, New York: Orbis Books, 1991).

consumer lifestyles (which cause more environmental damage than our mere existence).

Theological methods emphasizing the mediating role of social institutions and culture do not replace more poetic theologies designed to inspire a greater regard for the natural world. A careful inquiry into the sources of our values and the determination of social goods reveals how we need to adjust to our radically new situation. Our environmental problems do not arise out of biological or cultural necessity, but rather out of historical and social circumstances. The long gaze of theology, with a vision that sees across centuries, can discern the impermanence of social structures and values that many through history have taken utterly for granted. Institutions and ideals that evolved out of a world in which environmental stability could be taken for granted may no longer be useful in *our* rapidly changing world. Lightning-quick technological change means that these traits and ideas (including our concept of the individual, personal success, property, and selfhood) may have maladaptive elements in our time. Environmental theologies must be related more concretely to this complex social structure. They must address the powerful conditioning and the systems of meaning that motivate our consumer habits in the industrial world if they are to be successful in their aims.

In the next chapter, theology's concern with ultimate meaning will give way to the economist's more pragmatic focus on material things. Indeed the richness of what archaeologists describe as material culture certainly sets apart our age. Not only do we seem to do very little for ourselves, when compared with our distant ancestors, we cannot even keep track of what others do for us, or even from where the things in our daily lives come. How many of us know where the water that supplies our neighborhood was between the time when it fell from the skies and when it came out of our faucet (from what watershed or aquifer is the rainwater collected, in which reservoir was it stored before being piped to our homes)? Where was the food we ate this morning grown? Not many modern people in North America know where the banana and the grains in our cereal, the margarine on our bread, the sugar in our tea, the melon that we snacked on, and the countless other things typical in our diet come from before being delivered to our grocery store. How and where is the electricity that you are using right now generated? Where does your sewage go after it leaves your home? Where were your paper and plastic bags, the other packaging that you consumed, the glass in your windows, the materials used in making the furniture in the room where you sit, the components in your television, your ballpoint pen, your alarm clock, and all the other things that you used today manufactured? Where was the fuel that you burned today refined? Where were the cotton and other fibers in the clothes that you are wearing grown? Where were the filaments in your car's headlights made? Even if you live very simply, your life is connected to an international network of trade. The daily things around you have been gathered and combined from places around the world and represent the labor of an extraordinary number of people.

In the beginning of his short book on Confucianism, Herbert Fingarette describes magic as "the power of a specific person to accomplish his will directly and effortlessly through ritual, gesture, and incantation."[45] He explains further that "the user of magic does not work by strategies and devices as a means toward an end; he does not use coercion or physical force. There are no pragmatically developed and tested strategies or tactics. He simply wills the end in the proper ritual setting and with the proper ritual gesture and word; without further effort on his part, the deed is accomplished."

Fingarette is writing about religious ritual. This is what happens when a collection of individuals becomes the body of Christ in the shared meal of the Eucharist. It is true in more ordinary, everyday circumstances, too. When we go to the store to buy a new tire for our car, we do not do the labor of a Brazilian rubber tapper, or physically make the bands of Korean steel that support its construction, nor do we coordinate all the transportation necessary to bring the natural materials to a manufacturing site and the finished product to our neighborhood.

---

[45] Herbert Fingarette, *Confucius: The Secular as Sacred* (New York: Harper & Row, 1972) 3.

We only give the clerk money and everything is done for us. Surely the coordination of production and transportation by markets and prices is magic.

In our times, perhaps economists are right in their almost religious devotion to price as a cosmic regulating factor (a faith perhaps stronger than that of some theologians). In the twentieth century, markets and prices knit together a truly global civilization based on commerce. The specialization and productivity enabled by technology and organized by market prices seem to be the hallmarks of the modern age. Ordering our most complex decisions and guiding our most important policies, economics has been a faithful servant to the challenges of our time.

3

SOCIAL VALUES AND ECONOMICS

Kilimanjaro

Capitalism is a wholly new phenomenon in history...in the main it is not based on material and technological developments... but upon phenomena of a moral order... —Emil Brunner[1]

At 2:00 A.M. I had probably been asleep for only about half an hour when the guides broke my brief slumber for the final climb to Mt. Kilimanjaro's snowy peak. Although I slept wearing every single article of clothing that I had brought with me on my summer trip to Africa (including several pairs of cotton socks on each hand), my blood still felt the icy touch of the high altitude just as my head pounded from the change in pressure that accompanies 19,000 feet of elevation. The stars outside our hut pierced through the clear night sky like knifepoints through brilliant blue cloth and distracted me from the discomfort that had been the constant focus of my attention for the last twelve hours. The night air and the frigid silence were ideal companions as I first surveyed the broken rocks and porous sands that dwarfed the tiny hut that had protected us that night from the mountain's sharp winds.

After only an hour of climbing, the moon emerged from Kilimanjaro's flank and illuminated, in colorless detail and long shadows, the desolate lunar landscape that surrounded us. Ascending the scree slope, we passed over boulders and gravel-sized stones at a slow pace as we followed the switchbacks cut deeply into the side of the mountain and looked out toward the steep rock cliffs of our peak's much smaller twin across a desolate valley. A young investment banker and his fiancée suffering the blinding headaches and violent stomach pains of altitude sickness deserted our small party and retreated back

---

[1] Brunner, *The Divine Imperative*, 417.

down the mountain before 4:00 A.M. Reaching the peak just in time to see the red glow in the glacial snow reflecting the rising sun, we stretched out exhausted on long flat rocks. Far above the clouds, we seemed to be alone on our mountainous island as the sun broke through the razor-thin horizon and slowly painted the eastern skies with light.

Our illusion of solitude, however, could hardly have been further from the truth. Global climate change is melting the perennial snows of Kilimanjaro. Before it is gone, every effort will be made to exploit this place. The government of Tanzania recognizes Kilimanjaro as a marvelous business opportunity and profits generously at the expense of thousands of tourists who visit this mountain each year from all over the globe. High fees levied for each day spent in the park, required porters and guides, and other administrative fees ensure a high return on this natural resource.[2] Unfortunately, the crowds that visit the mountain with the help of erosion have left deep trenches where trails used to be and garbage in the mountain's most sensitive habitats. The government of this small equatorial country has had difficulty managing both the use of the mountain and its struggling economy.

The special ability of economics to manage, predict, and explain social scientific phenomena leads Paul Samuelson and William Nordhaus to describe it (on the first page of the most popular introductory economics textbook in history) as "queen of the social sciences—oldest of the arts, newest of the sciences."[3] Indeed, as these two authors continue to explain, we will "from cradle to grave and beyond run up against the brute truths of economics." The influence of economic theory in political debates, policy decisions, and academic course selections represents only a small sampling of the pervasiveness of this type of thinking. Our leading universities certainly must employ more economists than scholars from any other discipline. Economists

---

[2] For instance, park guards are required to deny all users entrance after noon, thus ensuring a high occupancy in the state-owned (and very expensive) hostel, which represents the only accommodation near the park's gates.

[3] Paul A. Samuelson and William D. Nordhaus, *Economics*, 12th ed. (New York: McGraw-Hill, 1985) 3.

Economics, Ecology, and God

swell the ranks of business schools, law schools, schools of government, and public policy, as well as the traditional departments in the social sciences. In our age, as the sun of theology sinks lower on the horizon and popular interest in philosophy wanes, economics represents our primary manner of understanding our relationship with the material world. Our culturally and historically peculiar association of price as equivalent to value marks the modern condition in which virtually all material things, from ancient forests, sacred burial sites, or stained glass windows, to modern art or artificial hearts, can be converted into money and exchanged. As the primary and formal study of the relation between individuals, societies, and the world, it represents particularly fruitful grounds for understanding the environmental crisis.

Similarities between the study of ecology and economics partly reflect coincidence and, to a large extent, indicate different but related approaches to many of society's most important questions. Thomas Carlyle's popular assessment of economics as "the dismal science" may very well be similarly applied to the study of ecology today.[4] With the effects of human activities increasing, both fields could also be described as primarily concerned with scarcity. Furthermore, these two words share a linguistic heritage that very few other word pairs can claim. They come from the Greek words *oikos*, for house or household; *logos*, which means word, logic, story, or study of; and *nomia*, which means law or rule. Since the beginning of our society's relatively recent concern for ecology, these two fields have intersected as economic principles have been applied to solve environmental problems and as ecology has been used to critique the outcomes of economic policies. Studying the basic assumptions of economics clarifies this relationship.

This chapter addresses the study of economics as an outgrowth from moral philosophy and theology. Within its methodological framework and assumptions lies encoded evidence of its ancestral background. The disaggregation of academic disciplines and increasing specialization has meant that students of these fields have not realized the contribution

---

[4] Although this statement of his is heard relatively frequently, he also is reported to have referred to economics as "pig philosophy" among his writings.

69

they could make to each other. After beginning with a brief definition of modern mainstream economics as taught in our universities, we will review a few of the assumptions upon which it depends. After this we will examine two classes of criticism for economics as it is understood today. Certain elements of this particular culturally and historically located vision of the individual and society may be inappropriate as we approach limits in our world.

How many economics textbooks begin with *caveat emptor*, arguing that the buyer should beware as she reads the lines that follow? While this standard introduction may not be as appropriate here, a short inventory of qualifications should make my direction and intentions clearer. Although theological approaches to economics in the past have primarily addressed distribution issues (the allocation of wealth between rich and poor), this will not at all be the focus of this discussion. The intersection of economics, theology, and ecology already represents a significant challenge without examining an even broader field of concern. Furthermore, since my interest lies in economics as taught by economists, not sociologists, distinctions between capitalism, Marxism, socialism, and communism will not be explored. I will similarly not address either the substance or the criticisms launched against neoclassical economics by institutionalists, the Austrian School, or any other specific sect within the community of economists. Many of the distinctions among these schools of thought are the source for divisive, ideological disputes that would only deflect the argument. Furthermore, in order to keep this argument simple, I will not describe the subtler, critical view of economics as it is taught to economics doctoral students. Instead this will be a set of criticisms based on how economics is taught to undergraduates. Graduate students have a much clearer understanding of the limits of their models; however, most ordinary people understand the topic in much simpler terms. Despite the conflicts within different schools of economists, many of them agree on much more than they might otherwise realize, and in many cases, these schools of thought share assumptions and oversights characterized by textbook economics. Although thinking in terms of these distinctions has formed the manner by which we perceive the world, these categories for understanding economics may also restrict our vision in many significant ways. Finally, this will also not be a comparative systems approach to economics. The extraordinary extent of environmental degradation in China, Eastern Europe, Russia, and Japan only indicates that all of our modern economies have the potential for extensive damage.

Political Economy

> The ideas of economists and political philosophers, both when they are right and when they are wrong, are more powerful than is commonly understood. Indeed the world is ruled by little else. — John Maynard Keynes[5]

This section is not intended to replace a more careful study of economics, nor to describe the field in full. It is not even meant to convey a sense of the primary issues that academic and professional economists face, but rather a brief history of the more formal ideas that have been so essential in the lives of ordinary people, normal citizens, consumers, and workers. Many subjects important to both theology and ecology will similarly be omitted.

Most importantly, however, I am not proposing that thoughtful economists necessarily believe all of the enabling propositions that follow, only that this is how economics is taught to college undergraduates. Since each major large American university may have as many as two thousand students taking Introduction to Economics each year, and since these basic propositions serve as guides to countless business decisions, they are important influences on how we understand the expansive network of global trade. Although economists typically speak to each other using journal articles as their medium, sections excerpted from introductory and intermediate textbooks introduce the qualities peculiar to economic thinking in a simpler way. I think that this is appropriate since what follows explains how ordinary people in

---

[5] John Maynard Keynes, *The General Theory of Employment, Interest, and Money* (London: Macmillan, 1936) 383.

modern societies perceive the social connections that make up what we call the economy.

The primary and accepted definition of economics as a field of study employed by virtually all of the introductory textbooks, and used as a general rule of thumb for practicing economists and ordinary consumers, concerns scarcity. Most economists accept Lionel Robbins's famous definition: "Economics is the science which studies human behavior as a relationship between ends and scarce means which have alternative uses."[6] Although some economists think that this sort of definition may be too broad, others, such as Gary Becker, argue that economic thinking can be applied toward social situations in which scarcity is not a factor.[7]

The economist Greg Mankiw seems to offer a similarly broad definition of economics when he writes, "There is no mystery to what an 'economy' is. An economy is just a group of people interacting with each other." Economics is concerned with human relationships and decisions-making. Mankiw explains that "people respond to incentives." Echoing this idea in their bestselling book, *Freakonomics,* Stephen D. Levitt and Stephen J. Dubner claim that "incentives are the cornerstone of modern life," while economics is, at root, "the study of incentives."[8] The study of scarcity and incentives in human relationships lies at the heart of what economists believe they are doing.[9]

Despite minor disagreements over the particulars of such a definition, making the best choices regarding the use of limited resources is the central economic concern. Economists also base their study on the ability of people to choose between these alternatives (Robbins writes

---

[6] Lionel Robbins and Baron Robbins, *An Essay on the Nature and Significance of Economic Science*, 3rd ed. (London: Macmillan, 1984) 14, 16.

[7] Louis Lévy-Garboua, *Sociological Economics* (London: Sage Publications, 1979).

[8] Steven D. Levitt and Stephen J. Dubner, *Freakonomics: A Rogue Economist Explores the Hidden Side of Everything*, rev. and exp. ed. (New York: William Morrow, 2006) 12.

[9] N. Gregory Mankiw, *Principles of Microeconomics*, 5th ed. (Mason OH: South-Western Cengage Learning, 2009) 147, 149, 151.

further that "the ends are capable of being distinguished in order of importance"). This scarcity means that hard decisions must be made as to how these resources will be used—that is, what, how, how much, and how many different kinds of goods will be produced, and the manner by which these will be distributed. The importance of scarcity (of wetlands, clean air, old-growth forests, ocean reefs, wildlife, etc.) in any discussion of the environment quite naturally attracts economists because of their confidence in models that clarify the tradeoffs involved when making decisions under the constraint of scarcity. Some economists have a fondness for glibly stating that economics exists because scarcity exists. One might say that economics exists because economists do.

Since the most striking thing about any modern industrial economy is its complexity, those seeking to understand it must work primarily with abstractions (of individual and group behavior). These simplifications form the basis of models designed to account for the actions of consumers, firms, and economies. Social scientists and entrepreneurs, the wizards of Wall Street and the captains of industry, then evaluate the usefulness of these models, extend their application toward other circumstances, and invent new ones. The many sub-disciplines of economics alone reflect the complicated nature of the study. These include: labor economics, monetary economics, welfare economics, comparative economic systems, industrial organization, economic history, econometrics, international economics, behavioral economics, etc. The primary division of labor in economics, however, is easy to grasp. Microeconomics addresses the level of the individual firm and consumer, while macroeconomics deals with these abstractions in the aggregate and examines the functioning of the national and international economy. These two areas of interest have dominated to different degrees since the formal study of political economy came into being over two hundred years ago.[10]

Economic history is primarily concerned with the history of economies rather than historical analysis of economic thinking as a

---

[10] Political economy split into economics and political science at the beginning of the twentieth century.

discipline. Economists have manifested more interest in the effects of railroads on modern industrial economies than in the subtle conflicts between the men who brought forth this study out of moral philosophy after the beginning of the Enlightenment. This reflects the scientific ethos of the field, which conceives of itself in relatively ahistorical terms, as an objective enterprise whose results depend entirely on fact, rational observation, and experimentation rather than on the inherited ideas of its earliest benefactors. Despite this scientific convention, economists do sometimes look back at their predecessors with pride, and this influence is felt through brief citations referring to the great works of political economy. However, the depth of the past's influence exceeds the power of anecdote. In their concern with efficiency, their choice of categories in studying society (for instance, the inputs to productive processes), their descriptions of how human beings make choices, and countless other central concerns, these first political economists have had an enormous impact on today's most intricate and complicated disputes. Through their invention of these ideas and models, these early economists participate in the policy decisions of today.

A very brief look at the humble beginnings of economics can illuminate some important factors in its evolution. Political economy grew out of the dusk of the Mercantile Age just before the dawn of industrialization in England. It traces its beginnings to the last quarter of the eighteenth century and a book titled, *The Wealth of Nations,* written by the now-famous Scottish professor of moral philosophy Adam Smith. Smith's pin factory example (which illustrates the benefits derived from the division of labor in productive processes) and the "invisible hand" (which coordinates optimal quantities of supply and demand through price) laid the foundation for modern economic thinking. We still often hear reference made to Adam Smith's notable comments (such as "It is not from the benevolence of the butcher, the brewer, or the baker, that we expect our dinner, but from their regard to their own interest").[11] These passages have a power over how we conceive of the social world

---

[11] Smith, *An Inquiry into the Nature and Causes of the Wealth of Nations,* 2:26–27.

that has long outlasted Smith's relatively long life. The counterintuitive claim that the self-interestedness of individuals will work toward the best outcome for all has been attributed to him on the basis of quotes such as these.

> [E]very individual...endeavors...to employ his capital...so...that its produce may be of greatest value.... He generally, indeed, neither intends to promote the public interest, nor knows how much he is promoting it.... [H]e intends only his own security,... only his own gain; and he is in this...led by an invisible hand to promote an end which was no part of his intention...By pursuing his own interest, he frequently promotes that of the society more effectually than when he really intends to promote it.

This rationalization of self-interest is distinctively modern and has come to have a life of its own. Today we view self-interest as the natural state of individuals rather than as a danger to community and its rules governing behavior.

Adam Smith is less often cited in his capacity as a moral philosopher than in his role as a political economist. He also argued that individuals ought to have a commitment "to the interest of the great community, (one) ought at all times to be willing that his own little interest should be sacrificed."[12] Quoted out of context, only half of Smith's ideas on the role of self-interest in society have come to wield an extraordinary power. "The butcher, the brewer," and "the baker", "the invisible hand," and "trucking and bartering" today have the power of a litany in their

---

[12] Adam Smith, *The Theory of Moral Sentiments: or, An Essay Towards an Analysis of the Principles by Which Men Naturally Judge Concerning the Conduct and Character, First of Their Neighbors, and Afterwards of Themselves* (London: Strahan, 1774) 217. Amartya Sen has argued that "the fact that Smith noted that mutually advantageous trades are very common does not indicate at all that he thought self-love alone, or indeed prudence broadly construed, could be adequate for a good society. Indeed he maintained precisely the opposite." Amartya Sen, *On Ethics and Economics* (Oxford: B. Blackwell, 1987) 23. For more on Smith, see Sen, "Adam Smith's Prudence," in *Theory and Reality in Development: Essays in Honour of Paul Streeten*, ed. Sanjaya Lall and Frances Stewart (Basingstoke, Hampshire: Macmillan, 1986).

frequent repetitions as justifications for extending policies favoring self-interested behavior.

Although the overwhelming sentiment in North America seems to suggest that economics merely diagrams (or was the means for discovering) the natural behavior of human beings and society, a more accurate view understands it as a system that has evolved (and been imposed) to address human problems. Human beings are not born with some intrinsic capacity for making markets, or with some natural predisposition toward the sort of self-interested behavior so frequently rationalized through references to the invisible hand. We do not exit the womb as readymade consumers. Adam Smith did not so much discover a radically new quality natural to human behavior so much as he described a different way of understanding certain elements of the human condition. His view is not the only one. Just like any other, it simultaneously broadens our attention (so that we can see that self-interested behavior need not prevent two people from benefiting in an exchange) and limits it (for example, to a particular sort of behavior dealing with commerce between equals that may be more rare in our actual everyday experience). His observations have directed our activity toward commerce and have helped to make our age unique in its especially focused attention on these matters. Since Smith's time, the evolution of economics in a particular historical and cultural context (expanding availability of resources from overseas colonies during a time of major technological, political, and philosophical change) has further formed the field and its most primary assumptions.

The miraculous result obtained through the intervention of "the invisible hand" mentioned above became the "Law of Supply and Demand" and was formulated graphically and mathematically, thus extending the power of the original observation. According to this understanding of human nature and society, the amount of a good produced, or supplied, and the amount demanded by consumers, will be brought into equilibrium by a freely fluctuating price. If there is a limited supply of a good at a certain price relative to that which is demanded, consumers will bid up the price until the quantity demanded again approximates the quantity supplied. If there is abundance in the quantity of a good relative to that which is demanded, suppliers will lower prices in an attempt to entice consumers to buy, until the price again brings the quantity supplied and the quantity demanded together.

This summarizes the mechanics of the revered paradox upon which much of neo-orthodox economics is based: individuals acting according to their human nature ("red in tooth and claw") as infinitely acquisitive and selfish will ultimately, and unintentionally, work out the best means of organizing production and consumption within a society. The mark of the time's prevailing philosophies and theologies—the new importance of individualism, doctrines relating to human sin, the Enlightenment idea of the universe as a mechanism, the deist belief in heaven and hell, etc.—lies indelibly imbedded within the primary assumptions of economics. Although more sophisticated, even the most complicated of modern mathematical models must make such basic assumptions about human nature.

The Economic Approach

> Even now, however, most economists do not perceive the full generality of their approach since they are reluctant to admit that economicness is embedded in human beings. —Louis Lévy-Garboua[13]

A funny thing happened on our way to the 1980s. After an unnerving economic roller-coaster ride featuring two oil price shocks and the puzzling new phenomenon called stagflation (that is, persistent inflation accompanied by stagnation in national output as measured by GNP), certain economic thinkers looked to apply economic ideas to a whole new range of problems. Economists who had long been only interested in money, labor markets, capital accumulation, prices, and interest rates suddenly perked up their ears and applied their familiar frameworks (such as supply and demand) to explain why people get divorced, or commit themselves to a life of crime, or why they decide to attend

---

[13] Lévy-Garboua, *Sociological Economics*, 99.

church or to have children. Gary Becker, an economist, wrote that children are "like durable goods" such as refrigerators, toaster ovens, washing machines, or blenders.[14] Marriage and divorce came to be described in terms of cost-benefit analysis. Some economists began applying the economic approach with gusto.

Elsewhere, Gary Becker writes, "Indeed, I have come to the position that the economic approach is a comprehensive one that is applicable to all human behavior," and goes on to explain that it is a useful framework of analysis for understanding "the evolution of language, church attendance, capital punishment, the legal system, the extinction of animals, the incidence of suicide," altruism and social interactions, and marriage, fertility and divorce.[15] He argues that the core of the economic approach is the following system of assumptions: (1) maximizing behavior, (2) market equilibrium, and (3) stable preferences, all "used relentlessly and unflinchingly." While many economists would disagree with applying economic assumptions in these areas, the power of these three assumptions seems to be one thing that most economists do agree on. Perhaps the best way of understanding what these assumptions mean is to review how they are presented in an intermediate microeconomics textbook appropriate for use among graduate business students, students of government, and undergraduates with a mathematics background.

Walter Nicholson, in his upper-division microeconomics textbook, suggests his own list of three general features shared by economic models.[16] Describing these may be helpful at this point to better understand the methods and assumptions of economics. Nicholson's textbook can be used as a representative example. He emphasizes the

---

[14] Children require higher maintenance and deteriorate less rapidly. See the following: Gary Stanley Becker, *A Treatise on the Family* (Cambridge MA: Harvard University Press, 1981); also G. S. Becker's *The Economic Approach to Human Behavior* (Chicago: University of Chicago Press, 1976).

[15] Gary S. Becker, *The Economic Approach to Human Behavior*, 9.

[16] Walter Nicholson, *Microeconomic Theory: Basic Principles and Extensions*, 3rd ed. (Chicago: Dryden Press, 1985). Although this represents an example from a microeconomic text, macroeconomics, does operate under the same kind of premises.

study of how individuals and firms act within an economy, or rather, the economy as a whole. Macroeconomists, however, work with many of the same enabling assumptions and will often take the same sort of approach in explaining their work to intermediate students. Nicholson's three general features of economic models include: (1) employment of the ceteris paribus assumption, (2) optimization assumptions, and (3) the distinction between positive and normative economics. The next section will study each of these in turn (dwelling on the second as the most distinctive of the field).

The second most important Latin phrase after *caveat emptor* ("let the buyer beware") for a student of economics must be *ceteris paribus* (or "other things being equal"). In order for economists to analyze the effect on a social system of changing a single variable, they must constantly seek to isolate the variables they are studying. For instance, to understand the effects of an increased gasoline tax on gasoline consumption, other changes that occurred over the period (such as a decrease in automobile size or a seasonal decrease in driving) must be treated either as irrelevant (and not affect the variable being studied) or statistically adjusted. This assumption works to simplify an extraordinarily complicated universe for the purpose of careful study. As with any assumption, something is both lost and gained as a result of this method. The technique of assuming a constant value for other factors mirrors the manner by which economics as a whole functions. An abstraction enables us to gain insight into one specific function within the economy (such as the gas tax). However, through this narrowing of our perspective, we necessarily lose sight of other important features of human behavior that may only be available through a more general view. *Ceteris paribus* both enables deeper study and changes how we attend to our work.

The other two characteristics of economic models better illuminate features of economics useful to this study. The first of these, which Nicholson calls "optimization assumptions," characterizes virtually every approach to economics. Each of Gary Becker's three features that define the economic approach (maximizing behavior, market equilibrium, and stable preferences) has been adopted in order to understand human behavior in terms of optimization or rationality. Economists study the maximization of profits by firms, and the maximization of consumers' well-being (called utility, a concept that arose out of the study of philosophy prevalent in those times). National economies maximize output, firms minimize costs such as taxes, and government regulators attempt to maximize public welfare. In order for such optimization to function, persons, families, firms, economies, and governments must be assumed to act predictably and simply. A legion of complicated stated or unstated assumptions thus characterize every economic model, and every branch of the economic project.

Human Behavior

> Modern capitalist societies, however richly endowed, dedicate themselves to the proposition of scarcity. Inadequacy of economic means is the first principle of the world's wealthiest peoples. —Lewis Hyde[17]

All of the social sciences—anthropology, political science, sociology, psychology, and economics—ultimately work from their own implicit or explicit answers to the question of what it is to be human. Embedded firmly in the bedrock of their most basic principles and methods lie the fossilized assumptions of what it means for a person to be better off, what constitutes a good society, what is necessary for human dignity and freedom. Although questions like these may not be explicitly raised as a part of most typical economic arguments, these issues necessarily constitute the backdrop for our discussions. While the market may make economics unique as a discipline, its distinctive vision of human being and society means that it is social scientific. The simple assumptions that embody this view of human action have been one of the primary reasons for this field's greatest advances and have given economic models a special power. Although these abstractions, which represent human behavior for the purpose of these models, may seem flat and one-

---

[17] Lewis Hyde, *The Gift: Imagination and the Erotic Life of Property* (New York: Random House, 1983) 28.

dimensional, they enable insights into the complex networks of social relations that constitute the economy.

Since the philosopher John Stuart Mill (1806–1873) redirected the emphasis of economics from the study of the nature and the causes of national wealth to a science of human behavior, economists have sought to describe a rational person (as have jurists, in their "reasonable person" standard) for the basis of economic models. These assumptions presume among many other things that people will act as rational *individual* economic agents, who know exactly what their (non-contradictory) preferences are (and can rank them). It is further assumed that individuals, as they acquire greater amounts of a particular good, will come to value that good less and less (thus leading to trade, which often is assumed to take place without cost). An economic "agent" furthermore has infinitely acquisitive tendencies and a high degree of willingness to work in order to satisfy these material wants. Economists recognize that this characterization of human being is a caricature, but justify their methodology by stating that models making such assumptions "seem to be fairly good at explaining reality."[18] The foundation of the economic approach lies firmly in the ground of natural law, in a theological notion of human being as individual in essence and perpetually corrupted by sin.

These assumptions make optimization possible. In his classical work *Mathematical Psychics,* published in 1881, F. Y. Edgeworth (1845–1926) writes that "the first principle of Economics is that every agent is actuated only by self-interest."[19] If this is the first principle of abstraction that characterizes the economic agent, the second is that people generally act rationally—that is, their actions manifest an internal consistency. A rational economic agent has internalized a list of goods always arranged such that if she prefers product A to product B, and product B to

---

[18] Nicholson, *Microeconomic Theory: Basic Principles and Extensions*, 10. An economist named Oliver Williamson somewhere refers to "human nature as we know it."

[19] Francis Ysidro Edgeworth, *Mathematical Psychics: An Essay on the Application of Mathematics to the Moral Sciences* (London: C. K. Paul, 1881) 16.

product C, then she will always prefer product A to product C. This list of preferences, as mentioned above, is relatively static according to most models since quick changes in the ordering of these goods would not allow for consistent or rational behavior. To further simplify their representation of human action, economists assume that economic actors are rational and that they work entirely independently. They seek to maximize their own well-being, or utility, according to their list of preferences without regard for other people or their preferences. A theoretical lead box makes an agent's preferences impervious to outside influence, unaltered by a loved one's list of preferences, and untainted by a desire to keep up with the Joneses.

In the conceptual world of abstract economic thought, there is little room for buying on impulse or habitual purchases or addiction, only for economic activity that reflects action based on simply defined, formal decision-making criteria. While economists may relax various assumptions (for instance, to study how a neighbor's purchasing decisions actually may affect a "real" person's own choices), this galaxy of basic presuppositions represents the norm that an economist will have in mind before beginning to develop an economic theory. Even economists who only address broader questions dealing with the wider economy have been trained in this framework, and most often will explain national phenomena with reference to these assumptions regarding individual behavior.

The Firm and the Economy

I have measured out my life with coffee spoons. —T.S. Eliot[20]

In the world of economic abstraction, the firm behaves much like an individual consumer. Just as the profit-maximizing individual agent plumbs the depths of her consciousness, manifesting perfect self-knowledge of her rational preferences without any traces of internal conflict, so do the members of the firm work in concord toward a single

---

[20] T.S. Eliot, "The Love Song of J. Alfred Prufrock," *The Complete Poems and Plays: 1909–1950* (New York: Harcourt, Brace and World, 1952), 5.

goal. Actually, the firm in many ways has an easier task than the individual, since a company needs only to maximize profit and does not concern itself with satisfying a long and complicated list of preferences (which specify an individual's utility). The challenge for the firm, according to most economic models, lies in its intermediary position. A firm must act simultaneously as a buyer of raw materials and labor hours while competing with other companies to sell its final product. Historically, the inputs to the production process have been grouped into three categories (land, labor, and capital). These categories for the purpose of many models are treated fairly interchangeably, despite the enormous differences between a machine-tooling lathe, a person who collects tolls on the turnpike, and an acre of rolling hills. According to these models, firms set prices on the basis of the amount of power they wield within a market and their production costs. Self-interested, rational firms maximize profits according to formal decision-making criteria, just as individuals rationally maximize their utility.

Macroeconomists study whole societies, or economies, and use similar assumptions in their efforts to simplify the complicated behavior of banks and governments, the masses of consumers and the unemployed, business and agriculture. In these models, the government seeks to create an environment where the market can exist (by regulating competition, preventing violence, and creating property rights arrangements). Furthermore, the government may, through various measures, seek to stimulate national output, lower unemployment and inflation, stabilize the money supply and foreign exchange rates, and benefit their citizens through optimal international trading arrangements. Although macroeconomists must account for a broader range of activities and motivations, they, too, use abstractions to simplify complexity and to draw conclusions that enable us to make difficult decisions. Like other economists, they, too, rely on abstractions that both enable their greatest insights and narrow the focus of their attention.

As a society, we feel comfortable reducing the complex intentions of individuals, firms, and governments to the profit motive. The counterintuitive results of the invisible hand and its ability to convert all of our self-interested behavior into the common good have become familiar in the two centuries since its first introduction. Describing human activity as rational and subject to formal criteria for making decisions seems to us like the most sensible way of understanding the social world. Similarly, the radical independence of persons, firms, and governments from the others that inevitably surround them does not seem out of the ordinary to a citizen of a post-industrial democratic society. Our familiarity with the peculiarities of the economic worldview makes its traits seem to be both invisible and universal. The assumptions underlying the economic approach that enable us to understand human behavior in terms of optimization have a long philosophical and theological history.

The third of Nicholson's general features of economic models is popular among virtually all of the introductory textbooks and explicitly distinguishes between positive economics and normative economics. Nicholson writes that "*positive* economic theories" are "scientific theories [which] take the real world as an object to be studied, attempting to explain those economic phenomena as they are observed A somewhat different analysis of economic theory is *normative,* taking a definite moral position on what *should be* done."[21] The economic ideal (as described in this chapter's opening) is not a thorough understanding of persons or societies in isolation, but the power to make predictions of the future and to make effective interventions in economic processes. Even economists who quite explicitly state that they are not in business to make predictions will make projections on the outcome of a trading alliance, a particular tax cut, a change in the money supply, or consumer confidence. Both positive economic advice (for example, that an increase in taxes of 2% will increase tax revenues by 15%) and normative economic advice (for instance, that the government has a responsibility to keep the level of unemployment below 4%) represent the type of recommendations and adjustments to the economy that social scientists feel define their endeavor. The detached scientific observer represents an

---

[21] Nicholson, *Microeconomic Theory: Basic Principles and Extensions,* 11.

ideal embodied in this distinction between cold fact and ideologically influenced recommendation.

Characterizing economic work as positive or normative represents an attempt to delineate boundaries, to distinguish between those issues that divide economists and those core theories that define them as a profession. For some, this distinction keeps the field intact despite the intense centrifugal forces that pull economists apart, which have made them famous for their disagreements. The normative element to economic thinking suggests one reason a newly elected president brings in an entirely different galaxy of economists to Washington. This distinction civilizes economic debate through its implicit insistence that economists actually do agree at some basic level despite the obvious outward tensions. It suggests that consensus exists, that economists are scientists as well as policy advisors, that the foundation of their work lies in the cold granite foundation of fact rather than the shifting sands of conjecture and ideology. The idea that there is positive economics suggests that certain eternal truths about social behavior have been discovered and will be always agreed upon, that certain economic propositions are not open to debate. It implies that verification by calculating proof and detached observation constitutes the significant part of the economic endeavor.

Theory and World

Although this introduction to the economic approach at best represents only a superficial glance in the direction of economic theory, it constitutes a significant section of this essay. From economics as scarcity to Adam Smith's now famous paradox, from the odd investigations made by economists into marriage, church attendance, and decisions to have children, to Walter Nicholson's three general features of economic theory, this chapter has focused narrow attention on the assumptions underlying economic thinking. References to the environment in the preceding sections are as thin as the air at the summit of Mount Kilimanjaro. Why has it been necessary to dwell at such length on the foundational assumptions of economics? Why should anyone be at all interested in the historical relationship between moral philosophy and political economy?

In our world of massive trade alliances and budget deficits, where personal and national success are defined chiefly in economic terms and politicians seek to persuade their constituencies of their economic savvy, in our time, during which single companies wield more power than entire nations and military striving has been in part replaced by fierce global competition, economic thinking has become habit. We understand our problems in economic terms. Both our personal goals and our international concerns have come to be shaped by the "economic approach." Despite this tremendous change in view and interest, which would seem altogether foreign to our ancestors, those assumptions that underlie this new perspective are only rarely explicitly acknowledged. We argue about improving America's global competitiveness, or about speeding up a sluggish recovery, or the budget deficit, or our personal finances, or the changing composition of our economy (from manufacturing to service), or about cost-benefit solutions to our environmental problems. Yet the assumptions that we bring along into these debates remain concealed to us.

When we think or speak about economic ideas, these assumptions are invisibly and implicitly part of the conversation. In describing a whitewater river, a granite mountain peak, or an old-growth forest as an environmental good, or in analyzing decisions about the material world in cost and benefit terms, we use economic language and assumptions without thinking about them. A complex network of ideas, an intricate web of hidden abstractions about human nature and the social good, about behavior, competition, and atomized individualism necessarily support any discussion framed in economic language. We talk about "the market demand for clean air" or a concern for wild geese, unpolluted water, or undeveloped land as if these were items inserted into an individual's long list of ordered preferences.

It is too easy for us to equate value with price and forget that the world as defined by economics is a utopia. Utopia literally means "no place." In the rarefied atmosphere at the altitude where the primary assumptions of economic theory reign unchallenged, self-reliant individuals produce the best outcome for society without even thinking about the effects of their decisions on others. In this ethereal domain, happiness comes easily, without the complexity that afflicts ordinary people in their attempts to understand themselves. In that world, material goods always will make the economic agent happier. We merely perpetuate our economic fantasy in adding "environmental goods" to the long list of industrial products that we assume will always make us better off. We never stop to wonder if more actually *is* better, never question the assumption that desire must necessarily remain infinite.

In the brief survey of economic assumptions above and the analysis that follows, I am not suggesting that we either could or should abolish this manner of understanding the world. I would rather have economists serving on the Board of Governors at the Federal Reserve Bank than botanists. I would prefer to leave my money in the hands of a banker trained in "the economic method" than one who managed my savings account relying solely on a special expertise in Romance Philology. I trust the projections of future interest rates by economists more than the predictions of tarot card readers. The next sections outline the limits of understanding environmental problems only (or chiefly) in economic terms. Furthermore, it is my intention that the reader will begin to develop a sense for both the usefulness and limitations of this system of thought. While the remaining discussion of these assumptions may be critical, it does not suggest that economics should be entirely displaced in favor of another method of making crucial decisions, only that our institutions perpetuate the flaws of their creators. This crucial imbalance has come to be written into the landscape of our world. The foundational assumptions of our social sciences affect the health of this planet; they have etched a deeply cutting script into our wilderness and have been drawn in long, straight lines across the countryside and deserts.

This attempt to summarize the relevant foundations of economics obviously does not do justice to the full extent of work in the field. It does, however, emphasize the important connection between moral philosophy and the basic assumptions that shape the manner by which economists, and all of us as consumers and producers, understand problems. Unfortunately, with the specialization of the various academic fields, economics has become relatively isolated from the disciplines from which it arose. Reexamining these assumptions offers theologians and others a special opportunity to lend their insights into the discussion. Powerful criticisms of theological methodology that have arisen in interfaith dialogue may have important implications for how economists understand their work. The economic approach, which itself represents a particular faith in human behavior, can be opened to other ideas of what it means to be human, to be a part of a social system that constantly acts on the material world. When we do this, we can begin to more self-consciously understand this powerful system of thought. The relevance of economics to the environment and the impact that such models have on the industrial world suggest a moral imperative for more carefully scrutinizing this formulation of our society's most accepted norms.

4

THE USE OF ECONOMICS

Introduction

> Let me say this before rain becomes a utility that they can plan and distribute for money. —Thomas Merton[1]

This chapter reviews the dominant economic framework that informs so much of our everyday thinking. It clarifies the implications of the economic approach, that peculiar but unavoidable means of understanding the world. It is not an argument against economic thinking, another outworn attack on that old straw man who so often has been the immobile target of renegade sociologists, union organizers, communists, and other persons of dubious intent. Instead this chapter outlines the edges of our formal and informal economic theorizing. It details the effects of these institutions. It represents their limits in a new context and evaluates the results of their primary methods of analysis.

However, these pages cannot speak without language; they cannot form and articulate thoughts without using the same speech that we have habitually used to understand questions of economic value. The words, lines, paragraphs, and sections here attempt to confront one of the oldest challenges of the human condition—familiarity. We have seen the economic landscape described in the last chapter so often, the contours of its gently rolling hills, the bordering fences that divide pasture from pasture, and the street signs (so crucial in an older village to a stranger's sense of direction), that they now escape our conscious notice. We take for granted that value is equivalent to price, that stable ownership arrangements are the cornerstone of democratic society. We

---

[1] Thomas Merton, "Rain and the Rhinoceros," in *The Norton Book of Nature Writing*, ed. Robert Finch and John Elder (New York: W.W. Norton, 1990) 545.

measure our well-being in terms of statistics such as inflation, unemployment, disposable income, and GNP, prepared according to familiar and trusted standards. The language and concepts that support our consumption and production activities are as important as steel mills, shopping malls, skyscrapers, subways, supertankers, and superhighways in our treatment of the environment.

Those hidden features of our economic thinking, which, like the purloined letter, sit centered in the foreground of our experience, could be categorized in any number of ways. One could group them according to the assumptions that they embody, the effects that they have on the world, the intent of those who benefit from them. They could be presented as they are studied by economists (the individual, the firm, and the macro economy), or as part of a more explicitly historical study, which addressed the assumptions in the order that they achieved almost scriptural status in their legitimization within the greater economic canon. Two sets of responses to the economic approach will be presented in the following two chapters. The present chapter studies how we apply the economic model (our use of its various frameworks). Chapter 5 is more global and addresses the shortcomings of the approach itself. It examines the central self-conceptions at the heart of our economic thinking, while this chapter emphasizes the effects of its individual assumptions.

External and Internal

> What is a cynic? A man who knows the price of everything and the value of nothing. —Oscar Wilde

This section inspects the long line of assumptions assembled with relatively little accompanying commentary in the last chapter. Economic thought is productive rather than descriptive. Its theories do not merely represent the world, they influence how we understand it. Rather than dwelling on a long and detailed further description of the economic approach, this chapter follows the implications of such thinking, the way it presents the world to us, how we use economic constructs to make decisions regarding our society and world. Learning the limitations of particular economic assumptions naturally precedes a more careful study of the frailties embodied in the whole system of thought. This first topic is introduced by explaining how environmental degradation fits into our economic thinking. A more careful study of the behavioral assumptions that underlie economic theorizing follows this. Finally, this chapter concludes with observations on particular economic assumptions, with a brief look at the difficulty of comparing goods and a short review of the implications involved in assuming that both growth and output can or should be unbounded.

In the language common to economists around the world, "collective action failure" and "externality" have come to be used almost as synonyms for environmental degradation. This usage originates in economic explanations for environmental tragedies, in the application of economic models as tools for understanding society. The stories we tell to explain the world around us become established in our language and describe much about ourselves. Theologians sometimes accuse each other of reworking God in their own image. Economists similarly create an explanation for environmental damage in the image of their own model. In both these cases, the values we carry with us as we begin our project become incarnated in the models we use. These models that make sense of our world then have a powerful influence on our understanding.

The last chapter explained that many economists define themselves and their field, their very reason for being, in terms of scarcity. Making the best use of resources and preventing waste represent perhaps the primary values for an economist. Indeed, economic theory leads us to regard these as principle goals of society, as two sides of the same precious coin. Waste happens when we irrationally fail to make the best use of our resources. This is not exactly the same as our everyday conception of waste as leftover, or garbage, and can lead to an ironic outcome. If the benefits of producing a good to society outweigh the damage of the pollution, it causes waste when we *prevent* pollution. In most cases, however, economics recognizes pollution as wasteful, as destructive to the well-being of individuals, firms, and economies. For an economist, pollution represents an example of the sort of waste that results from a collective action failure. In the tightly woven fabric of assumptions described in the last chapter, collective action failures arise from ownership crises.

According to the economic approach, since no one owns the air we breathe or the rivers that provide us with water, no one will care enough to protect them. This language articulates the view that if everybody owns something, then no one does. For a student of the economic approach, litter along the roadside, the harmful emissions from automobiles and factories, and the neglect of publicly owned parks and buses result from an ownership vacuum. The economic model emphasizes that individuals will only take care of what they own. Economists argue that if shepherds share the common use of a field for grazing, they will inevitably end up destroying it. Each shepherd, maximizing his own well-being, has an incentive to overuse the field since the benefits he receives from this behavior (a larger flock of sheep) accrue only to himself, while the cost of this behavior is shared by all who use the field. According to this logic (and the assumption that more income must always be better than less), each individual shepherd will continue increasing the size of his herd until the field is barren. This overgrazing that can occur when all the shepherds using a common field maximize their own well-being at the expense of others with whom they share the land is called the "tragedy of the commons." The shepherds, in maximizing their individual interests, end up destroying the very thing that makes their well-being possible.

It is interesting that this story assumes that no form of self-government has been devised to regulate this problem, that the group has not already decided to voluntarily limit individual use for the sake of the whole. It assumes that no other social mechanism or organization is in place to prevent the tragedy and that the shepherds have an infinite desire for more material goods.[2] Surely Pacific Islanders devised means

---

[2] Lewis Hyde explores the limitations of the tragedy of the commons (in his discussion of Garret Hardin's 1968 essay, "The Tragedy of the Commons") and the prisoner's dilemma game. Each of these models assumes that people are not

of conserving shared resources before the children of missionaries introduced them to capitalism. Later, we will briefly examine the tendency of economic systems to quickly destroy their own alternatives in developing nations. In this case, an enterprising economist unaware of the intricate social systems that are already in place, but genuinely concerned about the tragedy of the commons, may suggest a scheme based on ownership rights rather than on restraint. After the field has been divided up into parcels of property on her recommendation, returning to the arrangements that previously prevented its destruction is virtually impossible. Liquidating ownership rights after they have been introduced is infinitely more difficult than establishing them. In seeing the world through the lens of the economic approach, we both open ourselves to certain types of solutions and simultaneously blind ourselves to other mechanisms that may accomplish these ends.

This parable about sheep and the public common has been the primary model that economists use for studying the environment and interpreting how people act within groups. In a simplified form, it argues that individual profit maximizers will not share. In a system that exalts the individual, it should not be entirely unexpected that pollution is presented as a problem of collectives (a "collective action failure"). For many economists, pollution has been merely ignored as the friction that results when individuals quite naturally rub up against the material world. Many more of those faithful to the economic approach, however, are interested in the problem but describe it through stories (like the one above) that necessarily limit the field of their vision.

A study of how economics addresses phenomena explicitly defined as outside of its own scope can be particularly illuminating. No study of ecology and economics could be complete without mentioning the problem of externalities. Economists define externalities (or spillover effects) as nonmarket effects of consumption and production activities.

---

capable of communicating with each other and working out compromises, as if by nature people are incapable of making joint decisions. Lewis Hyde, *Common as Air: Revolution, Art, and Ownership* (New York: Farrar, Straus, and Giroux, 2010).

They exist outside of—that is, external to—the exchange relationship. The most popular introductory textbook referred to earlier uses the following definition. It illustrates the ease by which persons can become economic agents and how nonmarket processes quickly come to be regarded as incidental.

> An externality, or spillover effect, occurs when production or consumption inflicts incidental costs or benefits on others; that is, costs or benefits are imposed on others yet are not paid for by those who impose them. More precisely, an externality is an effect of one economic agent's behavior on another's well-being, where the effect is not reflected in dollar or market transactions.[3]

Incidentality must certainly lie in the eyes of the beholder, since the impact of nonmarket effects can be positively enormous. The brief quote does suggest how difficult it can be for those of us who have learned the power of the market to focus our attention on activities that occur outside of it. In peering at the world through an economic lens, we can often see only markets.

Economists differentiate the two species of externalities according to a simple rule: They are either good or bad. Since agents will not always be able to capture unintended economic benefits resulting from their actions, positive externalities will always exist.[4] Although the transistor invented by Bell Labs has a multitude of uses, we the beneficiaries of devices dependent on this technology will never pay the full financial compensation for its introduction. That is, we never pay the full value of what it is worth to us (or what we would pay if we were not already benefiting from it). Other commonly cited examples of positive externalities include the benefits I receive living in a society in which many were educated in private schools (although I have contributed little to them), or the pleasure I experience from the beauty of my neighbor's yard (despite not having ever aided her in her efforts), or the advantage of being surrounded by people who have been inoculated

---

[3] Samuelson and Nordhaus, *Economics*, 712.

[4] The rhetorical effect of the word "agent," the economic word for "person," reflects the philosophies prevalent at the time of its introduction.

against the flu (shots I did not have to pay for).[5] Although we should certainly be thankful for positive externalities, human nature means that we have a tendency to overlook our blessings. Neither economists nor ecologists, however, find these sorts of examples of nonmarket dependencies as interesting as negative externalities.

"Nonmarket interrelationships" of particular concern to most people include those activities that have negative effects on human well-being. These result in all the evils that environmentalists complain the most about: littering, air pollution, soil erosion, radioactive waste, oil spills, ozone depletion, over-packaging, water contamination, poisoned soils, etc. All of these result from interdependencies in which the sufferers of a particular negative externality remain uncompensated economically for their pain or inconvenience. This suggests an expectation that markets work things out fairly, that usually people are compensated for the suffering or inconvenience inflicted by others. Economists point out that while producers must sometimes endure their own pollution, they also receive the full economic benefits of this activity and therefore have an economic incentive to pollute. Unfortunately, according to such reasoning (the tragedy of the commons writ large), we the people of today have tremendous incentive to engage in intergenerational exploitation through our consumer lifestyles, enjoying the benefits that many generations following us will need to pay for.

Externalities include everything from the minor inconvenience of slow traffic on the road home from work on game days to the world's most pressing problems. Any exchange that does not involve us as participants, but whose results have an impact on our lives, is defined as an externality. Every market relationship in which we are neither the seller nor the buyer, but nonetheless influences us as bystanders, is included in this category. The rancid smell of factory smoke, loud noise

---

[5] If we have eyes to really see the natural world, we can receive an abundance of blessings for which we have not paid. Something is a positive externality only to the extent that some other market relationship made it possible for us to benefit. However, not all the goods we receive come to us through markets.

at a nearby construction site, bad tempers of those with whom we do not do business, an old rundown storefront, the cool air under a shade tree planted by the sidewalk, and a thousand other experiences outside of our life as economic agents also fit into this category. Even a relatively unimaginative person can recognize that the number and extent of nonmarket interrelationships exceeds the ones accounted for by the market. Describing these necessary facets of human life as externalities seems ironic in a world where such interactions predominate. As we begin to recognize that most effects of an exchange occur outside the market, we may be better able to cultivate a sense of humility about the limits and bounds of our understanding. Perhaps by referring to results derived within economic models or determined in economic markets as "internalities," we would be reminded that the application of economic theory has important limits.

Economists and theologians, in their professional capacities, understand pollution as differently as they do Christmas. Economists view environmental damage as the result of a collective action problem, as interaction that is external to the market exchange. Their sensitivities make them more likely to regard damage to the environment as a form of waste. To solve many such problems, they suggest more complicated (or rational) systems of ownership that convert public goods into private property in order to ensure that such goods will be better cared for and maintained. Economic agents will protect such goods against losses only if they regard this destruction as a personal infringement rather than as a more general violation against the well-being of all. Assuming that individuals will seek to acquire anything they can, and that they will exploit anything not yet theirs, will result in a different approach to the problem than operating under different assumptions.

Theologians, on the other hand, understand pollution as primarily a moral problem. They may be more likely to see environmental degradation as resulting from the speed by which technological change outstrips our socially formed system of ethics. As noted in the second chapter, our values and the metaphors we adopt to make sense of our world cannot always so easily keep pace with the quickly changing social situation. Theologians therefore tend to look at increasing the strength of those intangible threads that bind us together as a moral community responsible to God and creation. Chapter 2 enumerated only a few of the many programs designed by theologians to do this. Just as economists tend to see the solutions in the same way that they view the problem (in terms of self-interested profit-maximizing), so do theologians in their emphasis on moral suasion and responsibility. This special attunement to ethics often makes theologians uncomfortable with economic methods.

A theological solution to littering would not be to create a property right for all spaces subject to litter. Instead, theologians would be more likely to try to change people's moral evaluation of this behavior. In the case of littering, a tremendous ethical change has occurred during the last forty years, making this practice much more socially unacceptable. Although this particular example suggests one situation in which a theologian's view would have been especially useful, this does not imply that one ought to rely exclusively on either of these ways of understanding the problem. I am only intending to suggest that inherent in any way of looking at a problem is a tendency to recognize only certain sorts of solutions. Our models and our views simultaneously enable us and disable us. This suggests that a wide range of insights is a necessity in confrontations with a serious problem. The modern tendency to see the world only in terms of the economic approach limits our very ability to conceive of alternatives.

The Self-Interested Self

We are the hollow men
We are the stuffed men
Leaning together
Headpiece filled with straw. Alas!
Our dried voices, when
We whisper together
Are quiet and meaningless
As wind in dry grass
Or rats' feet over broken glass

In our dry cellar. —T. S. Eliot[6]

The conflicted interior world, the battles of the divided self that Sigmund Freud described in his life work suggest a fundamentally different alternative to the "economic person" who, like Atlas, supports "the economic approach." Disequilibrium lies at the heart of Freud's interior economy. The superego dreams of a universal brotherhood, the id longs for dependence, love, and union, while the independent ego purposefully seeks the guidance of reason. The strivings of our divided subconscious, according to Freud, remain radically inaccessible to us, and indeed to all others except the carefully trained psychoanalytic specialist. While many of the specific elements of Freud's anthropology have little currency today, the tenacity with which he questioned the accessibility of our own self certainly represents a contribution to how we view human beings. His great innovation is his observation that we are only dimly known to ourselves in our internally conflicted attempts to adjust between the ideal and the real. He taught us that we never experience our instincts, desires, and drives as they are, but instead only as we reconstitute these expressions of the unconscious in our conscious thought.

I do not mean to suggest that we should immediately begin revising economic theory to account for Freudian principles, only that our self-understanding as human beings has always incorporated a large number of very different perspectives. Many of the views that undergird our thinking about ourselves and society upon closer examination sound very odd. Just as the Freudian self lies almost entirely obscured by ancient myths ("fantastic realities beyond reasonable appearances; worlds composed of absurd conjunction—events that never happened and yet control those that do"), the economic agent is thinly transparent, her desires monotonous and obvious.[7] "Actuated only by self-interest," she

---

[6] T.S. Eliot, *The Complete Poems and Plays: 1909–1950* (New York: Harcourt, Brace, and World, 1952) 56.

[7] Philip Rieff, *Freud: The Mind of the Moralist* (New York: Viking Press, 1959) 138.

reveals her internal, hierarchically organized list of preferences straightforwardly to others through her behavior in the market (without the need for a trained psychoanalyst).[8] She is impervious to what psychologists call "context" or her experiences immediately before making a decision.[9] She is unaffected by "framing," or anchoring (the psychological influence of a price that has already been mentioned). She is rational in her risk preferences in a way that is unaffected by whether she projects an outcome to have a 90 percent or a 10 percent likelihood, or whether it is described as a loss or a gain. She always takes into consideration the time value of money (inflation) when she makes comparisons and decisions. Her infinite passion for goods is rigidly ordered and unaltered by loved ones or by any subsidiary desire to keep up with the Joneses. It leaves no room for making moral choices. The internal division fomenting conflict in the Freudian subject never affects the economic self.

But what is self-interest? Amartya Sen argues that a notion of revealed preferences (as measured by an economic agent's decisions in the market) may not get us anywhere. He writes that "it is possible to

---

[8] Edgeworth, *Mathematical Psychics: An Essay on the Application of Mathematics to the Moral Sciences*, 16.

[9] Behavioral economists point out psychological studies about context in which subjects who have heard words related to old age statistically move more slowly down the hall than those who have not. They also describe as "anchoring" the power yielded by the person who sets the first price in a negotiation. Behavioral economists and psychologists have also made new studies pointing out that a person's approach to risk changes based on whether they regard the perceived loss as a forgone possibility or a loss of something that they already have. Economic work on the psychology of saving has resulted in programs that have proven very helpful in changing people's habits and in recognizing the gains that we can achieve when we question assumptions about economic rationality. Economists George Akerlof and Robert J. Shiller write about money illusion, defining it as a confusion about inflation and deflation that leads to irrational decisions. Daniel Kahneman, *Thinking, Fast and Slow* (New York: Farrar, Straus, and Giroux, 2011). Akerlof and Shiller, *Animal Spirits: How Human Psychology Drives the Economy, and Why It Matters for Global Capitalism*, 12.

define a person's interests in such a way that no matter what he does he can be seen to be furthering his own interests in every isolated act of choice."[10] If revealed preferences are what an economic agent chooses, and those things that an economic agent chooses are her revealed preferences, this is equivalent to saying that people choose what they choose. Unless we carefully specify what self-interest is, our results will be worthless. In making this abstraction meaningful, it becomes necessary to exclude other important facets of human behavior from our immediate vision. In short, we must choose between an empty version of self-interest that includes all possible human action and a necessarily restrictive abstraction that draws meaningful distinctions between self-interested behavior and other kinds of action.

No one would argue that human beings do not act selfishly—they do. However, one cannot reduce all behavior to greed without seriously distorting the meaning of our everyday experience. In using a system of abstraction that equates well-being only with self-interested behavior, and which emphasizes it above all else, we necessarily blind ourselves to other very important components of human action. While these most certainly include altruism (and the sense of moral responsibility or concern for public censure that makes us refrain from antisocial acts like littering), other sorts of values also fall outside of this category. For instance, although in economic models being happy is literally everything, in real life we often choose freedom over greater pleasure.[11] Most of us, at some point, choose freedom from debt over greater consumption today, just as the ascetic chooses the pleasure of "no pleasure" in accepting disciplines such as chastity, obedience, or poverty (disciplines that, in some sense, may reduce her well-being).[12] Freedom

---

[10] Amartya Sen, "Rational Fools: A Critique of the Behavioral Foundations of Economic Theory," in *Beyond Self-Interest*, ed. Jane J. Mansbridge, (Chicago: University of Chicago Press, 1990).

[11] Sen, *On Ethics and Economics*.

[12] As mentioned in the paragraph above, the bounds of what is described as self-interest must be limited for the concept to have meaning. Some economists include various freedoms and altruism as elements in an agent's list of preferences (as a debt preference or a preference for a particular charity, for

from a compulsion to overeat, to smoke, or to drink too much is sometimes more important to us than the immediate pleasure of indulging. Economic models presume freedom and therefore, in many cases, overlook it. While this assumption minimizes controversy, it also limits the extent to which we can understand the constraints that we experience in our everyday life.

The fixed list that *homo economicus* carries around does not depend at all on anyone else's preferences. The economic person is an island, unmoved by care for anyone else's interests, indifferent to his neighbor's needs or wealth. While this radical individualism may be illuminating as a means of understanding the tendencies of markets, it may simultaneously make cooperative behavior more of a mystery. While the reasons for this individualism may in part lie in the mists of Western civilization's Christian past (a faith that emphasizes a universal and individual relationship between each person and God), the economic approach at times takes individualism to an extreme. The dominant economic model of cooperation is collusion between members of a cartel. To most economists, this exercise of monopoly power over a market seems almost like a moral defect. Very few models for productive cooperation exist in part because individualism represents such a dominant value in the fundamental economic frameworks. In using an economic model for understanding a problem, it therefore becomes difficult to see that wholes often represent much more than merely the sum of their parts. The long history of aggregate approaches to economics testifies to this. Although people cooperate as members of families or as communities, this feature of our experience is necessarily de-emphasized in the basic economic frameworks. The economic approach will be more likely to highlight competitive approaches to problems and to discount the possibility or uses of cooperative behavior. This does not suggest that we should become communists, only that the models that we use for making sense of the social world necessarily limit our responses to it.

---

instance). However, in doing this, we can no longer use the word "self-interest" in any meaningful way.

While equating rationality with self-interest obscures the moral nature of our decisions, assuming that agents have a relatively fixed set of preferences limits how we can understand learning. Describing what advertising does is therefore difficult for such a model unless we relax the assumptions regarding relatively fixed preferences. The billions spent globally on advertising suggest that people do either rearrange their preferences or that they can be made to actually desire more. Economists, of course, have models to explain advertising. However, economic training that emphasizes individual independence by assuming static preferences and infinite desires does draw attention away from a whole range of questions about satisfaction and desire. Again, in assuming that the acquisition of goods and services will always satisfy or, rather, make the economic agent better off, we are distracted from considering too seriously the malleability of human desire and happiness. It draws our attention away from the possibility of complacency, or any sort of special ambition, or contentment, or the power of fashion, or our especially human tendency to change our minds.

In economic models, individuals, firms, and economies all have a similar goal: maximization of profit or pleasure. Assuming that being better off must necessarily be equated with having more and that desire is infinite may have been sufficient in times when our mildest consumer whim did not have the power it does today. How does assuming the impossibility of fulfillment affect our view or our policy prescriptions? How does it influence our goals as a society? The values embedded in these models come to be written across our landscapes with bulldozers. Los Angeles continues to expand further out into the desert while its core rots. Nations clear forests (at the expense of future generations) to export timber in order to generate foreign currency. Economic models do not merely describe social life, they enable particular social arrangements, and they direct our attention to certain qualities of the human condition and inevitably play a part in forming us.

Commensurability

> Economics itself conceals a complicated system of desire.
> —Paul Ricoeur[13]

So far we have discussed the mechanical algorithms, the formal rules, that we use to model economic judgments as if these correspond to our experience of making decisions. Our ordinary use of the word "decision," however, suggests something far different than merely consulting an internal list of preferences. A sense of clarity, or ease, or obviousness in determining which action we will take often leads us to say things like, "I had no choice but to." This sort of usage implies that easy decisions are not decisions, that the nature of a decision is choice between two or more fundamentally incompatible alternatives. Some options cannot be easily compared according to a single simple standard, thus leaving us with a dilemma, a decision. Whether we would rather have five dollars or ten dollars is not a decision. Choosing between a job that pays ten dollars an hour in the town where we live versus one that pays twenty dollars an hour in a town a hundred miles away is the sort of decision much more typical to our ordinary experience.

Economists adjust for the complexity of real decisions through claims that our list of preferences embodies product qualities rather than existing as simply a list of products. Ultimately, however, the economic approach evaluates all goods and services according to one criterion, price. The creators of eBay made a fortune from the insight that, in our world, virtually all material things have a price. Grazing land in Argentina, a cold piece of concrete from the Berlin Wall, a lead statue of Vladimir Lenin, a rundown shack on the shore of Lake Michigan, memorabilia from old Hollywood films, a portion of General Motors, an idea for a new kind of brake lining, an elegantly furnished condominium on Fifth Avenue, a shipload of wheat from the Midwest—all can be compared and exchanged on the basis of price. The

---

[13] Paul Ricoeur, *Freud and Philosophy: An Essay on Interpretation* (New Haven: Yale University Press, 1970) 523.

market's powerful means of establishing a thing's value captivates us in the modern world. In equating value and price, it has profoundly simplified our notion of worth.

The question of value represents a central concern in the Greek tragedies. The plot of the Sophoclean play *Antigone* revolves entirely around the problem of competing and exclusive systems of values. The leading character, Antigone, chose to defy her uncle Cleon in her decision to bury her brother Polynices, who was killed as he committed an act of treason. The single-minded ruler Cleon, faced with a similar choice, decided that familial and religious loyalties were secondary and, in his regard for civic virtue as the highest good, reluctantly executed Antigone. The point of this example and the play is that most important determinations of value cannot be made according to a single standard, an elementary list of preferences (or the simple determination of value through a market). Economic theory in its calculus sets up problems so that they are not really decisions. The economic approach at a basic level has little room for choices between real alternatives that cannot easily be conflated through comparison according to a single standard. Real dilemmas, however, such as in *Antigone*, involve fundamentally incompatible alternatives.

All of this becomes particularly important as we deliberate about the value of environmental goods. Proposals to allow the market "to decide" seem never to go out of style. It is easy in our enthusiasm for economic magic to attribute to the market a special power to save the world. Many argue that as we deplete our environment, the law of supply and demand will naturally cause prices to rise, thus making sensitive environmental goods more inaccessible to further depletion. Such simple suggestions fall in line with the rationalization of self-interested behavior common to a simplistic and popularized reading of "the economic approach." Probably not many professional economists would make such a bare argument in favor of exploitation, or uncontrolled greed. However, the economic approach easily lends itself to distortions like this one. In working so closely with models in which all the factors are relatively interchangeable—commensurable—according to a price standard, it becomes too easy to overlook how many different ways we can judge value. The World Bank evaluates progress in the countries where it makes loans almost solely on changes in Gross Domestic Product. They make crucial decisions about national welfare on the basis of such aggregate statistics that simplistically represent well-being as the product of the price and quantity of goods (and services) consumed. In assuming that everything can be compared according to this standard, the benefits of clean air, open space, species diversity, a healthy living environment, indigenous cultures, beautiful surroundings, and the moral responsibility to provide for future generations are undervalued.

The fundamental problem with cost-benefit analysis as a tool for making environmental decisions lies in its dependence on human imagination. Ultimately, in deciding the value of various costs or benefits, some items will be better suited to our standards of measurement than will others. This sort of standard tends to exaggerate the value of those things that can be easily calculated, such as quarterly profits or Gross National Product, while undervaluing those things that cannot so easily be measured, such as the value of clear air, undeveloped forests, or healthy drinking water. Cost-benefit analysis obscures the interpretive nature of any such decision-making process. It conceals the extent to which we depend on a particular system of measuring, a standard for valuing objects and experiences.

At this point, though, we begin to get ahead of ourselves. The last several sections have discussed a few limitations of particular economic assumptions. They have examined how economic theory necessarily narrows our attention, limits the range of questions that we consider as we approach a problem. These presuppositions regarding freedom, cooperation, personal formation, material growth, and commensurability do not necessarily suggest that economic theories are of no use as we try to make sense of our world. I am not committed to proving that basic economic concepts are blatantly wrong, only that they represent one incomplete way of understanding ourselves and our world. These last two sections suggest that these enabling and necessary assumptions can be improved or qualified to better address environmental problems.

This has been the approach of economist Herman Daly and theologian John Cobb in *For the Common Good*.[14] They assert the need for working within this framework to make substantive changes that will strengthen our communities and heighten our sensitivity to the environment. Although they propose radical changes to how we conceive of these basic economic ideas, they direct their efforts to work within economics. The concrete suggestions that they make ultimately propose to redefine many of the central economic symbols. They offer an environmentally friendly version of economics that is compelling in its scope and in its practical approach.

Indeed, the basic economic frameworks certainly leave room enough for substantial revision. Economists can attempt to rework the enthusiasm for individualism embodied in these models. They can develop models that tell stories that incorporate cooperation or that offer better explanations of how people are formed by economic systems. They can stretch the assumptions that describe how people make decisions, and the goals and desires that drive them. Economists can even work on making assumptions regarding national goals and priorities more flexible to better account for environmental concerns in national income statistics. All of these feverish manipulations of assumptions, these radical reconfigurations of the models, however, will fail unless we can come to better understand how economics works.

The next chapter moves beyond individual assumptions to examine the functioning of the entire model. It addresses the economic way of thinking rather than specific theories or assumptions. It takes as its focus the basic self-conceptions that lie beneath applied economics, and even deeper than the theory that unifies the diversity of economic approaches. In discussing answers to the question of what it is we are doing when we do economics, we can see more clearly what theologians may have to contribute in this conversation.

---

[14] Daly, Cobb, and Cobb, *For the Common Good: Redirecting the Economy toward Community, the Environment, and a Sustainable Future.*

5

THE LIMITS OF ECONOMICS

Foundations

> I criticize the myth that science itself is an objective enterprise, done properly only when scientists can shuck the constraints of their culture and view the world as it really is. Science, since people must do it, is a socially embedded activity. It progresses by hunch, vision, and intuition. Much of its change through time does not record a closer approach to absolute truth, but the alteration of cultural contexts that influence it so strongly. —Stephen J. Gould[1]

Our system of economic ideas is a human language with its own distinctive grammar. Its goals, methods, field of study, contributions, and source of inspiration must necessarily remain subject to the constraints of human systems of meaning and the frailties peculiar to our condition. The place where we begin, our potential and the limit of our greatest aspirations in our formal or informal economic theorizing, is the same. So are the subject and the object of our economic thinking. Economics represents one class of stories we tell about ourselves. Its rules and grammar differ substantially from those that characterize fiction. However, these two languages each function to orient our lives, to give us a basis for understanding the world and for making judgments of value. Our acts of speaking and hearing these languages necessarily enable and precede the process of forming our ideas.

Science fiction as a bilingual genre embodies the values of both the literary and the scientific imagination. In perhaps his most famous series of science fiction novels, beginning appropriately enough with *Foundation*, Isaac Asimov articulates a social scientific fantasy. The novels record the memorable plans of psycho-historian Hari Seldon as

---

[1] Stephen J. Gould, *The Mismeasure of Man* (New York: Norton, 1996).

he uses advanced statistical methods and social theory to predict the future of the great empire encompassing all of known civilization. This sort of prediction ability had a special appeal to social scientists during the 1950s. Bondage to the fluctuations of a business cycle has always been particularly abhorrent to economists. In another book, Asimov describes the particularly economic version of this dream. His story, "The Inevitable Conflict," describes a distant future when computers coordinate all economic activity on the planet (and make all the appropriate decisions regarding optimization):

> [T]he Machines are nothing but the vastest conglomeration of calculating circuits ever invented, and so our Earth Wide economy is in accord with the best interests of Man. The population of Earth knows that there will be no unemployment, no overproduction, or shortages. Waste and famine are words in history books. And so the questions of ownership of the means of production become obsolescent. Whoever owned them (if such a phrase has meaning), a man, a group, a nation, or all mankind, they could be utilized only as the Machines directed. Not because men were forced to, but because it was the wisest course and men knew it. It puts an end to war—not only to the last cycle of wars, but to the next and to all of them.[2]

Macroeconomists during the 1950s and early 1960s similarly predicted a future in which the largest economies could be fine-tuned through interventions directed by massive econometric computer programs. Although no contemporary economist would even dream of suggesting that such an accomplishment could be possible, we should wonder why it ever seemed like it could be done. We should also ask how the root of this misconception has influenced the curriculum of MBA programs and important business decisions. These predictions about predictions represent a particularly poignant parallel relevant to this section on theories about theories.

Some macroeconomic computer programs have thousands of variables, representing everything ranging from the long-term rates on

---

[2] Isaac Asimov, *I, Robot* (Garden City NY: Doubleday, 1950) 198.

government bond issues, to the share price of various major companies, to the primary foreign exchange rates, key commodities prices, etc. The Federal Reserve and state and national governments use them to understand the functioning and complexity of large economic systems and to make important decisions about the money supply or projections of tax revenues, etc. Despite rapid technological improvements in computing power, however, economists today realize that the complexity of human behavior cannot be forecasted as accurately as we once dreamed it would.

The reductionist tendencies that assumed that collective behavior merely reflected the simple aggregation of individual action have been laid to rest. In the past, social scientists tended to believe that anomalies would either balance each other out or would have little effect on the overall system. Since then, the three rules popularly referred to as "chaos theory" have humbled those who over-exaggerate the possibilities of economic prediction: (1) simple systems behave complexly, (2) complex systems behave simply, and (3) vastly different systems behave similarly.[3] Furthermore, the tendency of economic systems to manifest an acute sensitivity to seemingly minor initial conditions (the butterfly effect) means that accurate long-term economic forecasting is as unlikely as long-term weather predictions. For instance, a manager arrives late to work after an argument with her spouse and, therefore, neglects to submit a timely order to decrease production. This causes an excess of inventory and a bank foreclosure that finally cause a serious loss of confidence in the region and high unemployment. Although this sounds like a fanciful story, it is impossible to make predictions in a world in which people have colds, where important documents get misplaced, or where decisions get put off because of vacations. A world where seemingly minor conditions come to have a monumental effect on a system fights against our most Herculean attempts at prediction. Those things that make our individual personal lives so uncertain similarly complicate our corporate life.

---

[3] James Gleick, *Chaos: Making a New Science* (New York: Penguin, 1988).

For too long, however, a few social scientists have boldly speculated in the spirit of the French mathematician Pierre-Simon Laplace (1749–1827) that, with enough time for calculation and enough data, they could predict the future. This way of understanding the world does not only account poorly for chance, it radically underestimates the functioning of human consciousness. While the bold predictions about predictions from the 1950s dissipated with the cold economic winds of the early 1970s, the tendency to think about the world in these terms still exists. Unfortunately, an overconfidence in economic principles and scientific infallibility can have disastrous consequences, especially as it begins to seem like there are no other options. Using a standard of rationality as the fulcrum from which to make global predictions often misses a simple point. Ultimately all understandings depend on human systems of meaning. They are constructed out of history by individuals with particular interests and do not merely represent objective observations of the world. The recent move within the social sciences since World War II toward quantitative methods may have the unintended effect of obscuring this dependence.

By the mid-1980s, the faculty of the economics departments in North America had much more daily contact with mathematicians and statisticians than with the other social scientists with whom they most often shared buildings. "Scientific management" in business schools displaced business ethics, and economists began to lose sight of the social element of this social science. Departmental course requirements reflected this in their heavy emphasis on quantitative courses, as textbooks came to refer more often to physics as a model than to the academic study of sociology or psychology (economics' closest cousins). Nicholson, who provided us with the framework used earlier to introduce economics, writes, "'Positive' economists believe that one reason for the success of economics as a discipline is that it has been able successfully to emulate the positive approach taken by the physical sciences rather than becoming involved in the value-conscious, normative approach taken by some of the other social sciences."[4]

---

[4] Nicholson, *Microeconomic Theory: Basic Principles and Extensions*, 11.

Indeed, much of the field's language has been borrowed, as have primary concepts such as the dominant concern with economic "efficiency" (from physics) or the description of consumers' perpetual desire to have greater amounts of material things as "monotonicity" (from mathematics). Philip Mirowski, in his work, argues that fundamental microeconomic concepts were appropriated directly from Newtonian physics (potential energy corresponds to economic utility, force to price, and changes in location to changes in quantities of goods).[5] As a human system of meaning, this emphasis has resulted not only from the "explanatory power" of quantitative models but also from humbler motives. Certainly, mathematics offers a sense of elegance and order to an otherwise messy study of human behavior. In some senses, it can make dialogue easier by converting judgments of value or morality into questions of mathematical correctness. It is easier to attain consensus on the solution to problems like "92 + 35" than on the precise effects of a change in the income-tax laws. In using physics as a model, economists sought to legitimate their own work, to bring it under the golden halo of the scientific principles that have so successfully transformed our world.

Some economists may lament that their field cannot hope to have the same successes in prediction characterized by the controlled experiments of physical scientists. They suggest that economics is handicapped by having to take into consideration a greater number of factors. Just as biologists must take into account physics and chemistry

---

[5] Mirowski points out that this has been a source for inconsistency and unnecessarily restrictive assumptions in economics. For instance, conservation of energy makes more sense than conservation of utility. Michael Sandel points out the tendency for economists (like Lawrence Summers) to speak as if altruism and love can be saved up so that they are available later. Sandel argues that we become more loving by being loving, not by waiting to love in the future. Philip Mirowski, "Shall I Compare Thee to a Minkowski-Ricardo-Leontief-Metlzer- Matrix of the Mosak-Hicks Type?," in *The Consequences of Economic Rhetoric*, ed. Arjo Klamer, Deirdre N. McCloskey, and Robert M. Solow, 117–145 (New York: Cambridge University Press, 1988). Sandel, *What Money Can't Buy: The Moral Limits of Markets.*

in their theories, some economists have argued that their work lacks the predictive power of the hard sciences because they must account for the variability of a host of other sciences.[6] By focusing on this hierarchy of rigor rather than the varying levels of dependence on human constructions of meaning, social scientists making this argument vastly overestimate their task and their potential.

Many who use economic models do not often confront the extent to which their problems, tools, methodologies, and subjects of interest have evolved out of a particular cultural context. It is not immediately evident from reading college textbooks that economics did not just spontaneously appear in the world without a childhood or a history or a family, in the way that the mythological Venus did. In our informal economic reasoning, political and policy debates, journalism, business literature, and ordinary conversation, we rarely cite the sources of our economic opinions (or consciously examine them). Similarly, we speak of these uses of the economic approach as merely our own insights into the eternal verities, as external truths or common knowledge, and rarely consider where these ideas originated. This kind of an ahistorical approach, blind to the complications of the human ego, may in part be the result of the high merit that social scientists place on objective observation. This value itself has a long history and makes new understandings possible while simultaneously limiting our openness to other views, to other important truths, to other measures of worth. Theologians' interest in history and questions about how we determine value would be useful in a society that takes economic truths as expressions of brute reality, rather than as the products of our creative imagination and its influence on the social and natural worlds.

---

[6] They argue that although chemistry must account for the statistical variability of physics, psychology must account for physics, chemistry, biology, and physiology. Economics must account for these plus climatology, botany, etc.

Civilization and Its Contents (and Discontents)

> It never occurs to most of us that the question "what is the truth?" is no real question (being irrelative to all conditions) and that the whole notion of the truth is an abstraction from the fact of truths in the plural, a mere useful summarizing phrase like the Latin Language or the Law. —William James[7]

The introduction of the economic approach as a tool for understanding divorce, childbearing, crime, altruism, church attendance, legal behavior, and other topics has been considered by many sociologists as an unwelcome intrusion, as an academic turf-violation. These other social scientists, in their articles, explicitly state that they are motivated in their criticisms of economics by this encroachment of "economic imperialism" into their "territory." The title of one of these articles, "Clean Models vs. Dirty Hands," sums up the substance of the counterattack. Sociologists argue that the abstract theorizing of economists (in their simple descriptions of human behavior, market-clearing equilibria, and social organization) lacks connection to often-messy reality. They assert that despite scholarly success, mathematical elegance, and the popularity and influence of precise frameworks, economists do not adequately describe the world. "Economists' core assumptions lead them to ignore the empirical world around them."[8] "Doubts have been raised as to microeconomics' capacity to connect with empirical reality."[9] Sociologists claim that a more inductive approach, one that first looks at the data and then forms hypotheses,

---

[7] William James, *Pragmatism* (Cambridge MA: Harvard University Press, 1975) 115–16.

[8] P. Hirsch, S. Michaels, and R. Friedman, "Clean Models vs. Dirty Hands," in *Structures of Capital: The Social Organization of the Economy*, ed. Sharon Zukin and Paul DiMaggio, 39–56 (New York: Cambridge University Press, 1990) 39, 45, 46.

[9] R. Swedborg, U. Himmelstrand, and G. Brulin, "The Paradigm of Economic Sociology," in *Structures of Capital: The Social Organization of the Economy*, ed. Sharon Zukin and Paul DiMaggio, 57–86 (New York: Cambridge University Press, 1990) 60.

would be more accurate than the economic method, which works from previously established frameworks (such as supply and demand) to establish deductive hypotheses.

Conflict between sociologists and economists, however, cannot be entirely explained as a series of border skirmishes over the territory claimed by each of these warring academic disciplines. Their historical origins, the political environments and issues that have shaped them, and their basic conceptions regarding human agency make reconciliation difficult. Sociologists have a tendency to see human action as overly determined by a person's social context, and economists in their foundational models understand the individual as entirely independent, as uninfluenced by the surrounding society. An economist has been known to defend economics by saying, "While economists show us how to make choices, sociologists show us we have none."[10] This difference in view sounds strangely reminiscent of sixteenth-century theological conflicts over free will and predestination. The extent to which human beings can change themselves still remains in dispute, despite the absence of explicit mention of God in these debates. Intellectual battles over freedom and self-determination have evolved but still remain with us—and still have an enormous influence on how we understand society.

Despite the distance between these two different social scientific languages, their divergent views share important values. Both sociologists and economists agree in their frequent appeals to correspondence between reality and theory as the test of scientific value and that the object of their endeavor is a disengaged description of the world.

These standards for validity sound utterly straightforward and indisputable. The familiarity of these principles, of this foundation for understanding human experience makes it invisible to us. We have difficulty thinking of academic work or business-related reasoning in any other way. It seems perfectly sensible for an economist raising an objection in a seminar, a CEO reviewing sales projections in a board

---

[10] Quoted from an unknown source in Amitai Etzioni, *The Moral Dimension: Toward a New Economics* (New York: Free Press, 1988).

meeting, or anyone else to argue adamantly that a particular theory does not correspond to reality. The rules that support the grammar of the economic approach make such a critique devastating. However, this type of argument has its own presuppositions; it depends on assumptions that may need to be questioned in a world where such decisions have a broad effect on society and our physical environment.

Ultimately, when we talk about social science describing the world or about a theory's value as only dependent on its portrayal of reality, we obscure important components in our reasoning process.[11] While the natural science framework of analysis exalts description, the value of social scientific study necessarily must transcend it. We are not interested merely in the factual nature of our observations but in their relation to human systems of meaning. Random facts like the proportion of employed to unemployed bricklayers in Toronto, or the average age of women who subscribe to *Newsweek* in Pella, Iowa, or the number of three-children families in Michigan only come to have meaning in a particular context. Even before we begin to draw conclusions, we use systems of categories (such as gender, employment status, vocation, geographical region, and family) that lift our work above mere description, that make our task so much more than a simple translation of a world of facts into a world of ideas.[12] To describe the world is to impose human standards of meaning. Although we cannot ignore the importance of accuracy, the ultimate criterion for validity cannot be limited merely to a judicious comparison of our theories with brute social scientific facts. The theories and facts, and our selves, are themselves constituted through systems of human meaning. There can be no objective arguments for objectivity and no empirical arguments for relying solely on empirical analysis.

---

[11] Richard Rorty, *Philosophy and the Mirror of Nature* (Princeton: Princeton University Press, 1979).

[12] There is "no neutral algorithm for theory choice, no systematic decision procedure which, properly applied, must lead each individual in the group to the same decision." Thomas S. Kuhn, *The Structure of Scientific Revolutions* (Chicago: University of Chicago Press, 1996) 200.

Our familiarity with the economic approach makes it difficult to explain how we actually "do" economics rather than how we "say" we do it. Before we discuss how value can be determined without relying so heavily on a comparison between internal (mental) theories and an external (physical) world, perhaps a short historical explanation of this tendency would be useful. Richard Bernstein argues that the root of this conception of social science and the human being originates with René Descartes's (1596–1650) sharp distinction between mind and world as described in his *Meditations,* published in 1641.[13] In this theological proof of God's existence, Descartes begins in the first meditation by radically doubting the existence of all things. Recognizing that there must be a subject who is doing this doubting (*cogito ergo sum* in the second meditation), he then begins to construct a world and a God based on the fundamental distinction between self and all else. His method of stripping away any thoughts of his family, culture, language, country, upbringing, likes, and dislikes by consciously forgetting everything (including "that I was nourished, that I moved about, and that I engaged in sense-perception and thinking") must have seemed odd in his own time.[14] Today, however, we recognize this process, in which we simultaneously become disembodied and separated from the very social influences that make us unique, as the scientific method. This view of our lives as lonely and isolated individuals, confident only in the existence of our own consciousness (certain of its contents and doubting all else), forms the basis of scientific thinking. What matters most according to this picture is the correspondence between model and world, theory and fact, idea and action.

---

[13] Richard J. Bernstein, *Beyond Objectivism and Relativism: Science, Hermeneutics, and Praxis* (Philadelphia: University of Pennsylvania Press, 1983). Descartes chose the following subtitle: "in which are demonstrated the existence of God and the immortality of the soul," and dedicated the work to the Paris faculty of theology.

[14] Rene Descartes, *The Philosophical Writings of Descartes*, trans. John Cottingham, Robert Stoothoff, and Dugald Murdoch, vol. 2 (New York: Cambridge University Press, 1984) 17.

Our theories of agency that define the human being entirely in terms of thought mirror the qualities of *homo economicus*. The idea of a rational, profit-maximizing individual whose preferences remain uninfluenced by any other person is quite naturally related to the self-perception of the disengaged scientist who merely describes the social world without reference to his or her self. These two Cartesian selves have perfect self-knowledge and can know the world without anything to mediate their efforts. The first of these calculates personal utility on the basis of perfect self-knowledge (of an internally ordered list of preferences), and the second evaluates personal theories only on the basis of their correspondence with the world. The same foundational anthropology that forms the cornerstone of our conception of the economic agent also supports our view of the ideal economic researcher.

There is something profoundly disturbing about this sort of criticism. We react emotionally to statements like those above. We distrust people who tell us that there could be anything wrong with the way that we understand the nature of truth or value. We easily dismiss people who suggest that a comparison between theory and reality is deficient and label them as relativists. We adamantly declare that without this standard, "anything goes." At this point someone might angrily exclaim that this means that merely saying a theory makes it true. Someone else might object that there will not be anything to prevent every quack with a half-baked hypothesis about the gold standard from receiving tenure at Stanford. Yet in the section above, I mentioned that the mistake lies more in how we "say" we do economics than in how we actually "do" it. The fact is, in general, quacks are not taking over the faculties of M.I.T., Harvard, and Yale. However, neither are the faculty members of these departments of economics gaining credibility for more accurately comparing a physical world with their personal, mental models. Indeed, none of us in our informal economic theories, our sociological hypotheses, or our theological speculations does this either.

We have become so comfortable as Cartesian selves that we cannot even imagine any alternatives. The pervasiveness of this means of understanding the world has become deeply ingrained habit, almost unavoidable except as we strain in our conscious effort to think in other terms. Ultimately our ideas gain credibility not because their direct relation to the world is always immediately self-evident, but because others accept them. Economists publish papers, attract students, gain influence among members of the business community, get academic promotions and political appointments, build coalitions, and alienate adversaries on the basis of the persuasiveness of their arguments. Again, many of us may find this sort of statement unsettling. We may want to simply reject those people who make such suggestions as ideologically motivated or hopelessly inept and confused.

The reason why associating persuasiveness with the standard we use for understanding truth may be frightening or sound foolish is further evidence of how difficult it is for us to transcend Descartes's dualism. We want truth to reside in some Platonic higher realm, beyond the influence of our frailties, untarnished by human weakness. We want to think that we experience the world directly, as Adam did when he first opened his eyes after his creation out of the dust.[15] We worry that to admit that there is no ultimate foundation for knowing why we know the things we know, is to be open to the manipulations of others. Without the familiar standard for judging truth from falsehood, we can see no alternative to the possibility that demagogues and sophists like the ones who play such a prominent part in Plato's dialogues will manipulate us, and the truth, with their lying speeches and their evil intent. Empirical verification of an external world with mental theories is the social scientist's mighty fortress in part because of these insecurities.

The West's Christian heritage has emphasized that each person has an independent, individual relationship with God. This is clear in devotional classics such as Augustine's *Confessions* and Descartes's *Meditations,* which propose an anthropology dominated by the distinction between a private, mental inner world and a public, social

---

[15] Charles Sanders Peirce used this metaphor to describe his quality of "Firstness." Charles Sanders Peirce, *Philosophical Writings of Peirce*, ed. Justus Buchler (New York: Dover Publications, 1955).

outer world. This tradition still has important effects on how we think. The dualism that separates mind from world, and the individualism that gives us a tendency to see persuasiveness as almost a private affair between persons, means that we understand human interaction as merely a discussion among minds. We ignore the importance of the standards that define communities and provide the necessary lens for interpreting the world. These standards form a system of rules that is not utterly rigid, but changes and evolves in the same way that grammar gradually does. We cannot function and we cannot meaningfully conceive of ourselves or anything else without such rules. They represent the invisible net that binds all the members of a community together. They construct the basis for any judgment of truth or value.

In economics, just as in the English language, consensus exists on a huge range of issues that build the foundation for further work. Agreement on statistical methods, on standards that limit the range of study, on what constitutes valuable results, etc. forms the basis for this grammar. Just as with English, these standards represent the product of human work, luck, imagination, and ingenuity. That the English word "chair" was a human invention, however, does not mean that we can meaningfully use it to describe a pencil. We cannot effectively use words in any way that we choose. Economics' statements are similarly constrained. Even though they represent a product of the human imagination, we have consensus on most issues governing their use. Other similarities between economics and language also exist.

The constraints of the world as it presents itself to us are similar to the physiological limits on the written and spoken word. Both languages have evolved out of a specific chain of historical events that have left indelible marks on our present practices. The Norman Conquest of England in 1066 has forever changed the English language, just as the political context and the scientific ideals prevalent in the first centuries since the advent of political economy have left their mark on our economic ideas. There are objective standards for correct economics just as there is consensus on correct English. Just as we cannot make up our own version of English, with its own intricate grammar, so we cannot merely invent our own economic approach, but must rely on the work that has been done before us. The grammar and rules that support English and economics change slowly. Disagreement exists in our usage of both these languages. However, a sturdy core of consensus supports our application of them.

Perhaps a specific example would be useful to my point. Even according to this understanding of truth there can be situations in which everyone believes something is true that nonetheless we would define as false. For instance, I could claim that 42 percent of children in my town do not receive more than a minimal level of nutrition in the food they eat before going to school. Due to a computer calculation error, this could be wrong. However, just because everyone in the world believes this statement, this does not make it true. Before anyone interjects that it is false because these figures do not correspond to reality, we should have a closer look at why we would call it an error.

In her book *Pilgrim at Tinker Creek,* Annie Dillard points out that only single-cellular organisms perceive the world as it is.[16] The philosopher Immanuel Kant (1724–1804) shows that human beings must always be limited by the very consciousness that enables their action. Although the world presents itself to us, we can never experience it unencumbered by the systems of interpretation established within community. What we see depends not only on where, how, and why we look, but also on the ideas we use to make sense of the world. In the example from the last paragraph, our language necessarily comes out of a community, just as do the concepts necessary for its functioning. A community determines what is necessary for adequate nutrition, who should be defined as a school-aged child, what are the limits of a town, etc. The community even has standards for the definition, usefulness,

---

[16] "…I see within the range of only about thirty percent of the light that comes from the sun…A nightmare of ganglia, charged and firing without my knowledge, cuts and splices what I do see, editing it for my brain." Donald E. Carr points out that the sense impressions of one-celled animals are *not* edited for the brain: "This is philosophically interesting in a rather mournful way, since it means that only the simplest animals perceive the universe as it is." Annie Dillard, *Pilgrim at Tinker Creek* (New York: Bantam Books, 1974) 19.

and interpretation of a percentage or any other fact. Different communities have different standards, which themselves vary by context for the amount, and specificity of data that we must have before projecting a final percentage for the entire community.[17] Ultimately, the computer error did not so much shatter the correspondence between fact and theory so much as it violated the standards set by the community. A community makes our hypotheses useful through its attention, and thoroughly irrelevant through its disinterest. The standards of this group, however, can make a statement false even without its conscious recognition of a particular error.

While truth necessarily requires that a statement must correspond with the world as it presents itself to us, we cannot even understand the idea of truth without a system of rules. The computer's calculation mistake could be so minor that the final result remains within the margin of error that is acceptable to the community interpreting this figure. In this case the community's rules may determine that a factual error, that a particular lack of correspondence with the world as it presents itself, is unimportant. In our concern for verifying our theories by comparing them with "reality," we often obscure the importance of the system of rules that guides both our observations and our actions. These various languages that we use to interpret our experience must necessarily direct our attention and influence the results of our work.

We certainly cannot merely say anything we want and expect it to be true. What we say must be (and may be) true is only the case within a certain context, within the language and standards of a particular community, which articulates particular rules about the world as it presents itself to us. An economist, a sociologist, and a theologian all describe qualities of the world through the important medium of a uniquely shared system of beliefs, assumptions, and ideas. You are not merely a lone individual looking out at the world. The world—that is, you and all that you have learned—looks out at itself. Words do not serve merely as labels for objects, they constitute qualities and

---

[17] The rules of statistics impose a uniformity to those standards and provide insight into the implications of our choices.

relationships, they participate in our creation and formation. There can be no such thing as reality in general, only a reality specific to a person and a community within a particular context.[18] Our interpretation of the world as it presents itself to us is woven so deeply into our community experience of that world that the two cannot be untangled. Charles Taylor writes that "we are aware of the world through a 'we' before we are through an 'I.'"[19] When we come to see that meaning is not something wholly private to an individual, but represents something that is shared within a community, we can see that truth does not lie in a stark comparison between theory and world. Value does not exist within objective qualities but as a construction of the community. We err in believing that self-knowledge and knowledge of the world exist apart from our experience within a community.

Interpretation and Ethics

> No less remarkable is the fact that the market renders its participants—including the most informed and observant ones, the economic experts—quite unaware that the enthronement of profit as the criterion of economic rationality can only be achieved by the exclusion of basically all considerations of morality or esthetics from the calculus of judgment, so that rationality refers only to the rules for profitable activity, not the rules for socially useful activity. That is why economists can converse about the efficiency of a firm but not about its social validity, and why they become irritated when soft-hearted people declare that an enterprise judged only by its economic performance is as seriously misperceived as a government judged only by its surplus or deficit. —Robert Heilbroner.[20]

---

[18] Meaning must be necessarily for or to a subject. That is why the notion of intrinsic value so important to the deep ecologists mentioned in chapter 2 should not be confused as something that exists without a subject.

[19] Charles Taylor, *Philosophy and the Human Sciences*, vol. 2, Philosophical Papers (Cambridge: Cambridge University Press, 1985) 40.

[20] Robert Heilbroner, "Rhetoric and Ideology," in *The Consequences of Economic Rhetoric*, ed. Arjo Klamer, Deirdre N. McCloskey, and Robert M. Solow, 38–46 (New York: Cambridge University Press, 1988) 42.

Why does it matter that the foundations for our work do not lie firmly rooted in reality, but rather in the conventions of a particular community and its experience with the world as it presents itself? Earlier in this section, I argued that the way we "do" economics differs from the way we "say" we do it. Unfortunately, however, both of these are intimately related. A view that understands the economic task as the verification of theories through comparison with reality ultimately distorts the results of our work. The accepted practice of referring to unmediated experience of both the internal and external worlds leaves out the possibility for other systems of interpretation (which embody their own distinctive values). When we cease to regard economic theorizing as mere description or as a process of verifying social facts, economic debate is enriched, creating the possibility for a much deeper understanding of our social relationship with the material world.

This verification/description method of understanding, which characterizes the economic approach, immediately suspects people who draw conclusions different from our own. The only possible reasons for disagreement under these rules are: (1) The other person simply does not understand how economics should be done; (2) Someone has made a calculation error; and (3) The other person is an ingenuous ideologue, blinded by inaccurate, dogmatic bias. People who offer different explanations of social behavior in our current model must necessarily be "out of touch" with reality. Recognizing that truth and value do not merely inhere as self-evident elements of our experience, that they must be determined through comparisons with a particular community's system of rules allows us to differ in interpretation. Difference no longer must necessarily be equivalent to error. When scientists no longer take simple, unadorned reality as the subject of their interest, they open themselves to the possibility of new insights from other communities of ideas.

The distinction between "positive" or value-free economics and "normative" value-laden economics (discussed in the last chapter), so central to intermediate economics courses, represents a similar sort of naiveté. Nicholson's distinction between positive and normative economics (common among many economics textbooks) obscures the extent to which a system of moral values must necessarily lie ingrained within any economic approach.[21] Most of these textbooks argue that economics can provide the student with a toolbox for solving social problems. This metaphor, however, may not be entirely appropriate since most tools do not distort to such an extent how we actually understand a project. Money, employment, interest rates, and profit are tools that we have ceased to regard as tools. Michael Sandel writes that this has become even more the case over the last twenty years as market-based methods for solving problems have squeezed out other approaches, as advertising has expanded drastically (for example, in selling naming rights to stadiums). This has implications for fairness, as what he calls the "skyboxification" of modern life means that more and more goods are coming to be available only to the wealthy (who can afford "concierge doctors," for instance), and people of various social classes have fewer opportunities for interacting with each other. When markets are used to solve problems that are not appropriate for them, they tend to corrupt important institutions and practices (he uses the examples of lobbyists who pay people to hold their place in line for important congressional hearings and the corrupting effect that paying mercenaries to fight wars has on citizenship). Sandel writes that "we have drifted from *having* a market economy to *being* a market society in which market values seep into every aspect of human endeavor."[22]

The economic approach common among the business community, policymakers, and academics simultaneously conceals and emphasizes particular values. A popular saying reminds us that to a man with a hammer, the world looks like a nail. These last two chapters have taken these moral values as their primary topic of interest in order to

---

[21] Nicholson writes that "*positive* economic theories [are] 'scientific' theories [which] take the real world as an object to be studied, attempting to explain those economic phenomena as they are observed. A somewhat different analysis of economic theory is *normative,* taking a definite moral position on what *should be* done." Nicholson, *Microeconomic Theory: Basic Principles and Extensions*, 11.

[22] Sandel, *What Money Can't Buy: The Moral Limits of Markets*, 11–12.

understand what we bring with us as we apply the economic framework to our environmental problems. The central concern with efficiency and waste, the positive consideration of competition as a means of overcoming sloth, the benefits of independence over community, the centrality of deterrence and incentive rather than moral suasion, and the importance of self-interest and the profit motive represent only a few of the presuppositions that cannot be disentangled from the economic approach. Becoming aware of the values that this view embodies should represent the first step towards a more responsible use of its insights.

We forget that our economic reasoning has an historical origin in a particular culture, that these assumptions are not universal. Although we may be able to describe the behavior of a medieval king as he finances wars abroad or a pygmy market in economic terms, we must remember that the participants in these activities would not draw the same conclusions that we do. They would not even use the same categories for explaining their action. For instance, Thomas Aquinas (1225–1274) drew a sharp distinction between value in use (which he called value) and value in exchange (or price), while modern economics assumes price and value to be equivalent. The commensurability of all goods and services represents a particularly unnoticed presupposition in industrial societies. Many anthropologically distinct societies also frown upon the accumulation of material things, and instead have important gift-giving rituals, such as the potlatch.[23] Particular concepts of the value and the nature of individualism, family, growth, property, market, utility, materialism, selfhood, fairness, leisure, quantifiable measures of well-being, productivity, efficiency, theft, interest, the good life, etc. pervade the most basic foundations of all economic predictions and assessments of worth.[24]

---

[23] Marcel Mauss, *The Gift: Forms and Functions of Exchange in Archaic Societies*, trans. Ian Cunnison (New York: Norton, 1967).

[24] All of these assumptions provide rich material for theological reflection on the nature of personhood, the world, and God (who relativizes the most absolute of our cultural understandings).

As mentioned above, our great familiarity with the accepted values of economic thought disables us by limiting our ability to conceive of alternatives. Although we may take our conception of rationality for granted, the process of incorporating this view into our culture was a long and painful one. All of the present economic powers have long memories of industrialization and literary records of the discord that accompanies this process. Charles Dickens's *Hard Times*, Frank Norris' *The Octopus*, and John Steinbeck's *The Grapes of Wrath* represent only a few examples of a whole class of literature devoted to describing the dislocation that occurs with industrialization. Transforming societies into economies, communities into markets, and people into consumers quite naturally involves a near total disruption of daily life. On the basis of all historical experience, this transition seems to be irreversible as economic development quickly destroys its own alternatives. A contemporary example elucidates the difficulty of adjusting to the economic notion of rationality.

In Kenya, among the Kamba, as with many pre-capitalist peoples, Western understandings of capital accumulation have been particularly difficult for governments and developmental agencies to implement. The strong social value of responsibility to an extended family results in the wide dispersion (among aunts, cousins, uncles, etc.) of any excess profit that a particular individual may earn. Any financial windfall from a particularly successful harvest or from a higher-paying job will be distributed among cousins who need money for tuition, uncles who require funds to pay for new shoes, grandparents who require expensive medical treatment, or distant relatives who have lost their jobs. Although economically "rational" people would accumulate capital for investment purposes, the social expectation that such wealth will be shared among family prevents this process, which defines capitalism, from happening. As Kenya slowly converts to modern economic practices, radical distortions in every aspect of social life change the spirit and face of the region.[25] Our atomized view of the individual and of individual

---

[25] With the increasing importance of the monetary economy, rural farmers, often heads of households, have migrated to the cities in search of employment,

responsibility, however, makes it difficult for us to conceive of rationality on any other basis.

Conclusion

The distinction between normative and positive economics does little to highlight the dependence of the whole field on human systems of meaning. The economic approach necessarily in its abstractions must make important choices about the relevance of various features of experience. The values defining and distinguishing the economic approach lead to analysis that highlights certain elements of social life at the expense of other important features. It has often been pointed out that neglecting to include environmental damage in measurements of social good (such as GNP) makes any policy based on such figures fundamentally biased. Economists, as have virtually all academicians in the West, built their entire field of study upon the assumption that human beings are essentially disengaged subjects. A strongly unidirectional sense of causality (people change the world without being changed themselves) results from this deeply ingrained assumption.

As discussed earlier, a particular view of human agency lies embedded within both the individual profit-maximizing subject of economic theory and its author, the disengaged researcher. The notion of an autonomous self arose out of the philosophical thinking of Descartes and Locke and became popular at the same time as the new emphasis placed by society at large on commercial activity and the accumulation of wealth in the seventeenth and eighteenth centuries.[26] During this

---

leaving their families behind. The cost of transportation means that they seldom visit their homes, thus causing further social distortion.

[26] Descartes saw the mind as absolutely separate from the universe of matter (which he understood as dead). By understanding truth and rationality as defined procedurally (in terms of the scientific method) rather than in terms of substantive belief, he laid the basis for the primary manner by which economics operates. Charles Taylor's discussion of the evolution of the Western concept of selfhood offers many insights into the origin of these views that have become so central to economic thought. Charles Taylor, *Sources of the Self: The Making of the Modern Identity* (Cambridge MA: Harvard University Press, 1989). Locke's

time, moral philosophy gave birth to economics. The ideal of scientific objectivity has, thus, been incorporated into economics since its very beginning. This objectivity, however, makes invisible both the extent to which social scientists remain influenced by the society that surrounds them and the full impact of their systems of thought on the societies they observe. This inflated sense of detachment from the world represents the source of persistent methodological errors made in the name of social science.

As a study of society, economics does not merely stand apart from the world it observes. It remains perpetually and unalterably influenced by its social context. In our economic thinking, we are all subject to a two-way formulation of the Heisenberg hypothesis in that not only is the field of our interest changed through observation, but we also are changed in this process. Economists, government policymakers, and the captains of industry must always remain subject to the powerful forces of social conditioning, to the weighty hand that is the spirit of the times. Lack of attention to these influences limits reflection on how economic study or activity alters the social world. In the effort to maintain a value-neutral, disengaged view, the economic approach has consistently minimized the effects of its study on the world. While its adherents have recognized that economics interprets the world, they have neglected the extent to which the world simultaneously interprets economics. The ideas of economists and the values embedded in their models do not merely describe the world, they necessarily alter it.

Part of the special appeal, the magnetic attraction we feel for these economic frameworks lies in their counterintuitive nature. We find something particularly arresting in models of society that so heartily contradict our conventional wisdom. The appeal of suggesting that individual self-interest will lead to the best outcome for the whole, or any other model that initially seems so opposed to everyday reasoning, captures our attention. Counterintuitive models give a special authority

---

understanding of rational management of the self implied that one could disengage oneself from the world that forms our opinions. It implies that we can live and act totally freely from our tradition and our prior experiences.

to experts, just as the phenomena they describe make specialists indispensable. These models appeal to us in a much deeper way than mere description of the world. Our respect for the orderliness of mathematical elegance in these frameworks and for their counter-instinctual results adds meaning and richness to our understanding of social life. Economics, with its focus on price, also may appeal to us because it appears to be more ethically simple. Markets do not pass judgments or ask whether some goods or desires are worthier than others. Although morality is clearly bound by tradition and culture, economics seems to offer a kind of universal way of determining value.

In his dialogue *Phaedrus*, Plato compares education to seduction and stresses the necessarily moral content involved in any type of instruction. Introductory and intermediate economics classes in business schools, law schools, colleges, and schools of government that teach economics as a value-neutral tool for policy obscure the ethical nature of these frameworks. While the assumptions undergirding the basic economic models appear to merely translate truly ethical decisions into mere utilitarian calculus, much more is involved in this maneuvering. Teaching that two entities can be made equivalent through price is to offer serious ethical instruction. When we suggest that boldly self-interested behavior on the part of individuals can actually work out the greatest good for society, we teach a code of values that, taken to an extreme, undermines itself. In educating students in the economic approach, we simultaneously inform them in an ethical approach that values individual, competitive solutions to our problems.

The breadth of this chapter has incorporated insights ranging from Antigone to Phaedrus, from externalities to ethics, from Descartes to Asimov, from the divided Freudian self to the maximizing (transparent and indivisible) individual, from the collective action failures of the industrial world to the community exemplified by the Kamba. We have reviewed, in brief, the place of freedom, cooperation, education, formation, and valuation within the economic approach. We have begun the careful process of archaeological excavation in our efforts to uncover the values concealed within its frameworks. We have strained to read these symbols that simultaneously reveal and conceal the world as it presents itself to us. Their characters have become clearer as we have learned the nature of this language's grammar. In this process of reviewing the familiar rules of everyday economic thinking, we have taken our first glance into the depths of its soul as we try to recognize the values that are hidden to itself.

6

SYMBOL

The Holyoke Range

A bird's eye view of the whole region east of the Mississippi must then have offered one vast expanse of woods, relieved by a comparatively narrow fringe of cultivation along the sea, dotted by the glittering surfaces of lakes, and intersected by the waving lines of river. He who succeeds in giving an accurate idea of any portion of this wild region must necessarily convey a tolerably correct notion of the whole. —James Fenimore Cooper[1]

Leaving behind an apple orchard painted white with thousands of spring blossoms, an hour-long walk through a young forest at sunrise brings me to the crest of the Holyoke Range. The waxy leaves on the oaks, elms, and birches have only just emerged like gentle green wings, while the wildflowers scattered at odd intervals along the Robert Frost trail have erupted into the magnificent colors so characteristic of spring in Western Massachusetts. From the tree-covered ridge, on this clear early morning, the wide valley in front of me gives way to the Green Mountains of Vermont. In the distance far behind, the skyscrapers of Hartford Connecticut rise out of a thick mist. The rational tools of economics cannot calculate the worth of these gentle mountains and thickly wooded hills. For me, their value is both evoked by their magnificence on this chilly spring morning and projected onto the rocky slopes and slender branches by my active imagination. The unbroken forests so familiar to James Fenimore Cooper (1789–1851), who filled them with adventure, left a permanent mark on my childhood and influence my experience of this place.

---

[1] James Fenimore Cooper, *The Deerslayer* (London: Richard Bentley, 1841) 4.

The New England preacher Jonathan Edwards (1703–1758) often retired to these mountains for prayer, solace, and inspiration during the Great Awakening. Riding or walking in these hills, he would often return with notes for his sermons and folios pinned to the outside of his jacket. In these same woods he found the "inward, sweet delight in God," "the calm, sweet abstraction of soul from all the concerns of this world." From a young age he found "God's excellency in the grass, flowers, trees; in the water and all nature."[2] His prayers rebounded off the same rock faces I see here. He watched the sun break the horizon over the same ridges that now stretch off into the distance on my right. I feel grateful for the sense of faith that draws me back to the wilderness. Many others have felt this way as they looked out over the broad valley in springtime.

The foundation for our ability to evaluate experience, to assign worth, and to make judgments lies deeply imbedded in our consciousness and itself serves as a screen that filters all of our perceptions. Our past experiences and feelings as we first step into this shady woods necessarily influence how we will see and understand this world under the patchy, not yet developed canopy of spring leaves. This complex process ensures that different people will always experience these forests in entirely unique ways. While some will notice the new shoots of poison ivy along the trail, others may be making mental estimates regarding the amount of firewood that could be collected per acre by clear-cutting. Perhaps insects and mosquitoes will prevent some people from even noticing the quality of light that changes as one moves into a stand of pines. Although we may not even be conscious of our evaluations, these determinations of worth necessarily remain part of our experience and represent a central concern in environmental policy and in the religious life.

Economics as a symbol system represents a family of ways to adjudicate between various individual judgments regarding worth. This system of thought, which we learn informally through our own

---

[2] Jonathan Edwards, *The Works of President Edwards*, ed. Samuel Austin (Worcester MA: Isaiah Thomas, 1808) 34.

experiences with the market and through more specialized classroom education, serves as judge and jury in these necessary decisions. Economists fondly speak about dollar votes and consumer sovereignty, about the entrepreneur's profit instinct and business flexibility to market demand as the optimal means of integrating individual desires and as a mechanism for calculating the greatest good. This view of a world where complex decisions are made accounting for a wide range of inputs is a very tempting vision of orderliness, social harmony, and organization. Such an explanation of economic behavior makes the market seem as if it exists naturally, that any other condition represents some sort of intervention or distortion into automatic social processes. This puts the burden of proof squarely on the shoulders of environmentalists who must then translate their policy arguments into unwieldy economic language, a grammar that evolved to effect entirely different goals.

As I explained in the last three chapters, the economic approach carries along a particular set of values into its application toward our modern problems. It has been profoundly shaped by the process of industrialism, which required its tools to make necessary social decisions and to pave the way for our technological progress. Within our society, markets wield a tremendous power, playing the primary role in assigning prices to everything from satellite launches to family farms.[3] Market processes gather consensus on crucial matters where little prior agreement can be expected. Initial accord on the rules governing economic systems leads to social harmony, a unity in our regard for the results of its methods. Mediating between the properties of objects and society, this system of symbolization aids in organizing and arbitrating between various notions of value according to its particular system of ideals. Despite its pragmatic usefulness, however, economic thought is not often defined in terms of symbol and symbolization. As explained in the last two chapters, typical characterizations describe the field in value-neutral terms, suggesting scientific objectivity rather than emphasizing the limited nature of its culturally and historically bound frameworks of

---

[3] How many things can we think of that are in no way compared or considered in terms of price?

analysis. We talk about the object of social scientific study as if it were merely an external world without recognizing the powerful nature of the symbol system that we created and which enables us to understand our experience.

The authority that we invest in economics as a means of understanding the world, however, frequently becomes lost to us in our reliance on its usefulness. Our blindness to the limitations of the economic approach, the tremendous influence on the societies that it has transformed, and our own confining self-perceptions all have worked toward making this symbol system second nature or unconsidered habit. Yet motivations justified by the economic approach contribute to the destruction of whole ecosystems. Its application in many circumstances as a panacea to a whole range of environmental problems suggests a second result of this habituation. Understanding the relation between the material and social worlds in chiefly economic terms has transformed our world in the most literal manner. The ideas embodied in our familiar institutions may be the primary barrier to the very quality of life that they were designed to enhance.

The meanings of the words we use reach back through the centuries and often can lend insight into how our ancestors perceived the world. Words never are wholly arbitrary symbols, but necessarily arise out of particular historical circumstances. Chosen for a reason, they often provide us with a glimpse of how another age chose to explain their experiences when these words were new, before they became habit. We rarely stop to imagine how our society understood the world in the ages before the basic terms for our commercial activities had been coined. Two frequently used Greek words form the source of our modern term, "economics." Household (*oikos*) as the primary social unit in Greek society and custom (*nomos*), or the human rules that organize and order the community, were both bound together in this word.[4] Ancient Greeks, such as Herodotus and Aristotle, did not so much regard *anomos*, the root for our word "anomy" or "lawlessness," as the opposite

---

[4] Henry George Liddell and Robert Scott, *A Lexicon Abridged from Liddell and Scott's Greek-English Lexicon* (New York: Oxford University Press, 2002).

of *nomos,* but instead opposed this term with *fusis,* which we translate as "nature."[5] This deep meaning of economics should serve to remind us that economy is custom and created out of the dust by visible human hands rather than a natural invention formed by divine invisible hands.

With this in mind, we can reconsider the role that economic categories and conceptions have on our understanding of society. Daniel Kahneman may be the first Nobel prizewinner in Economics to have never taken an economics class. He writes at length about many different reasoning errors. These range from not recognizing the way that we substitute an easy answer for a harder question to our inability to recognize the limits of what we know. In particular Kahneman discusses the tendency of the mind to overvalue what is immediately present and to jump to conclusions based on limited evidence. This phenomenon is so pervasive that he uses an acronym for it—"what you see is all there is" (WYSIATI).[6] Another not unrelated error of perception is to think that the world exists exactly as we perceive it, unedited by the customs (*nomoi*) that influence our consciousness. The usefulness of economic theories and methods has resulted in a proclivity to allow our symbols to become mistaken for the things that they represent (for instance, we frequently regard GNP as our goal and forget that it is useful only to the extent to which it approximates the well-being of our society).[7] The idea of economics as a system of rules and laws, as a particular grammar organizing the households (*oikoi*) of our world, was introduced in the last chapter. This chapter further develops this view by examining how these types of rules function within conscious thought. By examining the operation of symbols, we can come to better understand the foundations of these rules.

---

[5] This distinction between human nature (*fusis*) and human convention (*nomos*) represented an important element in *Antigone* also as the main characters worked through their various ethical dilemmas to discern which standards were of central importance.

[6] Kahneman, *Thinking, Fast and Slow,* 85ff.

[7] Theologians define this reification of symbols, this misplaced attention, as idolatry.

Allegory and Metaphor

> Without symbols nothing has intelligibility and form for us. Without them we grope in darkness. Symbol and reality participate in each other. —H. Richard Niebuhr[8]

We mistakenly describe economics as a study of human behavior, or as an examination of the nature of social systems, or as a survey of the effects of scarcity, or the design of socially useful structures of incentives. We should instead understand it as a symbol system, always enabled by and confined within history and subject to human meaning. This view makes the limitations of human consciousness clearer. Furthermore, this perspective provides helpful insight into our society's excesses and some of the causes that lie behind the extraordinary (and accelerating levels of) damage that has been done to our world's natural environment in the last century.

As discussed in the last chapter, during the late 1950s and early 1960s tremendous technological advances led some economists to hope that in the future enormous computer programs would be able to make accurate forecasts that could prevent fluctuations in the business cycle. Although the usefulness of these kinds of technology has been recognized in airline flight scheduling, computerized telephone switchboards, and millions of other uses, the complexity of our world means that such approaches, for economics, will always be limited.[9] The

---

[8] H. Richard Niebuhr, *The Responsible Self: An Essay in Christian Moral Philosophy* (New York: Harper & Row, 1963) 52, 157.

[9] Economists realize this. Although massive computer programs diagramming national economies exist, they have not offered very accurate predictions of future business conditions and their limitations are certainly acknowledged. A computer program could not have predicted the rise of Netscape, Yahoo!, Apple, Google, or Facebook. It would not have been able to forecast the second war between Iraq and the United States. Certain markets (for instance, oil and finance) show a particular vulnerability to what George Akerlof and Robert J. Shiller, after John Maynard Keynes (1883–1946), call "animal spirits" or changes in confidence that make them particularly volatile. Akerlof and Shiller, *Animal Spirits: How Human Psychology Drives the Economy,*

fluidity of human systems of meaning and the massive gulf between constantly changing symbols and mathematical variables make it unlikely that computers will ever be able to fine-tune social systems. Human constructions of meaning based on symbols represent phenomena of an utterly different nature than those described by the most sophisticated computer programs of today. Although some may still argue that our predictions of the future are limited by the quantity of the data that is available, the quality of these measurements also must be questioned. Human beings simply do not make decisions primarily on a rational basis. We are subject to "irrational exuberance," which leads to wildly overheated markets and to the kind of panics that cause runs on banks and the depressed global financial markets of 2008.

The attempts of classical Christian authors such as Origen, Augustine, Aquinas, Luther, etc. to formulate rules for interpreting biblical symbols preserved a distinction that could be useful to our understanding of economic symbols. Rather than emphasizing the difference between "literal" and "figurative" symbols (and obscuring the mixed nature of signs at both extremes of this scale), they wrote about the degree of variability in the connection between a sign and the object it represents. This sounds more complicated than it is. Ancient authors recognized that some signs are fixed more permanently to the objects they they represent than others are.[10] These more rigid signs, which refer to only one object, they called allegorical signs and contrasted with symbols whose meaning varied according to context. Allegorical signs have no importance in themselves but only serve as pointers to other things. Simple allegories are altogether different than symbols, which take on a life of their own. Only loosely connected with their referents, symbols have important value in themselves, they connote as well as denote, they express and evoke as well as refer. Symbols evolve with fluidity and describe a complicated world in which meaning is separated

---

and Why It Matters for Global Capitalism. See especially their arguments in chapter 11.

[10] Galatians 4:24ff offers a biblical example of allegory as a means for interpretation.

both from the object and the symbols that represent it. The relation between objects, symbols, and meaning results in an unending source of complication and creativity as we attempt to understand the world.

By focusing on the relationship between the symbol and the object (which it represents) rather than on the association between a symbol and its literal or figurative meaning, one can come to better recognize the complexity of human consciousness.[11] It is too easy when we focus on a distinction between literal and metaphorical signs to fall into the trap of believing that language and thinking involve merely deciphering literal signs, which stand concretely for other entities (and represent them completely). Symbols have meaning in themselves through both human attribution and context. They direct our attention to particular qualities of the world as it presents itself to us. In his book *The Responsible Self,* published after his death, H. Richard Niebuhr uses a helpful example to indicate both the prolific nature of metaphor and the discernment problems involved in segregating literal from figurative symbols.

> The words we use in any language, moreover, are so richly metaphorical that we cannot even speak about metaphors or try to limit their use without employing metaphors. Even when we speak about *literal* meanings, we use a metaphor. Consider John Locke's sober statement about figurative speeches and allusions, allowable in his view only when we seek pleasure or delight but not information: " all the *artificial* and *figurative applications* of words eloquence hath *invented,* are for nothing else but to *insinuate* wrong ideas, *move* the *passions,* and thereby *mislead* the judgment; and so indeed are *perfect cheats.*" He was unable to convey this information about figures of

---

[11] Jung's distinction between symbols and sign could be useful in this context. The theologian Paul Tillich has also done some helpful thinking on this topic. Paul Tillich, *Systematic Theology*, vol. 1 (Chicago: University of Chicago Press, 1973) 239.

speech without making use of nine or ten figures of speech or metaphorical words.[12]

The human mind is creative, constantly producing new forms of symbolic meaning. Philosopher and mathematician Alfred North Whitehead writes, "Mankind has to find a symbol in order to express himself. Indeed 'expression' is 'symbolism.'"[13] We cannot help but make fresh associations that bring various aspects of our experience into focus. Although some have described the history of language as the process by which often-used figurative expressions gradually calcify into literal ones, this ignores the transformation of literal words into metaphor, which also occurs in a dynamic language. Poetry reapplies literal meanings in new figurative contexts; it works through creating new associations (by generating new meaning for symbols). Poetry fails when those associations cease to make sense to the author's audience and when they become so familiar that they no longer convey any meaning. Symbolic action represents a function not just of language but also of consciousness. We are mistaken when we forget that economic symbols are also similarly productive.

In supposing that economic variables and signs (such as inflation, price, monetary velocity, interest rates, GNP, the share price for grain futures, mortgage-backed securities, unemployment, etc.) merely serve as placeholders, or stand-ins for activity that happens in the real world, we are making a fundamental error. These should not be confused with allegorical signs that have no particular meaning in themselves. Nor are they mere derivatives. These variables and the greater system forming the constellation that gives them their significance have a degree of independence from the things that they represent, which often goes unnoticed. They add human meaning and all its attendant

---

[12] Niebuhr, *The Responsible Self: An Essay in Christian Moral Philosophy.* John Locke, *An Essay Concerning Human Understanding*, ed. Alexander Campbell Fraser, vol. 2 (Oxford: Clarendon Press, 1894). Locke quote from ibid., 146. Italics are HRN's.

[13] Alfred North Whitehead, *Symbolism: Its Meaning and Effect* (New York: Macmillan, 1927) 62.

complications into our calculations. Although national output, exchange rates, inflation, unemployment, housing starts, the federal funds rate, etc. have precise economic definitions, the meaning of these signs goes far beyond the explanations offered in textbook glossaries.

The Triadic World of Language

> Just as we say that a body is in motion, and not that motion is in a body, we ought to say that we are in thought, and not that thoughts are in us. —Charles Sanders Peirce[14]

The relationship between allegorical signs and metaphorical symbols is important for clarifying how economic symbols work. Philosopher, logician, surveyor, and mathematician Charles Sanders Peirce (1839–1914) first described this means of understanding symbolic behavior in the nineteenth century. Peirce distinguished between cause/effect phenomena (which he called diadic) and symbolization (a triadic relationship).[15] The simple relationship between one billiard ball and another, the instinctual "fight-or-flight" response of a mountain lion upon hearing a sudden noise, and the physical reaction between two chemicals are cause/effect relations. Even Pavlov's dog, who salivated upon hearing a bell rung, according to Peirce would be merely reacting. For him, conditioning would be merely simple causation, a diadic relationship involving object and sign, but not meaning. The bell in this case would not function as a symbol, but rather would be a stimulus, an allegorical sign, a stand-in taking the place of an object. Symbols, on the other hand, have a special meaning in themselves as they reflect a greater whole.

This distinction between allegorical signs and symbols, diadic reaction and triadic relation, does not at all depend on the degree of a relationship's complexity but on the nature of the intermediate factor.

---

[14] Charles Sanders Peirce, "Some Consequences of Four Incapacities," in *Peirce on Signs: Writings on Semiotic by Charles Sanders Peirce*, ed. James Hoopes, 54–84 (Chapel Hill: University of North Carolina Press, 1991) 71.

[15] Walker Percy, *Signposts in a Strange Land* (New York: Farrar, Straus, and Giroux, 1991) 111–38, 271ff. Peirce, *Philosophical Writings of Peirce*, 98ff.

Local weather patterns, for instance, represent an exceedingly complicated example of cause/effect behavior. A cause/effect relationship may be very involved such that two objects simultaneously affect each other, just as a symbolic relationship can be relatively simple. Whether Pavlov's dog is conditioned to salivate upon hearing a bell, a siren, or a whistle does not materially matter. These diadic signs are allegorical in nature and correspond identically to those things that they represent. A (cause/effect) sign does not have meaning in itself, or apart from its function as a signal, and is therefore not a symbol. Peirce also described this kind of relationship as "secondness." The important elements of secondness include: (1) an object that is represented by a sign and (2) the perceiver. The sign does not convey any additional meaning.

Symbols, however, may stand for another entity, but they simultaneously have importance both individually and as representatives of a greater whole. They do not merely refer to that thing which they represent but also to the whole system of which they are a part. Therefore symbols have a fluidity of meaning that complicates our interpretation of them. Our linguistic symbols do not merely stand for the objects they refer to, but denote characteristics of those objects, actions, feelings, etc. and stand in a necessary and often complicated relationship with other symbols. The word "serpentine" in the phrase, "the serpentine river passing through Northampton," does not refer to serpents but merely to one perceived characteristic of snakes and the shape of the Connecticut River as seen from the Holyoke Range. This word derives its meaning from the context on which it depends and from those characteristics that it possesses (through acquisition as part of a greater system). Symbols working through context necessarily draw our attention to certain features of experience as part of our work in making interpretations. Peirce also described symbolization, in opposition to allegory, as thirdness involving the object (a river), the symbol (the word "serpentine"), and meaning (meandering or twisting or slippery or changing). For him, consciousness is a triadic phenomenon.

Each of the last three chapters has illustrated the extent to which symbols, and symbol systems like economics, serve to direct our attention, to draw out specific qualities of our experience, as consciousness screens perception and builds abstractions. In the example above, "serpentine" as associated with the river draws out certain aesthetic qualities of the river as seen from that wooded sweep of mountains. A sentence describing the industrial activity up and down the Connecticut River using the adjective "venomous" would bring our attention to a different quality of experience. Economic thinking works in this way also by using abstractions that both draw the focus of our concentration to certain qualities of our social experience and distract us from other elements of it. While individual symbols can be used to change the way we experience the world, different languages also similarly enable and distort our perception of it. Theology and biology draw our attention to different features of our experience through the stories and motifs that they employ to describe experience.

In the beginning of his book *Zen Action, Zen Person*, T. P. Kasulis describes how Japanese grammar promotes, and grows out of, a particular interpersonal dynamic that prevails in that culture.[16] Japanese sentences often do not specifically address the individuals involved in a discourse (Japanese people say "writing" with the subjects implied rather than "I write to you"). Kasulis argues that this grammar serves to de-emphasize the individual in societies that use this language, and that it instead focuses attention on the relation between people or among objects. This frequent omission of personal pronouns, and the subjects and objects of verbs, fundamentally alters the manner by which Japanese people understand experience. It concentrates attention on relationships rather than individual action; it reflects a long history of customs that govern how people understand each other. The effects of this grammar, and the various influences on it, can be discerned in political, familial, and religious institutions. Values promoted by a particular grammar seep into cultural forms ranging from artwork to calligraphy to table manners. These then influence language.

---

[16] Thomas P. Kasulis, *Zen Action/Zen Person* (Honolulu: University Press of Hawaii, 1981).

We are familiar with the notion that specific languages reflect various values embedded within their vocabularies and grammars. Many languages do not have the verb "to be." Northern European languages have more words for "snow" than Polynesian ones do. The French historically have imported fewer foreign words directly into their language. Instead of drawing another language's word directly into French, they substitute a newly coined French word. English has been long recognized for its idiosyncratic and irregular usages and its quick incorporation of words from other languages into its enormous vocabulary. The frequent invasions of Britain by the Saxons, Jutes, Normans, etc. have fundamentally altered the way we express and understand ourselves in English today. Today, we still sense that old, well-worn Saxon words (like "supper") are not equivalent to the sophisticated words of the Norman court (like "dinner"). This subtle difference in meaning and connotation, perhaps noticeable only to a native speaker, has been preserved even though these newer French words have been part of our language now for almost a thousand years.

Just as complicated declensions, rigid sentence structure, and frequent compound words make German a precise language, so does economics also have qualities that distinguish its ability to make sense of our experience.[17] Its power results in part because we believe that it is generally fair and objective, that its measurements of value seem to account for a reasonably wide range of personal opinions and that its application appears to result in a productive society. Despite the bias

---

[17] German is a relatively more inflected language, and this means that it includes more grammatical redundancy. In this whole section, I do not at all mean to imply that Germans, Polynesians, and French people think in a different way or that languages are fundamentally untranslatable. I only mean that different languages, vocabularies, and grammars make certain kinds of expressions more likely. Our cultural practices and values are not independent of the language that we use to express them. Steven Pinkner writes about just what can and cannot be claimed as arising out of the diversity (and similarity) of human languages. Steven Pinker, *The Language Instinct* (New York: W. Morrow and Co., 1994). This includes a section on the "Great Eskimo Vocabulary Hoax" on pp. 53–54.

that economics as a language exhibits in favor of the wealthy, many of us believe it to be more in accord with our democratic values than other alternatives.

The last three chapters indicated the extent to which the economic approach as a language draws our attention to individualistic competition as a means of satisfying an infinite personal and social desire for more. This language does not just enable us to achieve social goals; it plays a major part in determining what those ends will be. It even evokes a particular class of interpretations as to the degree of success that a society has attained in achieving these goals. The economic approach as a grammar modifies our experience. The last two chapters explain that this language does not merely reveal the world as it is, but rather serves itself as a perceptive filter coloring our understanding of social processes. We addressed historical values concerning waste, freedom, cooperation, education, formation, and valuation in particular. This system of thought and expression expectedly tends to regard the natural world as an input into productive processes rather than as having value in itself.

Unfortunately, its system of calculating value does not do a good job of accounting for the chilling beauty of the winter constellations in the clear southern skies before midnight. It has little capacity to assess the full worth of a foaming white river swelled with spring mountain rains, or the sudden quiet of a northern forest in fall just as the skies change after sunset from indigo to azure to black. It cannot measure the precise value of a massive expanse of wetlands teeming with life and sustaining flocks of Canadian Geese newly migrated from the north. Its precise statistics and numerous projections do not adequately value the dignity and diversity of life. Not recognizing this language for what it is, a symbol system that helps enable us to make sense of our social experience with commerce, but instead regarding it as a natural law of human and social nature, only makes it less likely that its tools will be of help in our efforts to care for the natural world.

System and History

> [The symbol] partakes of the Reality which it renders intelligible; and while it enunciates the whole, abides itself as a living part in the Unity, of which it is representative. —Samuel Taylor Coleridge[18]

Samuel Taylor Coleridge (1772–1834) emphasized the important link between the universal and the particular that takes place within the symbol. Although in one sense, this could be taken to suggest that the entire universe in some sense is reflected in a symbol, it is more helpful to see the relationship between the individual and the symbol system of which it is a part. Symbols, unlike allegorical signs, are bound not only to their objects but to a whole greater constellation of meaning. They derive their significance, in part, from their usefulness and relationship to the wider, often invisible, system of meaning. This relation becomes particularly obvious in economics, which ties together diverse phenomena through fairly simple basic frameworks.

The impossibility of extracting a single economic symbol and observing it independently from the whole can be observed in a single example. How could an economist suggest policies regarding the overall level of prices in the national economy, for example, without considering employment, which seems to increase with inflation? Inflation as a concept cannot be separated from GNP (which is often discounted for inflation) or foreign exchange rates (which affect inflation and which are changed by it as foreign factors influence domestic prices) or demand and supply (which determine prices individually and in the aggregate). Inflation as a concept can certainly not be understood as separate from all the other economic symbols and ideas such as recession, price, demand, long-term bond yields, the prime lending rate, the Consumer Price Index, economic rationality, federal funds rates, mortgages, etc. No other economic symbol can be considered relevant without this vast network of symbols and enabling assumptions. These abstractions have a tremendous amount of power as a system of symbols

---

[18] Samuel Taylor Coleridge, "The Statesman's Manual," in *Lay Sermons*, ed. Derwent Coleridge (London: Edward Moxon, 1852) 33.

that both forms us and itself is constantly revised to reflect adjustments in our own self-understanding.

We must never forget that symbols are defined by use and are not characteristics of things in themselves. The Consumer Price Index is not by nature a cause/effect sign, nor is it a symbol except in the way that we use it. This qualification contributes to the complicated and fluid nature of symbolic processes, which ultimately reflect both creative abstraction and historical location. In 1744 *Zedler's Encyclopedia* defined "market" as "that spacious public place, surrounded by ornate buildings or enclosed by stands, where, at certain times, all kinds of victuals and other wares are offered for sale: hence the same place is also called market-place."[19] Today we speak of market research, market shares, market socialism, currency and futures markets, market-clearing unemployment, market mechanisms, market demand curves, market value, market forces, marketing executives, free markets, market baskets of goods, marketization, monopoly markets, market failures, black markets, market prices, overseas markets, market economies, market equilibria, all as a result of a simple abstraction made by Adam Smith. Our use of this same symbol 250 years later indicates the extent to which this word has come to mean far more than a geographical location, as commerce and economic exchange have come to play a more dominant role in our lives. To regard our use of the term "market" merely as the best possible means of describing human behavior under conditions of scarcity is to neglect its history and its power as an abstraction invented by human ingenuity.

Consumption, evolution, entry, exit, equilibrium, capital, supply, demand, investment, saving, competition, labor, production, company, property, sale, maximization, rational agency, actor, equilibrium, collusion, etc.—all are other economic metaphors, each with a similar history. As mentioned earlier, in representing the economic approach as an observational science concerned only with making mental theories that correspond to an external world, we ignore the extent to which the

---

[19] Paul Ekins and Manfred A. Max-Neef, *Real Life Economics: Understanding Wealth Creation* (New York: Routledge, 1992) 7.

field and its results are both enabled by and confined within history. Economic symbols and methods originated and evolved in their own particular cultural and historical contexts and, therefore, will always bear the mark of those times and places. Furthermore, this process by nature must always remain open-ended. Although the allied nations participating in the Treaty of Versailles (which ended World War I) understood the economic significance of the treaty as the means of procuring reparations from Germany to rebuild their countries, we in modern times cannot fail to recognize the relation between the high reparations and the German hyperinflation that later aided in Hitler's rise to power. The historical significance of our policies and procedures by definition will never be complete and can be understood only after time has passed.[20] Economics as a system of human meaning will therefore be forever influenced by the past and eternally open to future revision.

All of our economic abstractions ranging from "junk bonds" to "M1 money supply" to "socialism" have histories describing a transformation similar to the changing use of the word "market."[21] Viewing economic symbols as "fixed" ignores the source and meaning that form the basis for our reception of these ideas. Our social scientific models emphasize the importance of the real-world objects (or phenomena) that symbols stand for. Frequently, however, the significance of a symbol is not in its allegorical or literal meaning so much as in the qualities it evokes. Economic symbols point both backward toward the concepts they represent and forward toward the meaning that people typically associate with those signs.

An example would be helpful to make this point clear. Although we have very precise definitions describing the denotation of these symbols,

---

[20] It has often been remarked that only in the last instant of the last human being's life will history become set.

[21] Obviously, we do not merely make up economic variables to suit our fancy. However, the process is a much more complicated one than merely describing how the "outside" or "real" world is. Again the complex interrelation between causal efficacy and presentational immediacy may be one means of understanding how these symbols come into being.

often their connotation must also be carefully regarded to understand their total impact. Recession and stagnation denote a decreasing or constant level of national output (usually measured by GNP, a calculation of a nation's total productivity). While employment and the overall level of well-being within a society (the quality of the environment, the society's culture and family life) could be improving and the income differential between rich and poor could be decreasing during a recession, the connotation of this one symbol suggests that the economic picture is grim. The meaning of GNP as a symbol transcends its denotation. It means more than the simple definition provided in the glossary of a college textbook. Political fortunes, the allocation of global development budgets, public confidence, stock market stability, international investment prospects, and hundreds of other measures will respond to the connotation as well as the denotation of recession. Often economic symbols express far more than they actually denote.

Advertising

> Our enormously productive economy demands that we make consumption our way of life, that we convert the buying and use of goods into rituals, that we seek our spiritual satisfaction, our ego satisfaction, in consumption. We need things consumed, burned up, worn out, replaced and discarded at an ever-increasing rate. —Victor Lebow (an American retailing analyst after World War II)[22]

During the lengthy and bitter trench warfare of World War I, which killed a whole generation of European young men, one would initially imagine that artillery barrages and sniper and machine-gun fire would constitute a fairly obvious (allegorical) signal of aggression. However, sometimes the timing, duration, and number of shells fired signaled to the enemies that these shots were part of an informal "live and let live" policy pursued by both teams of combatants. Machinegun fire at exactly

---

[22] Victor Lebow, "Price Competition in 1955," *Journal of Retailing* (Spring 1955), http://hundredgoals.files.wordpress.com/2009/05/journal-of-retailing.pdf (accessed 7 October 2013).

7 o'clock, no gunfire between 8 and 9 o'clock, or the repeated shelling of particular (and militarily insignificant) targets represented a covert system of communication initiated by the lower ranks in *ad hoc* self-preservation arrangements. Martial stalemate and the dearth of transfers in or out of any particular geographic region meant that both armies soon began to recognize combatants on the other side and to make these informal pacts to limit the deadliness of shelling and gunfire. These agreements were designed to seem like aggression to an outside observer, or a higher-ranking officer, and to simultaneously signal to the other side a continuing adherence to the practice of nonaggression.[23]

This custom illustrates three things relevant to this chapter. First, it suggests that symbols must be interpreted carefully, that even acts that seem obviously hostile can come to acquire an altogether different meaning. Human beings, with their richly creative imaginations, convert the most allegorical signs into expressive symbols. No particular action is symbolic or allegorical except with respect to context. Second, it indicates that while we often have a tendency to regard literal meanings of signs as more important than metaphorical meanings, often what a symbol expresses is more important than that to which it refers. In other words, our insistence on knowing the literal meaning of something is often misguided. In the example above, the peaceful overtures, or insubordination depending upon one's perspective, expressed through

---

[23] This example in its own context served to indicate which qualities in a relationship make cooperation most likely to work out. It is from a book on the prisoner's dilemma game that is so central to economic theory. Robert M. Axelrod, *The Evolution of Cooperation* (New York: Basic Books, 1984). The use of car horns represents another kind of ambiguous symbol. In Boston or New York City, honking your car's horn could mean anything from a mild sense of irritation to extreme anger. In Los Angeles the horn is used less frequently and indicates that the driver is angry. In Hawaii car horns are used most frequently as a means of saying hello to friends and family as one drives by. I have been told that in India horns are used in place of rearview mirrors as a means of letting the drivers in front of you know that you are behind them. Even in simple actions like this, meaning is not irreversibly fixed to the symbol. In more complicated cases (such as in analyzing literature), discerning meaning represents an even weightier task.

timely artillery shells would be entirely misread as literal examples of bloodthirsty violence. Finally, it reminds us that in regarding economic behavior, like buying or selling, as only an expression of self-interest, we may similarly be limiting what could be symbolic of a greater range of meaning. Theologians, who so often trade in intangibles, realize the importance of the expressive power of symbols and seek to understand how to make moral evaluations of symbols.

We make daily use of the economic approach as we try to understand the markets for new cars, used books, suburban houses, jobs in our field of work, groceries, and winter clothes without often considering the breadth of its influence on our society. Certainly, any reflection on the distinctive qualities of modern times must include frequent references to this institution as well as to our quickly deteriorating environment. Uncovering the role that economic thinking plays in this process is difficult in our society, which takes for granted its most basic methods. When we cease to regard our economic theorizing as merely our effort to interpret the world, we begin to discover how complicated this effort can be. In economics, both the symbol system representing the basic framework of analysis and the object of study are subject to interpretation. Neither the meaning of the behavior that we see in the supermarket, the mini-mall, or the bank, nor the meaning of the textbook that seeks to describe it is self-evident.

Perhaps advertising best illustrates this principle.[24] Nothing ages more poorly than advertisements. They inevitably convey a specific sense of temporal location and cultural presence. Advertising from an earlier time or another place must be translated in order to be effective, or even understood, by contemporaries. We regard the claims of ads for old-fashioned household gadgets, bicycles, and patent medicines like those printed in the early Sears and Roebuck catalogues as quaint. Our ancestors, the purchasers who were influenced by brash ads for these now-dated novelties, seem to us like gullible, unsophisticated consumers.

---

[24] I am indebted to the following: William Leiss, Sut Jhally, and Stephen Kline, *Social Communication in Advertising: Persons, Products, and Images of Well-Being* (New York: Methuen, 1986).

The insecurities that ads from another time sought to instill and exaggerate in their audience seem silly to us now.

Not only do the products (and the circumstances of their use), fashions, and technologies change, but also methods of persuasion have evolved dramatically. In the first two decades of the last century, advertising in print featured lengthy text and a photograph or drawing of the product. Through the middle decades of the century, the amount of text gradually decreased as pictures illustrating the benefits of using a product became more important than isolated product qualities. Rather than picturing the bottle of medicine, a corset, an automobile, or a clothes ringer alone, advertising came to show how these goods were used. The print advertisements started to display models in order to accomplish this end by including pictures of smiling consumers merrily enjoying these products.

The focus in attention shifted from the product to the product's use by gradually making context a more prominent part of the ad. The familiar advertisements of today have moved even further in this direction and project a lifestyle or a feeling, as the setting of the ad has become more important than the product or its use. Our modern advertising executives no longer strive to impart a large quantity of product information to their target audience. Instead they search for a single powerful message that will stay with a consumer. Using the language introduced above, these advertisers seek more to evoke a response, to produce a feeling, rather than to refer to particular products. Advertisements that do not even mention or picture the product no longer surprise us, as consumers have become more sophisticated in recognizing the meaning of subtle allusions to brands and manufacturers. When driving past a billboard advertising a European brand of drinking water, with the familiar picture of the Alps but without any print or picture of the product to explain the context, we congratulate ourselves for recognizing the product. By participating in this puzzle, we may lodge a desire for Evian water more deeply within our consciousness. Even with this increasing sophistication, consumers have become more sensitive to brands and branded goods. In the last decades, the importance of brand has increased tremendously in products such as children's clothing, athletic shoes, etc.

Advertisers attempt to link the projected lifestyle with product qualities and features in a more subtle manner than they did in the past. Advertisements of cigarettes and soda that only rarely include text today at one time had lengthy descriptions of their qualities. The trend has been a movement from selling product attributes to selling consumer benefits and image or lifestyle. This trend to move away from selling product attributes to selling consumer benefits and now lifestyle in the language of symbol is a change away from an emphasis on denotation to one based on the qualities advertisements connote. While advertising must both refer to a product or a brand and express, this latter quality (this evocation of feeling) that engages the creative imagination of the consumer has become recognized as the key to successful advertising. In the multimillion-dollar world of marketing, sophisticated executives understand that they are really selling intangibles associated with products and not physical goods. They know that their job is not to sell sports cars, but youth, a discerning taste, pride, adventure, sexual appeal, strength of character, sophistication, affection, conspicuous wealth, technological acumen, and ultimately, respect. Advertisers do not sell razors or even a good shave or soft, smooth skin; they sell a sense that their product will make its user more attractive to others. Perhaps that is why, in the past several decades, women have played such prominent roles in advertisements trying to "move" men's products.

Although we tend to privilege the referential, denotative, literal functions of symbols over the evocative, connotative, and figurative, advertising indicates that this may be as inaccurate as disregarding the metaphorical functions of economic signs. The expressiveness and the symbolic nature both of advertisements and the products they represent further complicate any understanding of economics as an observational science. Although many economists feel uncomfortable asking unscientific questions about the nature of desire, and if human beings really are better off only by virtue of having more things, this desire as expressed through our material goods represents an important part of the whole equation. Just as our formal mechanisms for understanding the social world are carefully constructed systems of symbols, so are our means for expressing our own desires, for making sense of our place within a greater social whole. Both our shared views on how we understand the world and our own consciousness operate by associating meaning with symbols. One might say that people today are not materialistic enough. The subject does not matter as much as what it connotes. We do not just want a beer; we want to seem young, attractive, and energetic. We do not buy clothing because we need more to wear so much as to make a statement or to keep up with a nebulous, ever-changing fashion goal to clarify our identity, to define ourselves. Economics as a symbol system makes sense of the complicated interrelation between things, society, and our symbolizing consciousness. It is a primary symbol system for understanding a symbolic world.

Conclusion

> It is the first step in sociological wisdom, to recognize that the major advances in civilization are processes which all but wreck the societies in which they occur: like unto an arrow in the hand of a child. The art of free society consists first in the maintenance of the symbolic code; and secondly in fearlessness of revision, to secure that the code serves those purposes which satisfy an enlightened reason. Those societies which cannot combine reverence to their symbols with freedom of revision, must ultimately decay either from anarchy, or from the slow atrophy of a life stifled by useless shadows. —Alfred North Whitehead[25]

How we regard economic thinking considerably influences how we care for the material world. Indeed, the distinction between economics as observational science and as a humanly constructed symbol system located in the historical era of industrialism could hardly have greater implications for ecology. In environmental debate it is not uncommon to hear arguments that free markets guard against over-depleting a resource or extensive environmental damage since the market will assign

---

[25] Whitehead, *Symbolism: Its Meaning and Effect*, 88.

higher values to these goods as they become scarce.[26] For others, faith in the invisible hand to coordinate our best interests has become a substitute for responsible care for the environment, or a means of rationalizing self-interested behavior, or a distraction from understanding pollution as an ethical problem. While the biased nature of an economic market in determining the allocation and production of goods sometimes is acknowledged with regard to its lack of adequate regard for future generations, and in its preferential treatment of the rich, most of the other guiding values implicit in this system of thought are only rarely recognized. As stated many times above, economic symbols participate in the promotion of an extensive system of values concerning individualism, responsibility, reward, work, family, government, justice, value, and worth.

The symbolic nature of economic thought quickly becomes concealed in itself. In our rapt attention to quantitative rigor, to statistical and mathematical elegance, this fundamental element becomes lost. Economics can never become more or less perfect than a perfect poem. This does not mean that we cannot make judgments of truth or value, only that these are made on the basis of a grammar that is a human creation. We use this system of human judgments to make sense of a human world of meaning. Even an economics with the sophistication of modern physics would be unable to transcend its symbolic nature. The invisible hand, and the principle that individuals all acting selfishly will work out the common good, should not be understood as decreed by natural law, but must be seen as a helpful metaphor for understanding various aspects of our society.

Regarding economics as a historically located symbol system rich in meaning, as a product of both the human imagination and our world's evocation, represents an important first step toward a truer ecological awareness. Mistaking economic judgments and measurements for objective descriptions of worth means these often-useful frameworks have acquired the powerful force of habit. Unless we begin to recognize

---

[26] For example, as wood becomes scarce, higher prices will force people to do without it, and to substitute some other less scarce resource.

this process of habituation, this enabling symbol system will become a disabling prison, walling us off from alternative possibilities. While well-suited to the beginning of an Industrial Age and to the commercial possibilities (and the opportunities for greater resource exploitation) that resulted from the Age of Exploration, many of the assumptions incorporated to suit these circumstances may no longer be appropriate in our time. Depletion of atmospheric ozone, the decreasing availability of clean water sources, the erosion of soil, overpopulation, the proliferation of greenhouse gases, forest destruction, species extinction, and persistent pollution are all increasing at record rates and to extraordinary levels. This makes our situation fundamentally unique in the history of the world.

Despite this, our abundance of faith in ever-continuing economic growth and our boundless pride in our systems of ownership have become our primary export to the former Soviet empire and the developing world. The lingering effects of the Cold War have crippled our ability to criticize and evaluate our modern industrial economic systems, creating momentum that blinds us to their symbolic nature. Recognizing our habitual misuse of economic frameworks and the dangerous effects of our reliance on their determination of worth is the first step toward reclaiming this symbol system and our society's freedom to include a broader range of criteria in our judgments of value.

7

PROPERTY

Northumbria

> The charming landscape which I saw this morning is indubitably made up of some twenty or thirty farms. Miller owns this field, Locke that and Manning the woodland beyond. But none of them owns the landscape. There is a property in the horizon which no man has but he whose eye can integrate all the parts, that is, the poet. This is the best part of these men's farms, yet to this their warranty deeds give no title. —Ralph Waldo Emerson[1]

Traveling alone across the green hills of England with only a giant rucksack, I felt like I was returning to a home where I had never been. The dew soaking the long green grass, the perpetually threatening sky, and the wonderful footpaths connecting the ancient villages of my mother's home country were true to her reminiscence. Without any specific plan or itinerary, my twenty-mile walks almost never led me to places of particular interest but instead took me rather haphazardly across the ordinary places that had been such memorable parts of my mother's childhood. In my life of change, the stability of villages like hers, which remained almost entirely unmodified over forty years, felt especially comforting.

One morning after a sunrise departure and about five miles of walking through flowering meadows filled with damp sheep, morning showers forced me to take shelter in an ancient stone chapel. Passing through the hedgerows that formed the border of the graveyard by the church, the brisk wind and sheets of rain against the small bell tower

---

[1] Ralph Waldo Emerson, *Selections from Ralph Waldo Emerson: An Organic Anthology*, ed. Stephen Emerson Whicher (Boston: Houghton Mifflin, 1957) 23.

reminded me of a scene from *Wuthering Heights*. Inside the sexton took time out from carefully polishing the pews to chat. He proudly pointed out the hand-carving of the pews (with little wooden mice carved into the sides) and told me the history of the church, saying that life in the village was slow. Without a hint of resentment in his voice, he said that he wished I could have come earlier in the summer before a rich American had bought all the church's stained-glass windows and shipped them in boxes to New Mexico. Tragically, in the latter part of the twentieth century, virtually everything has a price; everything seems like it is for sale. Since we learned to measure it, time itself has become a commodity. The enclosure movement that reshaped the landscape outside the church has not yet finished transforming this village or the world.

One of the most distinctive and globally influential characteristics of Western civilization over the past five hundred years has been an ever-increasingly complicated and expansive sense of ownership. While the prevailing concept of property varies tremendously across anthropologically distinctive societies and historical eras, the enclosure of the commons in England during the early 1500s marks the beginning of a major change in our Western view of ownership. Beginning with those rectangular divisions of village commons, fenced in to exploit profits from raising sheep, our understanding of the relation between property and commerce has changed radically.[2] As the Europeans first bought, sold, and divided wealth from mercantile voyages, they began forming the seeds that would later become the first banks, joint stock companies, building societies, and insurance companies. The Age of Discovery offered a whole new world filled with opportunities both for innovative forms of ownership and for converting mineral resources, human labor, and land rich with exotic crops into exclusive property. A second enclosure movement in England during the late 1700s and early 1800s signaled another radical change in trade relationships. Like the phoenix rising from its funeral pyre, the ashes of the Mercantile Era brought forth an Industrial Age, an era of the individual, and an explosion of

---

[2] The dispossessed peasants claimed that sheep were devouring people.

various ownership forms ranging from copyright and patent ownership to complicated joint stock and financial ownership.

Our most recent generations, however, have seen this tendency to create and extend exclusive ownership claims expand beyond all the limits of imagination. Diverse forms of communism created new types of state-sponsored exclusive ownership in all of the industries that it embraced within its powerful totalitarian grasp. Culture indelibly stamped out hundreds of different versions of property ideals as developing societies inevitably modified the very institutions that were unalterably changing them. As technological and scientific advances increased the pace of global assembly lines, and the intensity of work in product labs, property has begun to have a new meaning. Today one can own kidneys, soap-opera stories, junk bonds, derivatives, cellular telephone designs, parking spaces, phone lists, communications networks, currency fluctuations, reproductive material, musical tunes and jingles, mineral rights, development plans, parts of companies, bank loans or mortgages, electronic circuits, demographic data, satellites (remote sensing data, frequency channels, rocket launches, hardware, and software), airlines, airspace, airwaves, airtime, airports, pollutable air. A whole new vocabulary created in the last thirty years in part reflects the radical changes in real estate and finance (REIT, timeshares, etc.). In the amount of time that it takes to read this sentence, billions of dollars will change hands to buy and trade huge blocks of mortgages (GNMA, FNMA, FMC, etc.), junk bonds, derivatives, overnight money market accounts, or futures on everything from foreign exchange to home heating oil to wheat. None of these forms of financial ownership even existed thirty years ago.

Land, ocean, sky, glacier, broadcast frequencies, genetic codes, ideas, the moon, the minerals under our feet—all have been claimed—pieces of them all can be bought, sold, and owned. Cattle raised on rainforest grazing land in Brazil can be converted into money (through being sold, mortgaged, leased etc.). That money then can be used to buy a townhouse in Beverly Hills, a lead statue of Vladimir Lenin, a section of Bavarian forest, a Renaissance painting, a family farm in South Dakota, semiautomatic rifles, stained-glass windows from an ancient church in the English countryside, or virtually any material thing we can think of that is not controlled by a national government. The convertibility of virtually all material things represents the oddest feature of the emerging global society and yet we scarcely notice it. The copious footnotes and necessary copyrights and the overwhelming concern over plagiarism that accompany respectable scholarship represent only one example of a view on ownership that would have astounded (and probably offended) someone like Martin Luther or the Church Fathers who quoted pages and pages without citing authorship.[3] The oral poets of Africa, Oceania, the Americas, and elsewhere similarly would have been astonished at this feature of modern thinking. Perhaps one day the credits at the end of our movies will be longer than the films themselves.

Of all our economic symbols, the concept of property is, in practice, the most malleable. The notion of privatization (which describes the creation of new systems of ownership) no longer represents jargon that only economists understand. We have become very comfortable with more fluid notions of ownership.[4] Our comfort with this aspect of property and its familiarity in our everyday lives make it a good example of what economics means to us. As a concept closely related to our own linguistic sense of ourselves, the complex web of interrelationships between rights, value, price, the individual, money, nations, personhood, markets, etc., it suggests an excellent example of a symbol that represents both itself and the whole simultaneously. Its accessibility provides a wonderful opportunity for self-examination as our society continues to promote this particular framework of ownership as a global solution for the most complex problems that all societies are currently facing. This chapter considers what property means to us historically, legally, and as

---

[3] Although modern concerns over academic ownership of ideas may not be entirely commercial in their interests, they do reflect a very unique understanding of the individual.

[4] Deregulation (of shipping, airlines, long-distance service, etc.) during the 1980s made privatization a household word. With the opening up of the communist economies in the 1990s and the global financial crises of the first decade of the century this word's meaning continues to change.

part of our self-understanding. It raises alternatives and, at the end, discusses its relation to the environment.

Historical Background

> When one knows the use of weapons, he can use any weapon in accordance with the time and the circumstances.—Miyamoto Musashi[5]

> The past is never dead. It is not even past. —William Faulkner[6]

Just as we can imagine Miyamoto Musashi carefully evaluating the weight of his samurai sword before participating in mortal combat, we, too, should explicitly know our tool—that is, history—before beginning. During the twentieth century, the way society organized ownership provoked conflict around the globe and brought us to the brink of nuclear annihilation. To believe that scholars have remained uninfluenced in their work by the ideological struggles leading up to and fanning the flames of the Cold War is naïve. It may be hard for us to imagine now, but in the last century educated people seriously asked whether or not one should believe in private property. Ernst Troeltsch, in *The Social Teachings of the Christian Churches,* describes the issue of private versus community property as the primary focus of all early Christian writers who took up questions of ownership. Exclusivity and inclusivity have been our primary means of understanding property historically.[7]

As a symbol, property is both part of a whole network of symbols and a reflection of that whole. Its meaning continues to evolve over time. Construction on the Parthenon in Athens began in 447 B.C. Since the time when it was a temple dedicated to Athena, it has functioned as a treasury, a Christian church, a mosque, and most unfortunately, to store ammunition, which exploded on 26 September 1687. It is a

---

[5] M. Miyamoto, *The Book of Five Rings*, trans. Thomas Cleary (New York: Bantam Books, 1992).

[6] William Faulkner, *Requiem for a Nun* (New York: Vintage Books, 1975).

[7] Ernst Troeltsch, *The Social Teaching of the Christian Churches*, trans. Olive Wyon, vol. 1 (New York: Macmillan, 1931) 115–18.

miracle that so much of it has survived into our own time. Societies have not always valued preserving historical monuments and buildings, ancient forests, and various landmarks. The models of future cities in the world's fairs during the early part of the twentieth century displayed little concern for preserving cathedrals and other structures of historical interest. Although environmental change has always been a continuing part of the human condition, our modern environmental preservation movements similarly represent a fairly recent phenomenon.

Aristotle's distinction between human beings and the rest of the material world represents another influence on our modern conception of property. Although virtually anything may be bought and sold, human beings in the modern world may not be. The true roots of our contemporary conception of property, however, begin many centuries later. After a brief discussion of slavery, John Locke, in the second of his *Two Treatises of Government,* in summary form describes the most important elements of our modern notions of property.[8] Locke grounds his philosophy in the relationship between humans and God. He argues that although God originally granted "the Earth to the Children of Men to Mankind in common," "labor put a distinction between them." Since human beings "must of necessity appropriate" "the fruits and the beasts" of Earth for them to be of use, the concept of property was necessary to protect the labor that an individual invested. Every human being "has a property in his own person"; therefore, the result of labor should also be considered that person's property. If someone spends forty hours carving a stick, that person should own it because of the life that she put into it. Property was thus defined by usefulness and the extent to which someone invested labor into procuring it.[9]

In the three hundred years since this definition of property, it has represented a primary argument for Western European imperialism. Many early New England colonists rationalized their refusal to grant

---

[8] Locke, *Two Treatises of Government*, 283–91.

[9] It is interesting that Locke did not discuss inheritance in greater detail. Privilege rather than invested labor seems like a far more common source of wealth.

property rights to Indians on this basis. The Puritan divine John Cotton writes, "We did not conceive that it is a just Title to so vast a Continent, to make no other improvement of millions of Acres in it, but only to burn it up for pastime."[10] The earliest legal cases in the United States justified the confiscation of Indian lands because the original inhabitants of the land would not make the improvements that white settlers would. This is particularly ironic in light of the damage that has been caused by industrial development, ranging from soil erosion and pesticide poisoning to nuclear waste leakage and unattractive urban sprawl.

The final point of note from John Locke's treatise describes the limits in taking property. He argues that we should take only that which we can "enjoy" or "as much as any man can make use of to any advantage of life before it spoils." In an economic world with accessible markets, the demand for any natural resource increases beyond the amount one person or family can enjoy since individuals no longer gather merely for their own consumption, but with the intent to trade. As the industrial nations converted to capitalism, the new importance of capital accumulation and commerce made Locke's limit obsolete. This added demand provided the primary impetus for taking goods held in common and converting them into private property. The tragedy of the commons describes the incentive that individuals have to overuse a common good (for instance, to overgraze a common pasture).[11] Since individuals derive all the benefits from their use of a common good but share the cost of its misuse with all the others, an economic incentive exists promoting overuse. Most conversions of a commonly held good to private property are attempts to avoid this tragedy of the commons (economists and lawyers refer to this as internalizing an externality). The usefulness of private property as a means of preventing the abuse of commonly held property (rather than through the use of rules formulated in community or by authoritarian dictate) has seemed naturally attractive in an age of burgeoning individualism. All of our modern means of understanding

[10] John Cotton, "John Cotton's Reply to Roger Williams," in *The Complete Writings of Roger Williams* (New York: Russell and Russell, 1963) 46–47.

[11] Garrett Hardin, "The Tragedy of the Commons," *Science* 162 (1968).

property take this sense of the individual's primacy as a basic assumption. Regarding privatization as the only solution to the tragedy of the commons, in part, fails to recognize that common use without exploitation is possible, and both enabled and promoted by an ethical system that constrains those who share a common good.

Definition

> To change ideas about what the land is for is to change ideas about what everything is for. —Aldo Leopold[12]

The close relationship between our view of ownership and our understanding of our selves has a long history. In the Greek of the New Testament, "uparxo" means to be or to exist, and "ta uparxonta" means one's belongings.[13] In some senses, ownership is central to our understanding of being and existence. As mentioned earlier, the prolific nature of possessive pronouns and their wide range of usage in European languages mean that we refer to everything, from our hand to our heart to our ideas to our soul to our mind, as things we have rather than as parts of who we are. Philosophers of the twentieth century recognize that our being is interwoven with our possessions and that these exercise power over us.

Advertisers understand the intimate connection between what we own and who we are. In his book *Being and Having*, Gabriel Marcel writes that "to possess is almost inevitably to be possessed" and that "attachment confers power onto things."[14] Ownership also is a primary concern of Martin Buber's in his book *I and Thou*. Buber writes, "[W]hat has to be given up is not the I but that false drive for self-affirmation which impels man to flee from the unreliable, unsolid,

---

[12] Aldo Leopold, "The State of the Profession [1940]," in *The River of the Mother of God: And Other Essays by Aldo Leopold*, ed. S.L. Flader and J.B. Callicott, 276–280 (Madison WI: University of Wisconsin Press, 1992) 280.

[13] Bruce Manning Metzger, *Lexical Aids for Students of New Testament Greek*, new ed. (Princeton NJ: Theological Book Agency, 1969) 16.

[14] Gabriel Marcel, *Being and Having*, trans. Katharine Farrer (London: Dacre Press, 1949) 69, 164.

unlasting, unpredictable, dangerous world of relation into the having of things."[15]

Despite the power of these ideas, the lawyers' and economists' concept of property seems more important than that of philosophers and theologians. Like a mathematician using an x,y,z axis in graphing an object in three-dimensional space, the three different definitions that follow specify a location for our sense of ownership that will be helpful in clarifying how our legal/economic views of ownership affect our relationship with each other and the material world, including our natural environment.

In every culture that anthropologists have encountered, the problem of possessions has been addressed in a unique way. Despite the various norms in defining ownership, the overall qualities and features of such systems that Western cultures most easily recognize can be simply enumerated. One means of defining ownership identifies the agents involved as: (1) the owner, (2) the property, that which is owned, and (3) others affected by the ownership arrangement (these are people who are influenced but do not have control in the property right). This definition specifies ownership as the set of interrelationships between these agents and can be especially helpful for people socialized in a society that deemphasizes relationships occurring outside of market transactions. Ownership is relational, not objective. Property is not an inherent quality of an object but a system of relations between those who own it, those who do not, and those who regulate this relationship. Lying implicit within this definition is an idea of property as a right to exclude others from use rather than a view of property as a construction that enables people to capture the benefits of their labors.

Although an important introductory legal text states that "the emergence of new property rights" is an effort to "internalize externalities when gains of internalization exceed their cost," most lawyers focus primarily on ownership as a bundle of rights (or the possession of a requisite number of rights to constitute total

---

[15] Martin Buber, *I and Thou*, trans. Walter Arnold Kaufmann (New York: Scribner, 1970) 126.

ownership).[16] These rights are part of the reason ownership in our society is so complicated. They include: the right to buy, control, duplicate, improve, sell, destroy, transfer (to give as an inheritance, etc.), lease, restrict access to, modify, etc. These broad categories can be further divided according to the specific situation being addressed (land, genetic codes, and labor contracts function in very different ways). Few forms of ownership are unrestricted (we may own the land our house rests upon, but we still are not permitted to pour unrefined oil into the soil beneath it, or to convert our house into a drive-through fast-food restaurant). As these examples suggest, property rights can be configured in a tremendous variety of ways. This is the approach our society has taken to the problem of possessions.

Another means of describing ownership concerns the locus of control in various types of ownership systems.[17] Through this design, we can classify property in one of the following three ways: (1) Private—an individual right to exclude others from use; (2) State—also an exclusive right to control that lies in the hands of the individuals assigned by the government (this includes both democratic socialism, in which control is determined through elections, and the versions typically described as totalitarian communism); and (3) Common—which finds its basis in inclusiveness (i.e., the Old English Commons or our modern park system). This definition makes explicit the heart of ideological disputes that have been of such great interest in the twentieth century.

Finally, probably the most important aspect of ownership, ironically enough, relates to the difficulties inherent in describing it according to

---

[16] Jesse Dukeminier and James E. Krier, *Property*, 2nd ed. (Boston: Little, Brown, 1988) 52. Economic concepts have had a particular influence in our legal codes. The bundle of ownership rights that customarily accompanies the ownership of a vegetable shipment includes the right to destroy; interpreted loosely, this is not generally a right of ownership for most land ownership rights (in which one may have the right to destroy improvements but not the land underneath it). Similarly, land ownership rights have very specific rules regarding use, such as those in the form of zoning regulations.

[17] C. B. Macpherson, *Property: Mainstream and Critical Positions* (Toronto: University of Toronto Press, 1978).

any of the bases listed above. In any property relationship, the role of the agents involved or the locus of control can vary or overlap according to the individual right that is the focus of interest. For example, a landlord may have the right to buy and sell a piece of property, but a laundromat renting the property under the terms of a lease has the right to use the property exclusively (to lock the doors, to profit from business there, etc.). In this example, the local government also has claim to both the right to buy (through eminent domain) and the right to use (through zoning regulations). Furthermore, federal laws also protect the overall society's interest by forbidding the owner, the renter, and the state from creating impediments to common use through legislation limiting the bases for discrimination against others interested in laundry service or in buying the property.[18] In this example, both the principle agents involved (owner, property, and others affected), the rights related to the property, and the type of ownership control (private, state, common) vary according to the particular ownership arrangement that is being addressed. The nature of interrelationship inherent in property makes this the case in virtually any situation.

Most of those people who defend our current practices of ownership see private ownership as a personal right. Indeed, the original framers of the Declaration of Independence initially considered writing that all people have the right to life, liberty, and property. John Locke's proposal lies at the heart of disputes regarding property. According to this argument, exclusive property is the result of labor (or some labor investment), and that to deprive someone of their property is to deprive them of the fruit of their labor.

One counterargument to those proposing property as a natural right instead regards the glass as half empty, pointing out that very little of what most people own is actually the result of their individual labor. We have progressed far beyond the agrarian society in which labor (rather than acquired skill, capital investment, or available technology) is the primary determinant of income or wealth. Instead, they argue that most

---

[18] Price discrimination in this case is allowed, while discrimination based on gender, race, or religion is not.

of the "fruits of labor" mentioned above are those resulting from participation in a greater society whose earlier advances and current organization make these products possible.[19] Those framing this argument point out that, currently, the Western view of ownership sees it as a right to exclude others from possessions that were mostly accumulated not through individual merit or hard labor, but as a result of circumstance and as a product of interrelationship. They believe that those benefiting from interrelationships should be required to take responsibility for them in other ways.

Regardless of the extent to which one believes that our ownership arrangement is just, a general consensus agrees with the definition of ownership. Ownership for the modern person is the bundle of rights determining the relation between owners, physical property, and others.

Alternatives

[A] man is rich in proportion to the number of things which he can afford to leave alone. —Henry David Thoreau[20]

Although it may appear to be no great revelation, our understanding of the nature of property is quite unique over history and across cultures. Societies in the modern world still exist that do not make the same distinction that we make between persons and things. Anthropologists have made many of us familiar with mana, or the spiritual power that certain sacred objects possess according to some cultures in Polynesia and Sub-Saharan Africa. The potlatches distinctive of the American Indians residing in the Pacific Northwest, characterized by a radically different perception of the spiritual component of gifts, and lawsuits brought against the Department of Forestry, which cited arguments that

---

[19] One might argue that these benefits resulted from the historical configuration of property. At the same time, it is impossible to know which means of structuring property ownership is superior since another system of ownership was not tested (perhaps it would have had better results), and second, the current economic situation (a less agrarian, more mature version of industrialism) may require a different prevailing concept of ownership.

[20] Thoreau, *The Illustrated Walden*, 82.

land is sacred, each suggest a different means of determining what should be treated as an object. Understanding the manner by which societies conceive of this distinction is crucial in order to comprehend their view of ownership.

North Americans understand what it means to objectify another person. Behind this sort of statement lies a sense of the opposition between persons and things. The uniqueness of our modern conception of personhood (based on this distinction between object and person) is perhaps made most clear in the codes of Roman law up until 400 C.E.[21] Roman law made careful distinctions between various types of property on the basis of the manner by which an object is inherited. *Res mancipi* and *res nec mancipi* represented the crucial property distinction (as opposed to our distinction between things and people) and correspond to the difference between *res familia* and *res pecunia*. *Res familia* included the things of the household, such as immovable goods, children, precious things, certain slaves, etc., and required *mancipatio* (a solemn tie relating to handing things down) in order to be transferred to another owner's hands. *Res pecunia* originally did not fall under *mancipatio* and included food, cattle, sheep, money, and metals that the un-emancipated sons could trade. Roman legal distinctions and idol worshipping suggest that they probably considered some objects to have characteristics we generally assign to people (such as personality, agency, etc.).

Perhaps more interesting, however, is the manner by which Roman society also considered some people as having traits we reserve for objects. I am not intending to propose that slaves were treated exclusively as things (provisions that slaves could buy their freedom obviously meant that slaves were a special type of property), only that the relevant legal distinctions were not based on an object's "personhood" but on other criteria. These distinctions were based on Roman values emphasizing hierarchy and family, not on a modern distinction between

---

[21] My understanding of Roman law has been shaped by Mauss, *The Gift: Forms and Functions of Exchange in Archaic Societies*. Also, P. G. W. Glare, *Oxford Latin Dictionary* (Oxford: Clarendon Press, 1968).

persons (and their rights) and objects. This introduces a radical difference between modern views of private property as a right and those prevalent in the Roman world.

Other examples show a vastly different understanding of property and ownership across cultures. Tamati Ranaipiri describes hau, or the spirit of things for *Maori* people in New Zealand.[22]

> Let us suppose that you possess a certain article (taonga) and that you give me this article. You give it me without setting a price on it. We strike no bargain about it. Now, I give this article to a third person who, after a certain lapse of time, decides to give me something as payment in return (utu). He makes a present to me of something (taonga). Now, this taonga that he gives me is the spirit (hau) of the taonga that I had received from you and that I had given to him. The taonga that I received for these taonga (which came from you) must be returned to you. It would not be fair (tika) on my part to keep these taonga for myself, whether they were desirable (rawe) or undesirable (kino). I must give them to you because they are a hau of the taonga that you gave me. If I kept this other taonga for myself, serious harm might befall me, even death. This is the nature of the hau, the hau of personal property, the hau of the taonga, the hau of the forest.

To some this may seem primitive or superstitious or, at very least, strange. Yet cultures ranging from Scandinavia, Old Germany, the American Northwest, Melanesia, and Papua recognize an obligation in transactions that transcends mere physical exchange. Whether we interpret these practices as belief in the spiritual nature of things or as an honor ethic (which values honor over material possessions and trades it just as we would exchange private property), these constitute a fundamentally different manner of understanding the relationship between humans and the material world.

---

[22] Eldson Best, "Forest Lore," Transactions of the New Zealand Institute, 42:35. Quoted in Mauss, *The Gift: Forms and Functions of Exchange in Archaic Societies*, 14.

I am not suggesting that such views are universal or that our modern societies should begin to understand things as endowed with an inner spirit, merely that our concept of property may not be complete. Our understanding of the human being, as detached, as uninfluenced by the material world, may be a serious misperception. Although the historical documents on usury (the rules against lending at interest) sound positively silly in our world of money-market accounts, IRAs, multinational banking, and multitrillion-dollar deficits, the power of these authors' convictions is based on a fundamental assumption that entirely eludes us. Usury presumes that the manner by which we use money or relate to the physical world has a fundamental impact on our very sense of being in the world. Concern over usury presumes that people do not remain unaffected by material things, that our possessions and the way we use them influence us deeply. For people in these societies, property is not merely the product of our labor or the result of good fortune to be protected according to legal rights, but a primary factor in personal formation. For them, property does not merely affect how others perceive us, it changes the way we fundamentally are. Those who are concerned about usury believe strongly that how we use and regard physical objects or material wealth has ultimate relevance to God as the source of all meaning.

Conclusion

> No account of the uses of symbolism is complete without this recognition that the symbolic elements in life have a tendency to run wild, like the vegetation in a tropical forest. The life of humanity can easily be overwhelmed by its symbolic accessories. A continuous process of pruning, and of adaptation to a future ever requiring new forms of expression, is a necessary function in every society. The successful adaptation of old symbols to changes of social structure is the final mark of wisdom in sociological statesmanship. Also an occasional revolution in symbolism is required. —Alfred North Whitehead[23]

---

[23] Whitehead, *Symbolism: Its Meaning and Effect*, 61.

This chapter scrutinized a single symbol within the greater constellation of ideas relating to economy. It discussed our peculiar modern tendency to regard environmental problems as tragedies of the commons, resolvable only by devising more complicated systems of private property, by dividing up the whole into parts controlled by individuals. This resolution of the problem obscures the importance of ethical codes (and moral solutions to environmental problems) enforced explicitly as formal rules governing our behavior or implicitly as general standards (a personal sense of responsibility) that also constrain conduct and enable us to function in communities. Although the way objects participate in our sense of identity may not concern economists, this is important for the environment. The material world and how we use it is fundamental to our identity.

Our habit of thinking in terms of the "self-evidence" of rights as "inalienable" or as "natural" can serve as a smokescreen that obscures the extent to which our concepts of property and ownership have been constructed out of a particular historical context. For the sake of social and political order, perhaps they had to be considered in such a concrete manner. Indeed, from the time we are very young children, we are taught how to regard private property, and the special nature of those things we call our own. The purpose of the brief sections above is to illuminate both our dependence on one understanding of property (as a bundle of rights specifying a particular relationship between owners and others) and the extent to which this concept shapes and reveals our thinking. Unless we recognize that no historically or culturally universal concept of property exists, our vision with regard to the natural world can be nothing but severely limited. A connection exists between property as primarily the right to exclude others from use (with the intent of protecting common goods from overexploitation) and the effects of overconsumption on the environment.[24]

Most of the assumptions underlying both economics and property, in particular, initially were born out of the Reformation and the

---

[24] Although we are remarkably cognizant of being diminished as a result of losing our property, its other effects on us are not often noticed.

Enlightenment as means of promoting individual human dignity and worth. Reacting against rigid hierarchy, these thinkers substituted the disconnected individual for the, then, commonly held views that regarded humans as merely parts of a greater feudal scheme. With this purpose in mind, their ideas were very helpful and well suited to an Age of Exploration and the beginnings of the Industrial Age. As modern economies and relatively more democratic political systems developed, these ideas regarding individual autonomy and self-reliance became imbedded in them.

The influence of Protestantism on capitalism posited by Max Weber continues to be debated today.[25] Weber hypothesized that Protestant asceticism made possible the accumulation of capital for investment purposes that defines capitalism. Protestants substituted their work ethic for the unavailable monastic asceticism. This delayed gratification was one way of distinguishing whom God chose to save. He further argued that this distinct theology differentiated Protestants from adherents to other religions and was the reason for the West's relative affluence. Despite the controversial nature of these claims, most people do recognize that the Christian theology of individual sin and salvation has had tremendous effects on current views of community, responsibility, and subsequently, of ownership. A "[p]riesthood of all believers" replaced a prevailing view focused on community in which monk, noble, and commoner fulfilled specific responsibilities for the overall society. In emphasizing that all have equal and unmediated access to God, and that all Christians have similar responsibilities, this renewed emphasis on the individual has had a profound and lasting impact on our notion of human personhood.

Many of the dominant theologies of those times described God's nature as independent, detached, and unaffected, and thus, most certainly influenced those qualities perceived as necessary for the human

---

[25] Max Weber, *The Protestant Ethic and the Spirit of Capitalism*, trans. Talcott Parsons (London: Allen & Unwin, 1930). Robert W. Green, *Protestantism, Capitalism, and Social Science: The Weber Thesis Controversy*, 2nd ed. (Lexington MA: Heath, 1973).

exercise of power and authority. Douglas Meeks details the specific traits attributed to God that had the greatest anthropological effects on society's view of property as the following: (1) God as self-possessor, (2) God's property ownership as exclusive, and (3) God's freedom as manifested in an ability to dispose of property.[26] The concept of God in community or a God in relation to other beings, despite Trinitarian influence, did not capture the imagination of these early reformers. Although these thinkers could have chosen to preserve a stronger concept of community, they did not. As a result, North Americans value self-reliance and rights rather than responsibilities.

The emphasis on independent agency and individual autonomy (as a reaction to earlier feudalism) has done much to positively change the world, just as the importance of inalienable rights has fundamentally altered the way we understand other people. As mentioned earlier, we have difficulty conceiving of human worth or dignity apart from these rights, or the language that perpetuates this understanding of the human being. However, in disregarding the extent to which we are formed by our particular experiences, by our language, culture, historical location, possessions, etc., we neglect to recognize the way our desires, wants, and needs are also a product of these influences. A one-dimensional definition of fulfillment implies that we will be happier only with more things, when in reality, we can be happy only when our desire for material things matches the level we have actually attained. Recognizing desire as dependent on advertising, relative affluence (keeping up with the Joneses), the lessons we are taught as we grow up, and countless other influences is the first step toward realizing that a planet with forty times the resources of Earth is not necessarily enough to keep us happy.

In the United States there does not appear to be much concern about advertising unless it makes fallacious claims or targets its campaigns at young children. North Americans may be irritated by the number of advertisements they see, or interested in the ones that most capture their attention, or amused by the archaic ad campaigns in other countries, but

---

[26] M. Douglas Meeks, *God the Economist: The Doctrine of God and Political Economy* (Minneapolis: Fortress Press, 1989) 116.

they rarely stop to think about their cumulative effect. Consumption is such a tremendous virtue (it stimulates the economy, provides jobs, etc.) that advertising, which fans the flames of desire for more things, passes unnoticed. Yet, just as we are deprived by someone who takes something we have, are we not also somewhat diminished by having our wants dramatically expanded by Madison Avenue? Do we remain unchanged as we devote more and more of our energies toward acquisition?

Understanding property only in terms of natural rights neglects the important influence that property, and our desire for it, exercises over us. If possessing means being possessed, to what extent are we possessed by our desires for products that degrade the world?[27] Although mistaking material affluence for well-being might have been appropriate during a time when humans did not have the power to exercise much influence on the world around them, this error in a world of more than five billion people will not have such relatively benign effects. Our understanding of property in the industrial countries, which consume 80 percent of the world's resources, masks the relationship between desire and satisfaction, which become most important in a society in which the majority of people have their basic biological needs satisfied.

Constructing property arrangements may be useful as a means of avoiding the tragedy of the commons through the assignment of responsibility and reward. But it is only one possible solution to the problem of authority within society. In many respects, without knowing it, we have substituted the tyranny of things for medieval tyrannies.[28] This is only rarely made explicit in our materialistic culture in which the authority of priests and nobles has been traded for that of consumers, economists, and business magnates.

---

[27] Marcel, *Being and Having*, 69.

[28] Lewis Hyde's most recent book provides an excellent study of various kinds of ownership arrangements and the tendency of market systems to erode other alternatives. Hyde, *Common as Air: Revolution, Art, and Ownership*.

The quantity of consumer goods that Americans buy is astonishing.[29] Relativizing this modern idolatry, the worship of material growth and production, in today's world sounds to most like the worst sort of heresy. Imagine the national response to a politician who proposed that we should have a recession on purpose because the people of this country are looking for fulfillment in the wrong places, or because passing the ecological legacy that we inherited from past generations down to our children represents a more important social goal than exceeding the consumption levels of our parents. The only way politicians can currently sell environmental responsibility to the public in election campaigns is to argue that these regulations will create more jobs and allow us to have more things. Imagine the social effects of cutting the amount of time that people spend on the job in half (and thus returning to the productivity levels of earlier decades), simultaneously increasing employment rates while decreasing national output.

It almost takes the conflict between our understanding of economic well-being (as exceeding the output of past generations) and a vision of ecological sustainability for us to understand the influence that our ideas of property have on us. The right to property as a right to consume, produce, and pollute, and its centrality to our understanding of the material world show why it is important to have other individual and social goals. Perhaps we can begin to see ourselves as belonging to the world rather than seeing the planet as dead matter that belongs to us. Theology offers a way of understanding the human being, society, and the world around us that deviates from our economic anthropologies. The next chapter will examine in greater detail the role of theology and its contributions.

---

[29] Juliet Schor, *The Overworked American: The Unexpected Decline of Leisure* (New York: Basic Books, 1991) 108. Twenty years ago Americans purchased 51 million microwaves, 44 million washers and dryers, 85 million color televisions, 36 million refrigerators and freezers, 48 million VCRs, and 23 million cordless telephones for an adult population of only 180 million.

8

THE IDEA OF GOD

Desert

A man may not find wealth there,
    nor too much of food,
    but he often find himself,
which is more important. —Mary Austin[1]

Although the mid-day August temperatures can with regularity exceed 110 degrees, I typically began work in the fields outside of town during the cool of the morning before sunrise. On those long days, I would watch the sun rise over the Sierras and shine through the hazy air anticipating that in the next five hours temperatures in the alfalfa fields would soar. A huge portion of the water that poured out of our irrigation pipes soon would be sucked into the dry empty blue sky. Looking out to the nearby western foothills I could actually smell the water as it mixed with dust and poured out through ditches. The acres and acres of silent farmland around me could not be green during this time of year without this precious water.

While this valley is as dry as the Sahel it still provides the United States with almost one third of its fruits and vegetables (grown on the largest semi-continuous expanse of irrigated farmland in the world).[2]

---

[1] Mary Hunter Austin, *California: The Land of the Sun* (London: A. and C. Black, 1914) 174.

[2] California agriculture generated $43.5 billion in gross cash receipts during 2011. It consumes 80% of the state's water. Agriculture is the largest industry in this state whose GNP, if it were a country, would make it the seventh most productive country in the world. Most of this has been made possible by re-engineering the environment and by the construction of 1,400 dams and the largest two irrigation projects on the planet. California Department of Food

Without the providential gift of water that cascades down mountain rivers as snow run-off and some of the world's most massive water projects, the whole region would be little more than semi-arid. Most of the seasonal swamps and wetlands that were here for centuries during the winter rainy season have long since been filled as the water concentrated in these places has been distributed throughout the valley by an extensive network of canals. These massive civil engineering projects provide subsidized water to the large and wealthy western agribusinesses, which earlier in the century caused thousands of farms further east to go into bankruptcy. This cheap water, the long growing season and the enormous flat expanses of rich soil made these fields perfectly suited to the technologies which have automated much of modern farming.

Although the heat was uncomfortable for us, further south, in Death Valley summer desert temperatures could be deadly. Even in an air-conditioned car carrying an extra supply of water, desert travel can be dangerous. For me perhaps no two places in the world better exemplify our dependence on technology than these deserts. Yet, in the modern age few regions or cities could exist without the benefits of the transportation revolution that permits the concentration of such a large proportion of our total population in massive cities. Only one in ten people in the world lived in cities at the turn of the century, now more than half of the human race does.[3] This has been made possible by an agricultural technology revolution.

Some scientists believe that this era of substantial and sustained increases in crop yield has come to a close. In agriculturally advanced countries there is no longer a backlog of unused agricultural technology. As a result of this, and unsustainable aquifer depletion and other

and Agriculture, "California Production Statistics. www.cda.ca.gov/statistics/ (accessed 7 October 2013).

[3] In only a hundred years, America changed from being a predominantly agricultural society to an industrial society in which only a small fraction of the population works on farms. The mechanization of agriculture and the enormous global transportation network have meant that we are accustomed to supermarkets stocked with produce from around the world.

environmental degradation, "grainland productivity dropped from 2.1 percent a year from 1950 to 1990 to 1.3 percent from 1990 to 2008." As climate change continues to accelerate, food security will become a far more important issue.[4]

Friedrich Schleiermacher writes about our absolute dependence on God's providence.[5] This idea seems like a nearly constant theme in ecological theologies. The importance of technology in sustaining a global population of seven billion unevenly distributed people however, does not often receive the same degree of attention. Without the complicated networks of production and global trade, without the chemical processes for refining oil and the electrical generation facilities that heat our northern cities, without modern agricultural practices, without our expansive highway and communications systems and the many other technologies that we mostly take for granted, our society as it is currently structured could not survive. The social institutions we depend on include our concepts of markets, property, fair taxes, individualism, democracy, equality, the good life, etc. They provide the necessary foundations for us to function as a society. We have evolved to fit within a particular technological and social context just as we simultaneously played a part in creating that context. Now, even the most crucial changes made for the sake of our survival or well-being cannot be anything but painful.

Our habit of regarding the technological or sociological status quo as merely an (or worse, *the*) efficient response to the world around us rather than as a result of discrete historical processes may make change seem nearly impossible. The hundreds of towering dams constructed west of the Mississippi during this century, for example, were built in large part for political reasons not because they were the only or best solution for coping with the aridity of the western states. Our dependence on many of these water projects seems greater to us when we regard them as the only possibility for meeting our human needs than when we recognize

---

[4] Brown, *Plan B 4.0: Mobilizing to Save Civilization*, 8.
[5] Friedrich Schleiermacher, *The Christian Faith* trans. Hugh Ross Mackintosh (New York: Continuum, reprint 2009).

them as one solution that evolved out of the political and ideological context of the Great Depression.

Theology and Science

> A view of knowledge that acknowledges that the sphere of knowledge is wider than the sphere of "science" seems to me to be a cultural necessity if we are to arrive at a sane and human view of ourselves or of science. —Hilary Putnam[6]

Despite the importance of technology both as its serves to solve and create problems, many theologians, and scientists also, adamantly argue that science and theology have nothing to say to each other. Paul Tillich, one of the most notable theologians of the twentieth century at one time wrote, "Theology has no right and no obligation to prejudice a physical or historical, sociological or psychological, inquiry. And no result of such an inquiry can be directly productive or disastrous for theology."[7] Just as our historical circumstances created the economic symbols that we use, so do they also structure the types of questions we ask in our efforts to make sense of the world. The many conflicts between science and religion fought out during the nineteenth century led scientists like Stephen Jay Gould and theologians like Paul Tillich to segregate these two fields of thought. We try to preserve the sanctity of normative thinking by distinguishing and separating it from positive thinking. We look to save both the purity of scientific thought and the legitimacy of religious thinking by convincing ourselves that these two different ways of knowing have no common points of intersection.

While science may be of little help in making judgments on many specific claims about God (or about God's existence or non-existence), those things that we know about our world as a result of scientific advances do influence us as we seek to understand both the world, its ecology and its relationship to God. Our knowledge of the human

---

[6] Hilary Putnam, *Meaning and the Moral Sciences* (Boston: Routledge & K. Paul, 1978) 5.

[7] Tillich, *Systematic Theology*, 1:18.

condition and the universe we inhabit has changed enormously as a result of science. In some respects the various biblical authors tell very different stories about the world than what we are learning from modern geography, astronomy, geology, biology, psychology, physics, physiology, etc. Many facts taken for granted in the Hellenistic and Pre-Hellenistic worlds have been entirely disproved or at least understood in a fundamentally different way as a result of scientific advances. Whether we want it to or not, modern scientific thinking plays an important role in how we interpret biblical texts. These developments in technology certainly change how we understand God even if we claim that our theology comes to us during the quiet time we spend sitting in easy chairs reading scripture in the warmth of our study. Cultural changes also alter our understanding of God and theology. Our interests and emphasis in theological work cannot remain uninfluenced by the settled hand of the past or by the lively spirit of the present. In not recognizing the influence of these factors we disregard the extent to which theology is a human task and thus limited. We neglect to account adequately for our own fallibility when we begin attributing our very human ideas directly to God.

Similarly when we regard science as a mighty fortress impenetrable by theology we discount both the involvement of ethics with science and the important role of moral theology in forming how we make such judgments. Students in college during the Cold War had to decide what they would study knowing that almost ninety percent of the physics students would eventually end up working on some element of weapons design.[8] How one read biblical verses such as "I have not come to bring peace but a sword" (Matthew 10:34) and "all who take the sword will perish by the sword" (Matthew 26:52) had a tremendous impact on the direction of our scientific work. In a world of limits we must make

---

[8] K.C. Cole writes about the naiveté of physicists who believed they needed to be concerned only with technical problems and could leave moral issues up to elected officials during the early days of the nuclear era. K.C. Cole, *Something Incredibly Wonderful Happens: Frank Oppenheimer and the World He Made Up* (Boston: Houghton Mifflin Harcourt, 2009).

decisions on ethical grounds about where our research energies will be devoted, on the type of work to which we will commit ourselves. Questions about the nature of our experimental work (are we using ethical methods?), the outcome of our efforts (how will this technology be used?) and the value of alternative study (can my energy be best devoted to another area of research?) are too easily evaded when we draw a hard line between normative and positive, theology and science, value and fact. As discussed in chapter 4 the relevant scientific community makes judgments on significance, value and quality, they direct research toward questions which they consider interesting, all using criteria that are not a part of the formal scientific method.

Paul Tillich explains his position on the relation between science and theology arguing that theologians, as experts in "the ultimate concern," should not suggest that they can make privileged judgments in "matters of preliminary concerns."[9] Indeed, theologians and others should be wary of claiming divine support for their personal opinions (or their strictly institutional loyalties) and they should be especially attentive to the dangers of associating preliminary and limited objects and ideas with the Divine. While this warning may serve as a guiding rule for theologians, they must also realize that in being overly zealous to completely segregate science and moral theology they also make an ethical judgment. Choosing not to be involved is still choosing. In a world that regards science as the paradigmatic example of acquiring knowledge, where rapid technological developments constantly introduce new challenges to old ethical principles, theologians take great strides toward making their ethical pronouncements utterly irrelevant when they draw too bold of a line between themselves and the sciences.

Scientists want to separate theology and science to maintain the objectivity that they value so highly in their work. Theologians desire this same condition because they worry that scientists may start making claims about God (on the basis of research and new discoveries) that would undermine theological authority. However, when theology and science are entirely segregated there is more of a tendency for theology to

---

[9] Tillich, *Systematic Theology*, 1:12.

become irrelevant than safe from attack. The scientific project also is devalued when it loses access to the ethical resources of theological thinking. When positive and normative judgments are clearly divided, some questions of value inevitably get forgotten (as with the values that came to be concealed in the positive economic judgments described in earlier chapters). The role that our conceptions play in influencing our experience of the world means that at a fundamental level our perceptions are both enabled and disabled by our ethical principles. In drawing specific lines cordoning off different types of knowledge it becomes too easy for religion and ethics to become merely a private affair confined to arenas where their judgments have little meaning and even less influence. This segregation of science and theology cannot remove the role that ethics play in our perceptions and decisions. Such a distinction merely makes this important element of human experience more invisible to us. Neither our art nor our science can be disentangled from our life as moral agents. Since long before Plato, the idea of God or the divine has been intimately related to our understanding of ethics.

This chapter explains one way that theology might make contributions in efforts to protect the integrity of the natural world and the viability of those processes which sustain human life on Earth. The earlier chapters sought to describe the process by which social norms, especially economic standards, are formed over time and come to incorporate values within their very methods and assumptions which have an enormous impact on how we understand the physical world. This chapter proposes one view of theology's task in addressing the sources of environmental degradation. The next section illustrates the usefulness of theology to this project which at first glance seems to be relevant only to natural and social scientists. Theology matters because religion is an important part of many people's identity. Even for nonreligious people the values that have come to be embodied in economic and political institutions have deep theological roots. The end of this chapter reviews the contemporary meaning of the religious symbol idolatry and discusses how difficult it is to adjust ideas that constitute our sense of self.

The Role of Theology

> A help in answering questions: this is exactly the purpose of this theological system. —Paul Tillich[10]

Environmental theology is now a central concern in contemporary Christian thought. Major Christian denominations have made pronouncements on the issue and the American Academy of Religion devotes a section of its annual meeting to it. However, the public does not often consult theologians for advice in debates regarding environmental issues. Indeed, explicitly involving theology in such discussions in which economic and scientific arguments predominate, may seem very dangerous in a society that has become accustomed to an institutionalized distinction between the sacred and the secular. Despite such concerns, this sharp divide between church and state further prevents us from perceiving the sanctification of secular symbols as we transform them from means to ends.[11] The philosopher Michael Sandel argues that fear of disagreement has made people unduly hesitant to use religious or moral arguments in the public square. As a result markets have been making many decisions for us. "The era of market triumphalism has coincided with a time when public discourse has been largely empty of moral and spiritual substance."[12] In removing discussion of religion out of the public sphere, we add momentum to the already powerful tendency to give religious valence to economic and secular ideals. This is not to suggest that the state should sponsor a particular religion, merely that it already does sometimes promote secular ideals with a religious fervor. As Blaise Pascal wrote, "Men never do evil so completely and cheerfully as when they do it from religious conviction."[13] His statement does not necessarily suggest that we as a society are off the hook in our sharp division between church and state

---

[10] Ibid., viii.

[11] The US Constitution could be considered a kind of secular scripture and taxes as a tithe. The patriotism during the Olympic Games also reminds us of our tendency to deify the nation-state.

[12] Sandel, *What Money Can't Buy: The Moral Limits of Markets*, 202.

[13] Blaise Pascal, *Pensees* (London: Penguin Books, 1995), 153.

so much as it reminds us that a society's most powerfully held values always have the potential for causing the most substantial damage. In our society in which economic dogma can be espoused with a particularly notable fervency and single-mindedness this tendency should not be too quickly dismissed.

The brutal history of religious war and oppression among European peoples since the Reformation is not the only reason for disregarding theology as an aid in making social decisions. The decline in the status of religion, from the center of North American and European culture to its present role closer to the periphery, also has much to do with the theologies that have shaped our understanding of faith. In the two centuries prior to Charles Darwin theologians depended heavily on the argument from design. Theologians such as William Paley (1743–1805) argued that if one found a device like a clock in a field one would assume that it was made by a clockmaker.[14]It could not come into being on its own. The intricacy, beauty and complexity of nature for them implied the existence of God. For many Charles Darwin showed how we might speak about the way very complicated natural phenomena might have come into being without invoking God's role in their creation. This contributed to the opposition that people began to sense in the nineteenth century between faith and reason, religion and science. Theologians today, must recognize the influence of this history and that for many of our contemporaries the burden of proof in arguments relating to God rests heavily on the shoulders of the person of faith.[15] Theologians understand that today many find orientation in their lives without reference to any explicitly religious ideas or principles.

The disadvantages of employing theological concepts in public discourse however lie much deeper than the public relations problems experienced by religion in general. Many other limitations of theology at times also make it an unwieldy tool for this application. Perhaps the

---

[14] William Paley, *Natural Theology* (Philadelphia: Johnson and Warner, 1814).

[15] A better question would be to inquire into the nature of what we mean by the word "God."

most serious of these is the often-exclusive nature of this enterprise. Theological discussions do not long remain on the points which are agreeable to everyone, but by nature revolve around specific understandings of God, human and world that cause dissension. These conversations do not lend themselves easily to participants concerned only with objective thinking or scientific neutrality but usually dwell on ethical problems that are very difficult to resolve. The plurality of belief and disbelief make it difficult for a consensus to emerge. Finally, (as with environmental problems) the open boundaries of theology and the broad range of topics that it has historically addressed tend to make it difficult to maintain the appropriate focus. While discussing human nature, transcendence and creation may be necessary as we come to address the cause and extent of environmental damage, definite resolutions often are difficult in such a wide-ranging conversation.

Despite these shortcomings in applying theological thinking to environmental and economic problems, this approach can often be rewarding. Since the foundations of economics lie in the bedrock of moral philosophy and theology, philosophers and theologians could help in the debates regarding public policy and our most cherished assumptions about homo economicus. After two centuries of change in moral philosophy and economics, we have the opportunity to arrive where we started and to know the place for the first time. Theology can be useful to environmental debate in the following ways:

1. Natural law, as a theological or philosophical category, serves as the basis for many of the unconscious social scientific assumptions determining how important policy decisions are made. Although natural law arguments may or may not represent compelling forces acting on the thinking of many contemporary thinkers, principles based on this means of understanding the world have become built into our institutions and self-perceptions. As the scholars who formulated these assumptions, theologians are best trained for questioning these presuppositions and for proposing alternative views within the tradition that for historical reasons may have been discarded. (For example much of modern economic theory is based on a Hobbesian anthropology which views

human nature only as selfish, that people are "red in tooth and claw."[16] Other perspectives on human being may be helpful in modifying these assumptions and in building more flexible institutions).

2. Theologians, unlike members of the scientific community, have a unique tradition in addressing moral and ethical concerns. As discussed in chapter 4, by operating under the assumption that true objectivity was both possible and necessary for effective research, the scientific methodology itself has served to limit its ability to address the impact of socially constructed world views. By presuming that social scientists can stand outside of the social fabric, they have neglected to realize the full effect both of their work on the world and the influence of the particular social circumstances that formed them as individuals. Although very much subject to this limitation, theologians have recently begun to feel more comfortable being clear about the biases that their personal commitments introduce.[17] Theologians recognize that the object of their study, God, is not available to us in the same way that a particular physical object, like a tree, is. This has led to sophisticated thinking regarding the intangibles (such as meaning, responsibility, community, etc.) which serve as the backdrop for human motivation.

3. Unlike anthropologists who have experience in observing the various subjectivities of culturally distinct societies, theologians have always sought to offer prescriptive suggestions. Centuries of experience with the process of religious formation, and its explicit goal of changing world views, could have relevance as we seek to address global social problems. Catechism (or Christian initiation), monastic formation, the preparation of clergy, the experience of anchorites, all have helped theologians over almost two thousand years to become relatively well-acclimated to the possibility for radical human change. This heritage and

---

[16] I recognize that I am mixing Hobbes's philosophical metaphor (that "the life of man [is] solitary, brutish, and short"), with Tennyson's poetic one.

[17] Objectivity and relativity may not be appropriate concepts in many cases. Bernstein questions our tendency to immediately classify knowledge as either subjective or objective. Bernstein, *Beyond Objectivism and Relativism: Science, Hermeneutics, and Praxis.*

its particular interest in both formation and the resistance to formation, lengthy discussions over the nature of human freedom and agency, can certainly contribute to our understanding of the possibilities for change. The explicit mission of the church to build a "city of God" represented a vision of society that goes beyond a sociologist's concern for mere observation.

The power of meaning systems built on our concept of God and the centrality of religious symbols in our history and our collective experience represent further reasons for including the voice of theology in ecological conversation. For people of faith interested in these issues, religious understanding can hardly be segregated from other means of experiencing the world. The three categories above have been the model for earlier chapters and suggest several of the special insights that theology can offer in discussions of ecology and economics. While recognizing that the source and the effects of our economic sensibilities may not be enough to make a significant change in our attitudes and behavior, this strategy does undertake the first step in this process. The remainder of this essay addresses several more explicitly theological ideas that could be useful in reassessing our most cherished concepts of our societies and ourselves.

Virtual Theology

> But as important as technology, politics, law and ethics are to the pollution question, they are bound to have disappointing results, for they ignore the fact that pollution is an economic problem. —Larry E. Ruff[18]

The downtown districts of cities across the nation and around the world from London, Toronto, Hong Kong and Nairobi to Kansas City, New York, Atlanta and Houston in the last one hundred years have lost many of those differences that used to be so crucial in distinguishing them. Even in smaller cities such as Milwaukee or Sacramento, the giant steel

---

[18] Larry E. Ruff, "The Economic Common Sense of Pollution," in *Economics of the Environment: Selected Readings*, ed. Nancy S. Dorfman and Robert Dorfman (New York: Norton, 1972) 3.

and glass towers surrounded by four-lane one-way streets have come to represent the temples of the modern age. The city skylines of Europe and North America once dominated by cathedrals and churches today reflect our commercial interests in the lucid reflection of the setting sun against tinted glass. Our architecture reveals the primary values of our society.

Until Darwin, scientists routinely discussed the theological implications of their discoveries. Theology dominated the imagination of virtually all scientists, artists and thinkers through history to an extent difficult for us, as citizens of the modern age, to fully understand. For centuries, this system of thought formed the basis for all fields of knowledge, as its most trifling assumptions were regarded as absolute law. Virtually all thinkers in the Middle Ages, for instance, expended careful energy detailed theological arguments and appealed to the Bible often in intricate proofs which would seem entirely unnecessary to us. A careful study of the intellectual history of these centuries seems tedious to our contemporary minds. Their ideas appear cumbersome to us and burdened by the staggering weight of antiquated theological minutiae. Science was a branch of theology and drew conclusions both from inductive observation of the world and scripture. Rulers appealed to theology in order to justify all European government. Ideas like the divine right of kings had a power over even the most progressive thinkers that would be difficult for us to imagine today. Even the courts and their laws operated according to the stern commandments of biblical precepts. Rules governing the marketplace prohibited interest from loans on chiefly theological grounds. The power exerted by medieval theologians, abbots and bishops shaped the structure of social life for centuries.

The world of the Middle Ages seems strange to us. The sense of necessity that our ancestors felt about the central place of the Church with respect to both politics and the law, their constant fears about the eternal fires of hell, and their ever present interest in saints and miracles distance them from us. It is hard for us to remember that even in the Enlightenment, Sir Isaac Newton considered himself to be a person of faith first and a scientist second. He was motivated by a desire to describe a world subject to God's universal principles, not to create labor saving devices or to realize commercial gain. We may even have a tendency today to regard his devotion to theological problems during the latter years of his life as a distraction from his brilliant scientific work, rather than as an essential part of his overall system of thought.

We seem to have little difficulty in pointing out what we see as the peculiarities of earlier generations. However, realizing those qualities unique to our own civilization and time may not be so easy. No one in Medieval Europe could have imagined that the rules governing the exchange of turnips and carrots in peasant country markets would later come to be the primary principles for organizing most of the world's peoples. During those times they could never have guessed that in the distant future, civilization would operate not according to the values of courtly society, nor the standards which governed the church, but rather on those simple principles which were applied in the small country markets where feudal serfs exchanged vegetables grown on small private plots. Earlier chapters have reminded us of the power that the economic approach wields in virtually every aspect of modern life. Our tendency to regard economics as universal across history and culture only suggests the difficulty we have in recognizing how odd this manner of understanding our experience would seem to medieval lords or serfs.

In the twentieth century, faith in economic dogma and doctrine burned with the fire of religious devotion touching all the continents in the silent but no less intense conflict of the Cold War. People died with religious fervor on behalf of economic ideals. Mikhail Gorbachev and Deng Xiaoping, our modern equivalents to the Roman emperor Constantine who decriminalized Christianity, changed the political world as a result of their economic dreams and conversion. Even in the calm, rational discussion over free trade, the doctrine of comparative advantage evokes the fervency in our time that salvation by grace alone once did.[19] Economic doctrine whether reputable or marginal (including

---

[19] The theory of comparative advantage, in short, argues that in an international trading relationship, both nations will always benefit from fair trade (with the increasing mobility of capital and labor over national

such theories as comparative advantage, the invisible hand, the equivalence of price and value, the gold standard, supply-side economics, Keynesian intervention, marginal analysis, etc.,) plays an almost theological role in our society.

The quote that opens this section from Larry Ruff's article "The Economic Common Sense of Pollution" provides two important insights into how we understand the usefulness of economics as a tool for understanding our environmental woes. First, we can read it as a wise recognition of the important role that economic thinking plays in our treatment of the environment. Ruff clearly sees the powerful impersonal forces of the market in necessary opposition to a healthy environment. He points out that according to our market models pollution makes common sense as a means for a competitor to force costs onto others (by not paying for pollution abatement technology, etc.,) thus lowering cost and increasing profits. Second from this quote we learn that Ruff believes that economics is simply the way the world is. From this we can conclude that he believes that the market impulse necessarily represents a deep natural drive which cannot be explained or understood in terms of politics, law and ethics. In other words, economics is not merely a language, alongside of several others, for understanding our tendencies to degrade the environment. According to Ruff, economics is simply the way human beings necessarily are. In Ruff's world, economics does not represent a response to social life learned as a result of historical and cultural circumstance (and expressed through symbol) but rather a natural human drive that we have only recently come to understand in its complexity. This article's view of economics as the natural state of human society suggests that our economic presuppositions are about as

---

boundaries, this debate has become more complicated). This theory is the basis for most arguments against trade barriers. As with the invisible hand, this particular means of understanding trade has an almost religious following. Although I recognize the benefits of free trade, I find no compelling evidence to suggest that the balance of trade under these circumstances is always optimal, just as the operation of free markets does not necessarily assign a price equivalent to value. Arguments about NAFTA, the WTO, the European Union, the Euro, etc. keep this question constantly in our consciousness.

invisible to us as theological presuppositions were to the thinkers of the Middle Ages.

Economic thinking is the most compelling system of meaning in our time. Its universality and the energy that we devote toward achieving its ends make it far more important than almost any other means of making sense of the world. This system of symbols regards evil (such as inflation, unemployment, trade deficits, low output, inefficiency, theft etc.) as incarnated in chaos. It describes the human project as the creation of order in the world through the prevention of waste and the encouragement of productivity (similar to "be fruitful and multiply" in Genesis 1:28). Every month, quarter and year we publish new statistics which make news themselves, especially measures which economists expect to influence interest rates and thus bond yields. Our efforts to fight inflation or to battle the budget deficit or to compete successfully in world markets direct our energy in the way that military campaigns once did.

Extended payment plans, monthly car loan bills and long workweeks represent our modern sacrifice for the sake of our vision of meaningfulness. Shopping, once a purely utilitarian pursuit now is approached with the seriousness and devotion of a religious practice. Seven billion square feet (or 23 square feet for every man, woman and child in America) of our country has been converted into shopping malls. We make pilgrimages to the largest malls in Minnesota, Florida, Texas and Southern California that have theme parks featuring wave making machines and carnival rides in their designs. In a consumer society it makes complete sense that young people spend an extraordinary amount of their time in malls. High fashion has become popular even with our young children. Indeed they are formed like catechumen into consumers at a young age, receiving the final touches through their exposure to the media. Work at fast-food restaurants for the status rewards bought by extra cash is less onerous for young consumers than high school classes. Education in colleges offering degrees in accounting, advertising, business policy, financial analysis, marketing, corporate strategy, real estate and management science are means to commercial ends while student activities, including business fraternities and investment clubs, maintain a focus on profit-minded goals.

Profit and possessions, personal and national income, growth and development, production and consumption have become ends in themselves. Unfortunately this is no benign illusion. Even if the material needs of most people alive today could be adequately met according to this system of social rules, the requirements of future generations, the demands of a healthy eco-sphere, the hopes of other species and the preservation of beautiful wilderness certainly cannot be. These symbols have become habits of thought and have so much pervaded the other institutions in our society that few alternatives exist which can even serve to criticize our consumer culture. Universities have been quick to adjust to new demands for economic fluency through the employment of professional fund-raisers just as churches have in their progressively greater emphasis on increasing contributions by hiring outside professional consulting firms for advice on how to increase "market share."[20]

The symbols which interpret the commercial world have an unstated theological meaning for modern people. This system of thought provides us with orientation in the world. It directs our attention and shapes our desire. It assigns to us our most deeply felt goals. It structures

---

[20] "[A] prospectus of Stanford University's Institute for Higher Education Research states: 'Advances in economic theory and empirical analysis methods, developments in organizational behavior, and refinements of managerial technique have reached the point where we can hope to understand the complexities of non-profit institutions—including colleges and universities—to a degree approaching that for business firms.' William Massey, Stanford's vice-president for finance and a professor in the School of Education as well, says, 'Ever since I joined [Stanford's] central administration in the early 70s, I have become really fascinated with higher education as an industry where institutions with many interconnections interact in a kind of marketplace.'" This is reported in Robert Neelly Bellah, *The Good Society* (New York: Vintage Books, 1992). Examples of church growth consulting firms and endowed chairs established at seminaries for the purpose of increasing stewardship indicate the increasing influence that economic thinking is having on ecclesiastical concerns.

our perception of the world. It creates the context for our political and social experience, all without our conscious awareness of the profound extent of its influence. In the past, these functions were all part of our religious heritage as people looked to tradition to provide guidance for life's daily decisions. Perhaps in some senses, a society without a theology is not possible. Perhaps we need sublimated theologies to enable us to decide how we will commit ourselves. Through history the idea of God has been profoundly related to our understanding and experience of meaning and commitment. Through the ages, careful thought has gone into discerning what standards should be employed to judge how we can best devote our tremendous energies, talents and interests. The theological idea of idolatry as misplaced worship, as a mistaken devotion to temporary and fallible symbols, has been a helpful concept for making moral judgments about our commitments. However, before understanding the meaning of idolatry, we should be clearer about what we mean by God.

The Idea of God

> The chief rival to monotheism, I shall contend, is henotheism or that social faith which makes a finite society, whether cultural or religious, the object of trust as well as loyalty. —H. Richard Niebuhr[21]

In discussing the meaning of God within a contemporary, pluralistic context, we must make difficult decisions about the breadth and accessibility of our theological claims. Balancing between the specificity that clarifies any particular theological stance and the generality that is likely to include a broader audience becomes particularly challenging in efforts to address modern problems. Narrowly framed theological positions command a stronger sense of loyalty in a particular religious community and may be more suitable for expressing complicated ideas such as the relation between our cultural symbols and our religious self-perceptions. Despite these advantages, a confined parochial position

---

[21] H. Richard Niebuhr, *Radical Monotheism and Western Culture: With Supplementary Essays* (Louisville KY: Westminster/John Knox Press, 1993) 11.

does not seem appropriate as we seek to address global problems which by their nature require not only a deep commitment by a few people but serious attention from us all. This essay is the work of a Christian doing theology rather than an overtly Christian theology. It draws heavily on my own tradition for concrete examples. Because of my familiarity with it I can speak more authentically in both my criticism and admiration of this history.

Examining Christianity is a particularly important task since many of our ideas about capitalism and technology have evolved within the Christian context. For this reason, an understanding of Christian views concerning personal identity and responsibility, society, nature and the ideal cannot be ignored in identifying the cultural roots of our environmental destructiveness.

The theme that lurks quietly behind this essay's concern with environmental ethics, social scientific thought and the religious life is the question of commitment. The earlier chapters discussed commitment in terms of our natural environment, our tradition of thought, our social structures and our own self-conceptions. Chapter 1 asserted that our problems should not be understood in merely technological terms. We tend to underestimate the importance of culture in directing our desire. Chapter 2 briefly summarized the ways environmental theologians attempt to increase our regard for the natural world rather than to relativize our strong commitments to the social behaviors which degrade it. The middle chapters on the economic approach described the pervasiveness, intensity and history of one particular understanding of the relationship between human beings and the material things they want. Chapter 5 showed how our everyday use of economics as a symbol system influences our perception of the world. It is not simply a blandly objective study of scarcity. Each of these sections emphasized that we understand, experience and express our desires and commitments through the medium of symbols. These symbols both enable and limit our ability to assert ourselves.

We cannot think in any other way than through symbols. Describing these various commitments in terms of symbol and metaphor does not imply that they are not real or that they are mere illusions. Instead, it helps us to understand how our consciousness works, how our imperfectly expressed desires remain inaccessible even to us. The idea of symbol enables us to realize the social and historical nature of our institutions and our very selves. Environmental theologies must not be judged simply on the grounds that they are metaphorical but rather on the effectiveness of their symbolic power and their appropriateness to the situation. Their shortcomings result from an incompatibility with the more dominant system of symbols that express our social desires, not from their symbolic nature. Similarly, arguing that economics works as a set of imperfect metaphors, rather than merely as a collection of facts, does not suggest that it has no real world use. Pointing out the metaphorical nature of our experience does not put into question the reality of that to which a symbol refers, such an observation merely reminds us that the symbol is not the thing in itself. As symbol generating creatures, our world extends far beyond the realms of our conscious sense perceptions. This capacity represents the source of our most deeply held self-deceptions and our most profound achievements. It should not be disregarded in our theological efforts.

In one sense, "God" is a word. In another, it points to something that far transcends the possibilities of our immediate experience. What do we mean by the word "God" as a symbol that refers beyond the limits of even our imagination? How does it enable us to better understand our relation to the physical world and to each other? Ordinary people quite often wonder whether God exists. Many professional theologians, such as Paul Tillich, argue that this is not the right question to ask. Such theologians would claim that "God is not an object among objects" and offer a lengthy discussion about ultimate concern or meaning or Being or ground or existential possibility. They may claim that God does not exist as an object but does exist as that which makes all objects and consciousness of them possible. For these theologians, God even makes it possible to ask whether God exists. Too often, heated arguments over God's existence lack any definition of what either side means by God. Each disputant takes for granted that we have universal consensus regarding the attributes that this word brings together and the entity to which this ancient word refers. We agree on so little else, why should we expect uniformity in our conceptions of this word's meaning? Before proceeding to explain the relevance of sin, salvation, idolatry or any other theological idea, one must begin with a clear conception of what we mean by the symbol upon which these secondary concepts rely. We must be clear about our idea of God, even in our awareness of its limitations as an attempt to articulate that which cannot be adequately expressed.

Although we may or may not choose to debate about the existence of God, we certainly agree that there is such a word. The word God exists as part of a larger symbol system that we call the English language, which would not be complete without it. At a basic level the word God points toward something that agnostics doubt, something that theists believe in and atheists reject. We can find the word in books like the dictionary, we can use it in conversation as a means of expressing an idea, and we can recognize it as something important to others or ourselves. We hear the word when someone stubs a toe, as part of a marriage ceremony, on the radio or television and yelled out by street corner preachers waving worn bibles and staring with wild piercing looks at passing businessmen. We understand what it means to take "God's name in vain" or to "swear to God" or to "pray to God." Although some modern people may find it peculiar that missionaries, monks and ministers devote their lives to God, virtually everyone we meet has a rough idea of what this means. No one would be confused by this sort of profession of faith in the way that one might be if instead she heard a person declare that "eggplant pie with two inch bolts is my favorite train station in bumble bee." Although not everyone agrees with a particular statement of faith, they have some understanding of what it means. It does not sound to them like nonsensical babble. The word God exists. It has a long history and is familiar to everyone.

A second observation about the word God, is that it does not refer to something that we can experience in the same way that we perceive particular eggplants, bolts, train stations and insects which all appear in definite times and places in our lives. Even accounts of the most immediate mystical encounters indicate that experience of God is both unusual and beyond human control. For this reason, Karl Rahner states that the word God refers to part of humanity's spiritual and intellectual existence rather than to ordinary experience.[22] This does not reject the possibility that God is as close as the human heart or as distant as the furthest reaches of heaven. All this means is that the symbol God, does not refer to a tangible thing that always lies immediately at our disposal, in the way the oak tree outside my window does, but to something that we cannot understand in its completeness. If we want to explain our religious tendencies to someone else, we cannot merely point to God, and expect that other person to experience the same thing we do just as we cannot explain our decision to get married by merely pointing at love.

This symbol does not refer to something that lies under our control but rather to something that directs us. It is an odd symbol in our language. We use it to express the idea that in the sentence structure of the universe human beings are not always in the subject position. We use it to describe how the universe makes use of us. In some senses it subverts the whole idea of utility. Perhaps this aspect of the symbol is what makes it so powerful in any conversation about the environment.

The central theological idea of faith arises chiefly out of the sense that God's nature is accessible in an altogether different way than the objects of ordinary experience. Control, a central theme in our earlier discussion of economics and the environment, means something different here. Theologians point out that human beings cannot manipulate God. The word God not only refers to something not immediately available to all people's perception. God is an entity that ultimately transcends the possibilities of our ordinary experience. Friedrich Schleiermacher sums this up in describing religion as a "sense and taste for the infinite" or as the experience of absolute dependence on

---

[22] Karl Rahner, *Foundations of Christian Faith: An Introduction to the Idea of Christianity* (New York: Crossroad, 1982) 45.

something beyond us.[23] When we speak of God, we often mean something that we cannot experience in its entirety. While infinity and transcendence may not adequately describe this aspect of God, they represent popular means of expressing the vastness of the divine.

Third, God represents a standard of worth that looms beyond all of our measures of value. The symbol we use for it can never be adequate since it refers to something that is not a thing. It gestures toward that which can never be symbolized and which, by definition, transcends and enables all of our faculties. People of faith must either be satisfied with an inadequate symbol or have no way for expressing what they mean by God. Many devout Jews recognize this tension through a tradition which reserves a name for God that is not spoken. Perhaps this practice makes it less likely for religious people to mistake their idea of God, as represented by symbols, for that to which the symbols refer. As a symbol, the word "God" means that as soon as you understand it, that which you understood is not it. Although virtually anyone can recognize God as a word, it points toward something that most agree cannot be adequately represented. It is a symbol that both stands for a greater entity and reminds us that no symbol can adequately express its nature.

Theologians usually speak about this aspect of God in terms of idolatry. They point out that the idols we make are usually not little statues. They use the word idolatry to describe our very human tendency to mistake our ideas of the divine for God. It also names our proclivity for directing commitment toward inappropriate objects of devotion. Our efforts in seeking a promotion or the all-league bowling trophy, to rebuild an old automobile engine or to be an agent of world peace, to raise perfect grandchildren or any of a thousand other worthwhile projects become idols when we invest too much of ourselves and energies into them.

The idea of this second sort of idolatry serves as a guide to the proper expression of our desire, it provides a standard for orienting human activity. We use the idea of God to judge the quality and morality of our

---

[23] Friedrich Schleiermacher, *On Religion: Speeches to Its Cultured Despisers*, trans. John Oman (New York: Harper, 1958).

thoughts and action in the world. The inseparability of theology and ethics has been central to the western tradition since the beginning. The first scriptures according to Judaism, Christianity and Islam are the Law (or the Pentateuch). Although believers still feel uncomfortable with the prophets' call for justice, they recognize religion as central to our moral lives. From Moses to today's liberation theologians, from Adam and Eve's first transgression in the garden to modern concerns with environmental justice, our vision of God can never be complete unless it is related to standards for human conduct. The various biblical authors reinforce our deeply held sense that the idea of God must always be related to moral good. This does not exhaust the meaning of God; it is only one way that we make use of the concept in our daily lives. An idea of God grounds our ethical understanding just as such an idea may ground our picture of the universe, our sense of meaning and purpose, etc. This tradition dictates that all human action must be related to God when we attempt to form an evaluation of ethical worth. Even patriotism, mother love, regard for family, friends, job responsibilities and aging relatives cannot be considered as absolutely good, but must be understood in relation to God in order to make judgments about moral value. Even the noblest of motives may become an idol for us.

This essay suggests that our social scientific views and our understanding of the relationship between human beings and their physical environment has a persistent quality that makes them almost second nature. Taking notice of our often-unexamined love of progress and our habitual association of wealth with well-being can be accomplished by using the old-fashioned notion of idolatry. God stands as a point far beyond all our striving, relativizing our activity. The idea of God reminds us that even in our sometimes-noble efforts to provide material goods for others and ourselves, we may still miss the mark. The limits of our interest and concerns may still be drawn too tightly.[24] In

---

[24] The Puritan theologian Jonathan Edwards writes that human beings commit themselves only to "private systems." Only God is dedicated to the whole. Jonathan Edwards, *The Nature of True Virtue* (Ann Arbor: University of Michigan Press, 1960).

looking to an ultimate, we begin to recognize that even the preliminary concerns that we regard most highly should not become our primary ends. The idea of God allows us to expand the limits of our compassion beyond our self-interest. This sense of an ultimate allows us to broaden the circle of our concern beyond the boundaries of human society to include a greater interest in the natural world. Our deeply held respect for institutions and the ideas which underwrite the economic approach, and our profound attachment to material things as extensions of our selves can easily come to replace our devotion and commitment to a higher good, to God, the creator and sustainer of the world.

In building new coal-burning power plants to increase our electrical capacity, or chemical factories to produce more brightly colored throwaway plastic containers or new roads opening up pristine wilderness regions to development, the bottom line has little room for concern about our environment. The profit/loss calculations used to make decisions about such projects consider only the wealth of our stockholders, with little interest in their broader affects on those downstream and downwind. Americans have been notoriously unconcerned in the past about the effects of our enormous building projects on the beauty of the places where they were constructed. In the United States, we have not perniciously set about to make our country ugly. Our environmental degradation has been the result of efforts to procure prosperity.[25] Unfortunately, relentlessly pursuing any single social goal, such as material prosperity, can quickly become a dangerous idolatry. Even if we were able to implement a single policy that maximized every person's welfare, this still would not be enough. Our environmental efforts may in large part result from our desire to make the world habitable, comfortable and beautiful for human beings. The idea of God allows us to imagine an ethical imperative that demands a concern for other creatures and the world that is not merely an instrument for a greater human good.

---

[25] Even our military toxic and nuclear wastes were generated out of concern for defending the country from foreign attack.

A fourth observation regarding our use of the word God relates particularly to this point. While God represents the fulcrum providing the ethical leverage necessary for human society to function and the ultimate that relativizes all preliminary concerns, we often understand this word in very personal terms. The Christian tradition uses personal metaphors like father, shepherd, lord, master and king to describe the divine, just as the famous ceiling of the Sistine Chapel stands in a long line of art that represents God in human form. We speak of God's wrath, joy, love, honor, compassion, faithfulness, justice and creativity as if God were merely another agent among agents. Environmentalists have pointed out that the devastation of nature arises precisely out of this tendency to create a religion and a God in our own image. They have adamantly argued that such a view may be the underlying presupposition behind severe environmental destruction done for the sake of minor human comforts and financial profit. Theologian James M. Gustafson in his *Ethics from a Theocentric Perspective* describes the extent of anthropocentrism within the broader Christian tradition:

> The dominant strand of piety and theology has focused on the grandeur of man, on the purposes of the Deity for man, and primarily on the salvation and the well-being of man… Indeed, in some cases the divine purposes seem to be exclusively oriented toward human benefits: the salvation of man is claimed to be the ultimate intention of God… Religion itself becomes excessively anthropocentric, Ptolemaic; God is thought to exist and act almost exclusively for the benefit of man. The Christian story, beginning with the Apostle Paul, has intensified this concentration.[26]

Gustafson accurately enumerates the dangers lurking behind the idea of God. Our human limitations make it far too easy to project our hopes and desires on to this symbol even though it refers to a person that resists being bent or manipulated. The symbol 'God' has been used through history to exclude others and to legitimate oppression. It has been invoked as a justification for our deluded sense of self-righteousness

---

[26] James M. Gustafson, *Ethics from a Theocentric Perspective* (Chicago: University of Chicago Press, 1981) 109–10, 88–13, 78–93.

and as a rationale for terrible cruelty. Through threats of damnation it has been used to frighten people into submission. The idea of God has been subject to the same forces which lead to the manipulation of any other symbol. We may feel tempted to use this symbol as merely another means of satisfying our isolated ego. Although that which the symbol represents may not be at our disposal (in the way that the oak tree outside is) the means by which we express that transcendence can be subject to our error and our devious self-interest. It becomes too easy to proclaim that the universe and God exist for human benefit, rather than the more challenging claim that humans reach the height of their potential in serving God and caring for creation.

Does this mean that environmentalists must dispense entirely with all personal adjectives for describing God? Should prayers in church be addressed merely to an impersonal force which through observable laws brings extraordinary diversity into being from nothing? In what ways does personal language about God extend our understanding of reality?

In a commentary he wrote on Gustafson's theocentric ethics, Gordon Kaufman mentions the dangers of taking a concern with an anthropocentric God too far.[27] For Kaufman, our understanding of God must adequately account for those positive human qualities that seem relatively distinctive:

> [F]or example, self-consciousness, intentionality and choice, language, imagination and creativity, the ability to take responsibility for ourselves and our actions, the desire to make and keep promises and other personal commitments, the capacity to live together in love and loyalty and forgiveness in communities governed by freedom and justice.

Just because associating the idea of God with various human characteristics can be misused does not mean that we should dispense with any efforts to relate personal qualities with the divine. Adopting a

---

[27] Gordon D. Kaufman, "How Is God to Be Understood in a Theocentric Ethics?," in *James M. Gustafson's Theocentric Ethics: Interpretations and Assessments*, ed. Harlan Beckley and Charles Mason Swezey, 13–35 (Macon GA: Mercer University Press, 1988) 28.

misanthropic conception of God or a view that does not adequately account for our human qualities may salve our consciences, but it will not be true to our experience in the world or to the word God, as we generally understand it. Historically we conceive of God in human terms in part because God makes possible those qualities which we especially value and which we associate with being human. A primary function of the idea of God, locates the center of concern outside of our ego. Our very humanness seems intimately related with this ability to put aside our selfishness. When we hear someone say "God is love" we understand that God makes that human quality of transcendence possible in which our interest moves beyond the limits of our self. According to this understanding of human life and love, sin is the "closed-in-ness" that works against the generosity or the imaginative ability to consider another center of concern other than ourselves. Sin represents that self-involvement that makes it all too easy for us to lack love.

Just as an idea of God permits us to transcend ourselves and to love each other, so also does it enable the self-reflexive posture necessary for recognizing anthropocentrism. How could we even see any alternative to relating all things to human good if we did not have the imagination that allows us to transcend ourselves enough to notice the interests of other existing beings? An ability to consider the idea of well-being from another creature's perspective represents a broad leap of the imagination across the moat separating humans from the rest of creation. In a sense, our very condition as human beings, as anthropos, limits our ability to truly avoid anthropocentrism. The idea of God allows us to extend the boundaries of human compassion beyond human society. It permits a more disinterested benevolence and the virtue of desiring a good that may even contradict what is best for oneself. In making a case for an environmental ethic this sort of imagination is a crucial element. It enables us to see beyond ourselves and to examine the welfare of other people, other societies, other generations and other creatures. This possibility to transcend ourselves truly does make us creatures in the image of our creator.

Understanding the idea of God as one which creates the conditions for our best human qualities, our love, loyalty, affection, compassion, generosity, and yet not distorting that symbol to serve parochial human interests, is the difficult challenge that we face in using theological language to address social concerns. As we try to balance our misanthropic reaction to past religious abuses with the anthropocentric bias that narrows and limits our view, the possibilities for future misuse of this symbol cannot be denied. Nothing human can remain entirely uncorrupted and free of fallibility. Even our concept of the divine may mislead us. Despite this possibility however, the very idea of God represents our best chance for judging the soundness of our hopes and desires, our actions and institutions. This symbol's value in pointing us toward the transcendent reminds us of the fallibility of all our ideas, achievements, social structures and symbols. It warns us of our tendency to devote ourselves to idols, to misdirect our talents and energies. Through the ages it has served to orient and direct human lives by enabling us to transcend the limits of our ego and to reach out to a greater community of concern.

In brief, the symbol God refers to something that is not an object among objects and not at our disposal. It serves to direct our devotion, to orient our lives and to make possible the very transcendence that allows us to be most fully human. The idea of God forms the foundation for powerful theological concepts such as faith, idolatry, hope and sin. These theological terms express and measure our commitments to the beliefs, values and actions that represent the heritage of our culture. They provide an outline for understanding the relation between human beings and the physical world that surrounds us. They give us the critical distance necessary to evaluate a consumer culture. These terms and the idea of God that supports them offer a means for determining the legitimacy of our faith in markets. They can help us to question much of what we take for granted. In our theological thinking we should not only be inspired by a greater appreciation for creation but we must also learn to connect our environmental ethic with the deeply held social values so relevant to it.

The next chapter considers the relation between this idea of God and the complex notion of culture developed through the rest of this essay. It proposes one possible system of types that can clarify the connection between our cultural and religious symbols as market metaphors become increasingly important around the world. In this context theologians must be clear about how the ideas forming our experience of the market and the material world can be understood in relation to God. While the idea of God directs our devotion, ultimately we commit ourselves to God. In this commitment lies the possibility for transformation.

9

GOD TRANSFORMING CULTURE

Interlude

> To the attentive eye, each moment of the year has its own beauty, and in the same field, it beholds, every hour, a picture which was never seen before, and which shall never be seen again. The heavens change every moment. —Ralph Waldo Emerson[1]

It takes time to really learn a new place, to begin to recognize the seasonal relation between sky and horizon marked out by the setting sun in evening and the rolling constellations of stars at night. Every distinct geographical setting seems to have its own smells, its own pace, its own winds changing with time and season, its own particular version of spring, its own landscape dominated by features unlike any others. Even the skies and clouds circling the globe take different shapes according to place and season.

Newly arrived in the tropics three months before, I had adjusted only recently to the sweet fragrance of ginger, eucalyptus and guava born up to the high mountain passes by the comfortable trade winds. The lush jungle vegetation and the odd assortment of botanical survivors from long ocean journeys that flourish in the quiet green highlands called the Pali (the Hawaiian word for cliffs) seemed like an odd contrast with both the vast stretches of alabaster concrete high-rise apartment buildings of downtown Honolulu below and the expansive warm oceans that surround this remote island. After breaking a thinly threaded spider web at the point where the Kapalama Trail narrows, I passed first through a stretch of bent and gnarled ironwood pine trees and then through the dusty but fragrant ruins of an old eucalyptus forest, until I finally reached the open country above. Although these ironwoods were

---

[1] Emerson, *Selections from Ralph Waldo Emerson: An Organic Anthology*, 28.

originally planted in tight chevrons, with the point at the crest of the ridge, to serve as windbreaks and to prevent erosion, both they and the eucalyptus trees have almost entirely choked out the struggling native vegetation. The original sandalwood trees that dominated these slopes before Captain Cook first visited these islands were destroyed long ago for export. The popularity of its fragrant wood, used as furniture and incense in the Far East, has led human beings to harvest it almost to extinction in every habitat that supports these beautiful trees. In the shade of the overgrown eucalyptus forest one can still make out the template, the long ditch dug in the shape of a ship's hull, which was used to measure out how many trees would fit into the holds of the trading ships.

The larger koa trees that also were a part of these original forests have long since been cut to make furniture. Burned as fuel by wood burning ships and destroyed by cattle grazing, the smaller koa trees have retreated to higher elevations. Walking along the ridge's spine beside a line of towering Norfolk Island pines through clumps of pili grass I feel the cold mist of the fog as it blows through the Pali and I smell the sweet dampness of the jungle vegetation and the rich muddy soil in the valleys below. According to ancient legends the first human being was born on the mountain peak above this ridge. The island's first temple, or heiau, in the sacred valley below once sheltered the sick and infirm. It served as a refuge for the persecuted but has since been converted into an eighteen-hole golf course. Only a few of the palms and other trees from the botanical garden that once thrived at the top of this valley have survived the manic growth of plants introduced to the islands during the last one hundred years. Further up and to my right stood the place where Kamehameha I, the first king of the united Hawaiian Islands, drove his enemies off a cliff in a bloody battle which decided the political fate of this island of Oahu nearly two hundred years ago. Down below in the valley to my right, the last monarch of the islands, Queen Liluokalani was inspired in part by a type of lehua blossom found only in the upper reaches of this valley to write "Aloha 'oe" a song that for people around the world still evokes fantasies of this beautiful tropical island paradise.

After walking along the same slippery trail every day for three months I came to know each turn in the way until I could safely pass through here even in the darkest of nights. This gives me more leisure to watch the brilliant sun set through shredded pacific clouds behind the shadows of the dark green mountains on the western side of the island. After a dazzling flash of sun in ponds and irrigation ditches, the valley darkens gradually until the underside of the clouds begins burning with the bright colors familiar to these islands. The stark volcanic outcropping where I admire the panoramic view, which stretches from the beaches of Waikiki to the serious navy-gray ports and airstrips of Pearl Harbor to the power and waste treatment plants on the southwest coast, became a regular stop on my daily evening walks. At this place which crowns a ridge between two deep valleys, far above city and ocean, I stop to reflect with gratitude on the beauty which surrounds me and those who walked here before me.

This landscape cannot be reduced to fit into the margins of this page. Enumerating the smells, sounds, sights with every zephyr or drop which blows down the Pali to touch your skin is not adequate to the actual experience of this place. While a perfect knowledge of the scientific name of every plant and animal, or an encyclopedic historical memory would make this experience richer it could not exhaust the meaning of this place. Although the whole idea of economic thought is reduction to a single standard of value, a sense of place or faith is hopelessly lost in this transaction or this translation. This place does not exist in order to preserve species diversity. Religious faith is like this also.

Most of both the defenders and detractors of religion tend to speak in terms of a *need* for faith. Some write that we need some kind of faith in God as the foundation to support the weight of our ethical systems or as the ground of being or the source of consciousness. Others argue that people need faith in God to overcome alienation and despair over the apparent meaninglessness of their lives. Some assert that we somehow lack completeness without God. Other people adamantly declare that faith in God is a projection of our own fears, that we invent the idea of God because of our yearning for a greater fairness that eludes us in an indifferent universe. Liberation theologians and the proclaimers of impending apocalyptic doom often seem to understand God only as the needed comforter of those suffering under injustice. Some others believe that those in power need the idea of God to justify themselves in the eyes of those who serve them. The otherwise dissimilar writings of great thinkers like Kant, Hegel, Feuerbach, Marx and Freud regard the idea of God in relation to human need.

Although many explain religious life on the basis of need (described in theological, philosophical, anthropological, political, psychological, ethical or any other terms), others hear a voice suggesting a different source for the religious impulse. As I look out across Nu'uanu valley below me from my vantage point on Paki's Peak my reaction to the goodness and the beauty of the scene stretched out all around me is a deeply felt prayer rooted in a celebration of God's gifts. In many people's experience, we simply *have* faith without any prior consideration of the question of need.

This faith cannot be simply reduced to and explained by the idea of need. Gratitude is not always marked by the specificity of its cause or even its object. My response in gratefulness—the impulse that makes me feel an overwhelming sense of thanksgiving for the goodness experienced in creation—represents a different sense of faith than that described by philosophers of religion. It arises not out of weakness or common sense or suffering or humility or logic or fear but out of profound gratitude. This sense and taste for the infinite, this impulse that enables us to recognize goodness and beauty, seems to arise without any thought of need. I have included these paragraphs written in the Santa Monica Mountains, the hill country in the Machakos district of Kenya, Mt. Kilimanjaro, the Holyoke Range in Massachusetts, the green hills of Yorkshire, California's Central Valley and the Pali as examples in an attempt to convey the importance of this intangible gratitude.

These accounts remind us that the value of neither nature nor faith can be reduced to one thing. Meaning in these domains is cumulative not reductive. Each of our careful observations and our articulated responses add meaning to the universe. Each person contributes something entirely unique to our species' experience of awe and mystery in the face of the creative powers that we see around us.

Any program that reduces religion to either need or even gratefulness alone, for the purpose of either criticism or apologetics, inevitably fails to adequately capture what faith means. By isolating our understanding of the religious impulse only to the expression of thanksgiving we discount the importance of the ethical commandments that hold true even in our most desperate moments of disbelief. Part of what makes those times when we perceive beauty notable is that occasional sense of despair and emptiness that also inevitably arises as part of our ordinary lives. Last chapter's definition of God as an ultimate point of reference which relativizes all our human endeavors cannot be derived simply from the sense of awe and beauty that we experience on the tops of mountains. Neither are the customs, art, liturgies, music, doctrines and all the more tangible elements of tradition merely the natural result of only a vague sense of gratefulness. This type of raw religious experience does not provide clear direction in making the theological or practical decisions necessary for a church or community to function. The sense of the infinite, the apprehension of the divine is not usually self-interpreting. We require more than just this to build institutions and traditions.

Seeing religion only in terms of human need, whether for self-actualization or moral confidence, slights the role of an important source of religion, the spontaneous impulse to give thanks for the goodness and beauty in which we are immersed. Reducing all religion to need ignores our sense that we each stand as important elements within a much greater whole, that another perspective on creation and its meaning exists than our own. By defining faith chiefly in these terms it becomes too easy to make God into merely a heavenly servant or a cosmic judge and to forget those moments in the day when our natural response to joy is thanksgiving. The greatest danger of expressing the religious impulse entirely in terms of human need is the tendency for religion to then become a mere instrument for the attainment of human desires or justice. Arguing that faith grows only out of a human need risks the danger of mistaking religion for a crutch that holds up the church or a load-bearing wall that supports our universe or a necessary piece of the puzzle that makes reality all fit together. The spontaneous religious sense disrupts any such pretensions. Perhaps in this apprehension of beauty and goodness lies the seed for both our appreciation of faith and our respect for the nobility of the wilderness. In any effort to understand God and nature, accounts of the sense of transcendence we experience in creation are not simply incidental.

This brief interlude steps back from the task at hand to clarify what religion means in a larger context. In seeing the role of religion narrowly as a possible instrument for accomplishing even the noblest goals for social or environmental justice, we miss the real meaning that faith has for people. Religion is not merely something that we break up into categories and analyze, nor is it merely something we derive systematically on paper. We do not think religion so much as it happens to us. Religion does not define itself as simply one of many interests, as a hobby like stamp collecting, gardening, knitting, model railroads and baseball but as something that constitutes the believer's life. The nature of religion is that it cannot be extricated or considered apart from the strong claim that it exercises on its adherents. Alfred North Whitehead once wrote, "You *use* arithmetic, but you *are* religious."[2] Religion happens to us, then we respond through changes in our actions. In discussing the relationship between the environment and theology we must be cautious lest we come too close to declaring religion as merely a means to a cleaner world. We must always be careful to remember that religion is not merely a tool for social change. In our bold claims and our outrage against the rapid destruction of the wilderness we must not reduce religion to simply a more emotional version of morality.

Religion is not just a tool for fashioning a more beautiful and carefully tended environment. However, caring for the natural world

---

[2] Alfred North Whitehead, *Religion in the Making: Lowell Lectures, 1926* (New York: Fordham University Press, 1926) 15.

should not be regarded as simply a means to a future religious reward either. In associating salvation with a healthier ecosphere or claiming that we act as stewards of the environment to gain God's favor we make creation into a tool for our own spiritual advancement. This sort of program seems destined to construct golden calves out of ourselves, to make our own well-being into an idol. It slights the importance of this world and all of the suffering and beauty, the love and deception, the gentleness and cruelty that we experience in our lives. Perhaps new theologies that propose a radically immanent idea of God are a means of over-compensating for theologies of the past which were too quick to exile God beyond the far reaches of our world. When we make a radical separation between God and world we often tend to see the universe as merely an instrument, a means for procuring divine favor rather than as the continuous outpouring of the divine nature. When the divide between God and world becomes too great, human beings have a tendency to regard the world as a creation made entirely for themselves, a cosmic theme park where we can be perpetually at play. The relation between God, world and person seems more complicated than can be described according to a simple reward model. Not everything can be easily reduced to the scientific version of means and ends, causes and effects. If we are to make the necessary changes in our societies to improve the quality of the natural world we will have to do this because such an adjustment is both good in itself and worthy of our commitment. People of faith as different as Søren Kierkegaard, Augustine of Hippo, Luther, Erasmus, Theresa and Anselm have reminded us that moral action should not arise merely out of the hope for future reward. The idea of God as described in the last chapter enables us to discern how we are to devote ourselves independently of future reward. That sense of gratefulness or thanksgiving for the gifts of creation pushes us to care for our world more than any hope of future reward pulls us toward a stricter ecological ethic. We seek to care for our environment for its own sake.

Objects

> The primal human act,... and a model for all human acts, is an informative, creative act which transforms a world that is merely objective, set over against us, in which we feel lonely and frightened and unwanted into a home. —Frank Lentricchia[3]

> There is no such thing as an inanimate object. That is to say, there are no objects in the human realm of being without meaning and then no objects that do not somehow become animate within the processes of human interaction and individuation. —Chris Abel[4]

If the world and the objects in it are not to be understood as either playthings or tools for proving our dedication to God, what are they? Does it make sense to talk about the intrinsic value of things? Can our understanding of God and dignity be helpful to us as we make decisions about how we are to build our world and change the way we perceive it? How do theologians and economists differ in their understanding of objects?

We project mind into material objects for our comfort and to extend our selves. The world we remade presses back on us. The cosmos we touch continually alters us through the sensations that make their stamp on the malleable tin of our personality and physical being. Someone made the chair where you sit and built it with your height and the tasks you perform in mind. Two feet higher or lower and it would be wholly unsuited to the duties for which it is most often employed. It almost seems as if sentience and consent—its sturdiness, its relatively smooth

---

[3] Lentricchia is summarizing Northrop Frye's system. Frank Lentricchia, *After the New Criticism* (Chicago: University of Chicago Press, 1980) 24.

[4] This comes from Northrop Frye's *The Educated Imagination*. Both of these quotes were taken from the exhibit "WHAT if anything IS AN OBJECT?" at Harvard University's Fogg Art Museum during spring 1994. Chris Abel, "Architecture as Identity," in *Semiotics 1980* (volume 5 of The Annual Meeting of the Semiotic Society of America). Ed. Michael Herzfeld and Margot D. Lenhart (New York: Plenam Press, 1982) 10.

surface, its shape, stability, size and substance, perhaps even its beauty—
were built right into it by design. Perhaps you sit at a desk that has a
surface that makes writing easier and less tiring. It may even have
drawers that act like borrowed hands holding photographs, letter
openers, pens, tape, envelopes, etc., which, although distant from your
consciousness now, may soon be needed. Our bodies conform
themselves to the physical world which surrounds us, but so does our
sense of consciousness.

Press your feet against the floor, examine the carefully stretched
leather of your shoe or the gently molded shape of your sandal and feel
the thoughtfulness of its maker and the imagination of its designer who
considered your comfort as it came into being from the fabric of
creation.[5] Its shape, texture, color, weight, size and all the other features
of its design were considered carefully with you in mind. The materials
from which it was constructed were chosen for you. If you are not
wearing shoes note how the carpet or floor was also shaped smoothly to
accommodate your foot and the considerations of your eye. Notice the
book in your hand as an object rather than as a collection of ideas, the
thin leaves of paper that you now read, the quality of the light that
makes this activity possible. The ink on this page, arranged to make each
character clear, fulfills its purpose by passing unnoticed. The words they
form, your chair, desk, trousers, windows and pencil were designed for
your comfort, use and appreciation. All of the books lining your shelves,
the histories, poetry, science and literature were written and bound to
extend your faculties of consciousness, your perception and sensitivity to
beauty. This happens just as your reading glasses extend your vision, the
walls function as another layer of skin, the clock or calendar makes more
precise your sense that time is passing. Your pen preserves your
conscious thoughts and extends your memory and voice making it
audible a thousand miles away or in future centuries.

We live in a world of animated objects. The things we build reflect
the sensations that have made their impressions on us. We create these

---

[5] Elaine Scarry, *The Body in Pain: The Making and Unmaking of the World*
(New York: Oxford University Press, 1985).

objects out of material at hand and imagination to accommodate the world to our sensitivities. We formed them to make the universe friendly to our desires and comfort. These physical things—words, poems, furniture, carpets, computers, pencils, books, windows and all the material culture that constantly surrounds us—represent the residue of our transitory thoughts. They stand as visible evidence of our quickly passing consciousness, as reminders of the creative powers made possible by mind.

Made objects provide the leverage that extends the functioning of our own bodies and all of our capacities ranging from our eye-sight to our imagination, our hearing to our memory. Through them we refashion a world which is constantly creating and re-creating us. Bending the substance of the universe we craft it into a product that embodies our own sensations and ideas, an object ultimately more suited to our senses than that with which we began. The things around us represent a complicated mix of created gift and solidified consciousness. Our ideas come to be repeated in the material world, communicated or translated as physical things. These objects themselves then provide the very possibility for future creation. Just like children playing with sticks in the woods, we make our toys and they in turn participate in re-making us. As Jonathan Edwards insisted, "children should be made to understand *things*, as well as *words*."[6]

An ancient Zen parable tells of a tiring monk who in the course of rowing upstream against a rapid current felt the edge of his boat hit gently up against another boat. Growing more irritated as the unseen boat continued to tap against his without moving out of the way and yet stubbornly unwilling to yield himself, the monk finally turned around to face his hitherto unseen antagonist. Intending to reprimand the captain of this other rowboat he instead turned to see that the other boat had gotten loose and was floating without anyone onboard. At this point the Zen monk laughs at his earlier irritation and the hearer of the story realizes its moral. All the people we meet are the empty boats pushed

---

[6] Sereno Edwards Dwight, *The Life of President Edwards* (New York: G. & C. & H. Carvill, 1830) 475–76.

215

here and there by the currents and winds that influence them on the river of life. We understand that our irritation with them is as silly as the monk's sense of fury directed toward an empty boat.

But does this really describe our experience with objects? In real life our knowledge that any particular thing has no agency, no will or inclination does not prevent us from reacting emotionally to it. We expect objects to be conscious of our needs. We slam doors that insensitively cause us pain by pinching our hand or foot; we pound the hot plastic dashboard when our cars obstinately refuse to start. The destruction of our life's possessions by flood or fire affects us more powerfully than the lists of casualties caused in foreign wars or by distant accidents reported in newspapers. Although we may feel that it is silly to love faded photographs, old family furniture, favorite books and clothing worn soft through use as if these were appropriate objects of affection, we do. We animate the physical things in our lives. We always remain capable of recognizing the consciousness that enabled them to come into being and we feel gratitude that they were made to impress us through the medium of experience.

If made objects betray a hint of the conscious thought that makes them suitable to our use what are natural objects? How are we to understand the meaning of a nautilus shell, a thundercloud, an orangutan, a maple leaf, or a formation of sandstone? We are close kin to nature. The beaver's lodge, the veins on an oak leaf, crystal branches of ice on a window are not entirely alien to us. The beauty of nature surprises us; the connections between various phenomena train our capacities to perceive. Despite this, in comparison to the world of objects that we have made for our use and comfort, we see in nature something relatively more indifferent to human purposes. At the same time, there seems to be meaning in the diversity of phenomena that we experience in nature regardless of its relative independence from human designs.

Commentators often quote Henry David Thoreau's memorable line that, "in wildness is the preservation of the world."[7] By this perhaps he means that when we re-make the world by building consciousness into it, we also lose our ability to see God as clearly through it. The otherness we experience in indifferent nature partly constitutes the humanness of everything else. Our social scientific tools cannot comprehend this important source of the very humanity they take for granted. The objects of the world not made by us carry no evidence of this consciousness and yet they may provide the basis for it.

Perhaps the previous chapters have missed the mark in explaining our environmental problems too simply in terms of a sharp distinction between objects and persons. Embedded deeply within both theological and economic thinking lies a concealed philosophy of objects as they relate to people. Both promote a system of morality that depends on this distinction. The economic approach regards objects and services simply as 'goods' (collectively perhaps these are the highest good) that provide well-being to persons. According to this view objects are always commensurable. Even if they cannot be converted into an object with greater value (raw materials change into components which are assembled into final products), they can certainly be traded for something else. Persons determine the value of objects through market processes that coordinate and make explicit any particular thing's relative worth.

To use the language of economics, for a theologian capital and labor can never be regarded as fully equivalent or interchangeable. Theologians regard objects as distinct parts of God's good creation. Despite their value, things can never be the highest good whether they are produced in high-tech, dust-free automated factories or by the providence guiding evolution and the migration of the first coconut

---

[7] "The West of which I speak is but another name for the Wild; and what I have been preparing to say is, that in Wildness is the preservation of the World. Every tree sends its fibres forth in search of the Wild. The cities import it at any price. Men plow and sail for it…" Henry David Thoreau, *The Natural History Essays* (Salt Lake City: Peregrine Smith Books, 1989) 112.

trees to a distant Pacific island. Despite the goodness of creation and the objects in it, these can never represent the highest good. Furthermore, for theologians, the evocative power of objects as symbols means that human beings will be forever in danger of treating objects with the respect that should be reserved for God. The unique and direct relationship between each individual person and God, is distorted by our distractions and our devotion to idols. When we direct our energies and talents, our creativity and our hard effort chiefly on behalf of objects, when we endow them with a consciousness of their own, we fall short. We love those products that provide us with comfort. We desire their reassuring help in our daily life. However, these human things, which seem to embody consciousness and care, have come to threaten the very existence of wilderness and of all those things and creatures which are related to but stand beyond the immediate notice of human beings.

Market Culture

> The fact is, that shopping is the chief cultural activity in the United States. —The Director of the Southshore Seaport Museum in New York City[8]

Earlier chapters showed how theology can be used in considering the relation between the social symbols that we use to express our desire and the ethical principles that we use in evaluating our action. They introduced the idea of God as an ultimate standard of worth which directs us and provides us with orientation as we decide how we should commit ourselves. In this sense our personality in part comes from God who helps us to imagine the world from the perspective of another, to transcend ourselves through love. God widens our sense of concern beyond the boundaries of our selves (or our families and country) and helps us to overcome our tendency toward self-centeredness and self-absorption. The last chapter and this last section described idolatry as the proclivity to misdirect our energies, to commit ourselves to the wrong endeavors or to invest ourselves too much in any activity. The

---

[8] Schor, *The Overworked American: The Unexpected Decline of Leisure*, 108.

power that the market and its values have over us in modern times may qualify as idolatry. The economic approach (in its simple formulations of human nature as mere selfishness, etc.,) discussed in earlier chapters exercises a dominion over our consciousness that may not be appropriate given the limits of our world.

Simply realizing that markets are not natural, but the products of particular historical contingencies arising out of specific cultural contexts may take us a long way toward recognizing their impact on the natural world. Environmental catastrophe seems much less inevitable when we see that our most destructive behavior does not arise out of some primal drive that necessarily propels us to continue producing and accumulating the very products which destroy our world. In coming to this conclusion however, we must also begin to take responsibility for our actions and to recognize that ethics and not just economics must be employed in our efforts. Treating our social symbols as sacred or worse as natural is idolatry. This theological notion represents the first step toward relating our sense of the religious impulse to powerful social customs (such as our everyday economic reasoning). The remainder of this chapter will be devoted to another means of connecting our theological symbols with our common cultural symbols.

Human beings have a tendency to naturalize our cultural creations and to make these values and ways of understanding the world into our gods. Theologians in the twentieth century confronting this problem have focused considerable interest on God and culture as distinct entities. H. Richard Niebuhr in particular made this a primary distinction for understanding God's action in his book *Christ and Culture*. The following sections adopt a modified, truncated version of his famous typology in an effort to clarify the relation between our social symbols and our theological ones. In Niebuhr's first chapter he describes our almost religious devotion to secular values in the following terms.

> The antagonism of modern, tolerant culture to Christ is of course often disguised because it does not call its religious practices religious...because it regards what it calls religion as one of many interests...The implied charge against Christian faith is like the

ancient one: it imperils society by its attack on its religious life; it deprives social institutions of their cultic, sacred character; by its refusal to condone the pious superstitions of tolerant polytheism it threatens social unity. The charge lies not only against Christian organizations...but against the faith itself.[9]

Elsewhere Niebuhr claims that the relation between faith and secular culture is not a struggle between belief and disbelief but rather a battle between faith and faith. Our commitment, devotion and action all are at stake in this perpetual contest. Niebuhr introduces the problem of Christ and culture as a question continuing in different forms throughout history and becoming manifest as, "the problem of reason and revelation, of religion and science, of natural and divine law, of state and church, of nonresistance and coercion."[10] For our purposes here we will broaden the scope of his question to the problem of God and society. In doing this however, the problem remains largely the same. How can the often-radical demands of the devout relate to the broader cultural environment? How should people of faith understand and live with market culture; how should they render to Caesar that which is Caesar's?

The categories or types of relation between God and culture did not simply fall down from heaven on to H. Richard Niebuhr's desk. They did not appear in a mystical vision. These types merely represent the broader trends that make sense as we examine our historical experience. We never apprehend any of these categories in its pure form but we do recognize elements of each type in various times and places throughout history. These aids help us to make sense of the complicated relationship between religion and society in the West.

Before introducing the first category, 'God against Culture,' we ought to consider what we mean by culture. Although we may not often think of it as such, this word represents an important symbol that reveals much about the spirit of our time. In our generation the idea of culture constitutes a crucial tool that we use to understand age, race, leisure,

---

[9] H. Richard Niebuhr, *Christ and Culture* (New York: Harper, 1956) 8.
[10] Ibid., 10.

class, labor, gender, nationality and even sexuality. We do not so often hear about the culture wars any more, but we still debate about what is at stake as we evaluate our shared artistic and political life. Kathryn Tanner outlines a history of how this word has evolved through modernity.[11] What culture means has changed over time. It has gone from being an affirmation of class privilege (high culture) to a rationale for imposing a single system of practices on all societies (colonialism) to a means of affirming the differences that exist among various groups of people (multiculturalism). We use this word in all of these senses today.

Originally perhaps the idea of culture was intertwined with the ideals of chivalry. The cultivation implied by culture represented both the privilege and the responsibility of the nobility. Over centuries this ideal of refined tastes and habits began to apply to other classes of people. During the European Age of Exploration culture referred to universal standards of civilization by which societies could be compared and judged. Western European nations justified the imposition of their often-despotic rule on colonies by appealing to this ideal of culture as an embodiment of universal goals for human flourishing. Culture as refinement is exactly what Europeans of this time considered the rest of the world to lack.

The idea of culture represented a primary symbol defining the Romantic Movement. In that age the idea of culture was best expressed through the German notion of *Bildung* or self-cultivation through intellectual and artistic expression. Initially culture was associated with the recovery of Greek and Roman classics and considered universal. Over time however this changed. As a result of thinkers like Jean-Jacques Rousseau and Johann Gottfried Herder, culture came to be associated with the indigenous practices of a particular society, the folkways that were in constant struggle against forces of international homogenization.

In a few centuries the meaning of culture changed from an aristocratic and hegemonic notion of an absolute standard for human behavior to a celebration of human particularity. Anthropologists in the

---

[11] Kathryn Tanner, *Theories of Culture: A New Agenda for Theology* (Minneapolis: Fortress Press, 1997).

twentieth century have contributed much in this last regard by using the word culture to avoid qualitative comparisons between different societies. Rather than making normative judgments about relative worth, social scientists have used the idea of culture as a way of seeing these societies as merely different rather than better or worse.

In this chapter, culture should not be associated with cultural elites, with folkways or with value neutral social scientific comparisons. For our purposes, culture should instead be understood as the systems of habit that structure our social world which in turn largely determines the kind of nature on which we depend.

Earlier chapters introduced the Greek distinction between nomos (custom or human law) and fusis (nature or natural powers). Culture as the "artificial secondary environment that man superimposes on the natural" corresponds to nomos and incorporates "language, habits, ideas, beliefs, customs, social organization, inherited artifacts, technical processes, and values."[12] Culture, according to this understanding, is always formed socially through human efforts. It represents a system of values that differ widely and must be, to some extent, rethought by each new generation. Culture includes everything from the socially learned desires and needs that may cause environmental degradation to the technological skills and governmental structures that further mediate the relation between human society and the material world. Despite our tendencies to regard markets as natural, they are an excellent example of culture.

God Against Culture

> By "Society" modern science means, and rightly, primarily the social relationships which result from the economic phenomena. —Ernst Troeltsch[13]

The first of these types we will call 'God against culture.' This category emphasizes the tendency of certain religious groups through history to

---

[12] Niebuhr, *Christ and Culture*, 32.
[13] Troeltsch, *The Social Teaching of the Christian Churches*, 1:32.

radically reject the dominant norms and values of their societies. Examples include the relation of the early Christian church's martyrs to the Roman Empire, the third century exodus of Christians into the Egyptian desert, the Puritans in New England, the monastic and sectarian movements that across religions and through history have endeavored to extricate themselves from broader society to form their own version of the city on a hill (Mt. 5:14). This view includes those who reject any hint of culture's authority. Often the people who best represent the "God against culture" type are reacting to a situation of extreme suffering and repression which further exacerbates the desperately strict division between the children of light and the children of darkness.

Religious socialists, anarchists and separatists aiming to remake our industrial society into an environmental utopia all could be included in this category. Indeed the tone of several sections in the earlier chapters of this essay could be read as the sort of total rejection of consumer culture that this position demands. Radical environmentalists look to religious faith for their warrant, exemplify this critique in their rejection of material and technological progress as necessarily destructive. In reviewing the statistics recording the tons of toxic waste released into our air, water and soil, in witnessing the wholesale degradation of the few remaining wilderness areas and in taking note of the social disruption caused by utterly reprehensible industrial pollution this position may initially seem to make sense. At times the situation seems so hopeless that this answer appears to be the only ethical response. Perhaps the only reason this sort of position was not summarized among the nature theologies mentioned in chapter 2 is that its exponents are too busy acting, to take the time to write theologies justifying their position. For these people the justice of God seems entirely distant from the values and norms of consumer culture.

H. Richard Niebuhr in his chapter on this subject includes his first responses in a section entitled "A Necessary and Inadequate Position" and sums up both the necessity and the futility of drawing a line of demarcation that so sharply sets apart God and culture. Such a distinction is necessary because too much pressure exists on religion to become merely a variant form of culture by accommodating to its demands. The attempt to live up to the often-challenging ideals of religious faith certainly should not be slighted. Through history the radical response of withdrawing from the dominant society, or from a particular religious community has often made an important ethical statement which has fundamentally altered both groups. Despite the essential role that these groups play in reforming religion and society, H. Richard Niebuhr concludes that this position is inadequate. Historically he argues that the most radical of those who saw their religious faith as necessarily antagonistic with culture could not succeed without those who could better integrate the two.[14] The successes of the most radical of believers through history were made possible by successors who could make culture and God relevant to each other.

Evolution has built into our physiology not just the possibility for culture but the total dependence on cultural expression. We cannot survive and function as human beings apart from the culture in which we find ourselves. We depend on it for our language, history, economy and social order. The illusion of a total independence from the secular world is particularly dangerous in our day. Merely withdrawing from the system of technology, society and economy will not be enough. The global dimensions of the problem make a global approach to it particularly necessary.

Niebuhr's second and perhaps more profound point is that our understanding of God and the culture that surrounds us cannot be so discretely disentangled. The anthropologist Clifford Geertz calls human

---

[14] Niebuhr uses the following example: "Not Tertullian, but Origen, Clement of Alexandria, Ambrose, and Augustine initiated the reformation of Roman culture. Not Benedict, but Francis, Dominic, and Bernard of Clairvaux accomplished the reform of medieval society often credited to Benedict. Not George Fox, but William Penn and John Woolman, changed social institutions in England and America. And in every case the followers did not so much compromise the teachings of the radicals as follow another inspiration than the one deriving from an exclusive loyalty to an exclusive Christ." Niebuhr, *Christ and Culture* (New York: Harper and Row, 1951) 67–68.

beings "incomplete animals" who are finished by culture.[15] God calls us as beings who have already been profoundly formed by culture. In our encounter with God, we cannot simply put aside all of our past experiences. They have become an inextricable part of us. Even in despising what we may see as the extravagance of consumer culture, we can only do this as consumers, as people who have been exposed to millions of advertisements, who have been surrounded by others who always yearn to have more. Every economic reformer most likely spent a significant part of his or her life either affirming the standard economic measures of well-being or surrounded by others who do. We cannot help but possess the same qualities that we criticize. There can be no person who is not the product of these historical and cultural circumstances. We can never hope to fully transcend the conditions that have made us. Even in our strong reaction against our culture and its ecological brutality, we still embody its values and understand the questions in the terms that it has provided for us. The earlier chapters have been filled with examples of how tightly moral philosophical and theological thought have been entwined with our economic views. The theological roots of our notion of the individual as a being in unique relationship with God, our sense that we should "be fruitful and multiply" (Genesis 1:22), the importance of fairness and justice within our market arrangements (especially the right to profit from our labor), the distinction between person and object so important to property arrangements and countless other examples should remind us that the boundary between culture and religion is not so clear. This membrane is permeable from both sides. Our religious ideas influence our culture just as our cultural ideas influence our religion. Certainly the culture that surrounds us limits our choice of religion making it highly unlikely that a white Pentecostal family in Arkansas will give birth to a Hindu, or that a family in Bangladesh will have Quaker in-laws, or that a couple in Moscow will find that only Buddhist families live in their apartment complex. As our culture becomes more diverse it is even more important

---

[15] Clifford Geertz, *The Interpretation of Cultures: Selected Essays* (New York: Basic Books, 1973).

to recognize the extent to which our religious identity is related to our cultural identity.

Niebuhr concludes his chapter on Christ against Culture with four theological objections. He points out the tendency, in radically separating religion and culture, to denigrate reason in order to exalt a more religious sense of divine revelation. He also mentions the inherent problems involved in focusing on sin as primarily a problem for those outside the community of faithful believers. We all realize that human weakness exists among members of even the holiest communities and yet this sharp division of religion versus culture, us versus them, seems to make the sins of others more obvious than our own. Finally, in distinguishing sharply between God and culture, certain aspects of culture (that we happen to associate with our own religious or environmental views) inevitably come to be mistakenly regarded as God-given certainties. This element of delusion can lead to disastrous consequences. By being conscious of this tendency we can avoid the blinding self-righteousness that characterizes too many extremist proposals. In our awareness of the pervasiveness and fluidity of our culture, perhaps we can be slower to condemn and more conscious of our own environmental responsibilities. The next of Niebuhr's types over-compensates for this radical distinction between God and culture by seeing the two as too closely associated.

God of Culture

Save the Planet. —Hard Rock Cafe advertising slogan

Correcting the strenuous antagonism of the last type, this category replaces the certitude of a God and a culture entirely and perpetually at war with a vision that makes these two almost indistinguishable. Those who fit into this type see no conflict between religion and society. They cannot distinguish between the ethics of faith and the rules that enable society to function. They believe that the divine purpose works itself out through the culture which has been so influenced by religion through history. Those espousing this view are not likely to be social radicals. They justify their cultural inheritance as the outgrowth of religion.

Indeed culture and God as the last section reminded us, are closely related. The very words that enable us to hear, express, understand and even conceptualize faith grow out of a cultural environment. The etymology of our religious words like spirit (which derives from an earlier form of the word for wind) certainly indicates that religion would have no life apart from culture. We cannot imagine either humanity or religion without culture. Culture provides the concrete features that religion necessarily needs, just as religion provides a justification and a description of the deepest human drives that make culture worthwhile. Jewish and Christian ethics with the philosophical tradition of Greek culture form the bedrock which grounds our notions of democracy, fairness, equality, the good life, community, family, beauty, value, just government and all the unspoken assumptions that enable us to function in our daily life. Even in reacting against the past, secular society reflects the theological values of our ancestors.

This has been a frequently recurring theme throughout this essay. Our most secular ideals and values—those supporting the rules that govern how our society functions and thinks—arose out of an extended heritage of theological thinking reaching back through the ages. Perhaps the reason why our economic values so closely approximate a virtual theology is that these ideas grew out of the theologies that prevailed when they came into being. A mysterious unstated god lies concealed behind our modern understanding of the individual and her relation to the world. The individualism that our market societies require grew out of a theological reaction against medieval hierarchy. Reformers like Martin Luther (1483–1546) and Huldrych Zwingli (1484–1531) undermined feudal society by emphasizing a new source of authority and a means of interpreting faith that looked more to individual inspiration by the Holy Spirit than to a hierarchy of church leaders. Out of these humble conflicts over the meaning of scripture and authority arose our modern conception of the self as distinct from society. For modern people, perhaps the self may be even more important than society since actual selves can be identified and experienced in a way that abstract entities such as humanity cannot be. The most basic presupposition of market culture, that fundamentally the individual and not the community is the unit of concern, grew out of an ancient theological struggle over scriptural authority.

Perhaps another example of the close relationship between God and culture may better illustrate how we find the source of our deepest values in the history of both. Some environmentalists and some theologians have criticized Christianity for being too spiritual. They argue that believers burn out too much of their energy in thinking and worrying about the heavenly realms and that this leads them to be indifferent about the environment. This criticism in the West itself arises out of a sharp division between spiritual and material, and from a Christian heritage of the incarnation which affirms the material world. In this case both the critics and the criticized make claims on the basis of a shared tradition that values the material world so highly that it proposes that God became a discrete part of our physical world in Jesus. As mentioned in chapter 2 it seems much more likely that Christian affirmation of the material world naturally leads to a technology and spirit of accumulation rather than to a harmful neglect of the environment through disinterest. Again, the physical world affirmed by Christianity seems to be an important part of our modern market culture.

The "God of culture" has been a persistent theme throughout this essay as we have looked beneath the values supporting the economic approach common in our everyday life to the theological ideas that brought these into being. This God of culture however, cannot be endorsed without sacrificing the most important elements of what we mean by the idea of God. Lynn White's condemnation of Christianity as responsible for environmental disaster has as its primary supposition the belief that God and culture are coterminous, that they cannot be disentangled. He views the strands of our cultural heritage that are responsible for this destruction as equivalent to our religious history. His claim that our ecological blunders find their source in the Genesis 1:28 command for human beings to have dominion over creation reflects both his recognition of the profound interrelationship between God and culture and his very modern and dim view of dominion as necessarily destructive. However, in seeing culture and God as equivalent we fail to account for the profound discontinuity between religious morality and social behavior. After all, while certain biblical verses do seem to authorize human dominion, many more sections command that human beings should love each other. Despite the centrality of these commands, people through history have remained notoriously unaffected by the ethical precepts demanded by their religious traditions.

For this reason, ultimately the "God of culture" can never be adequate. The idea of a transcendent God which we discussed in the last chapter can never be too closely identified with culture. God cannot be understood simply as another object but represents a principle that enables people to transcend themselves through love. In humanizing us by making it possible for us to broaden the circle of our concern, God is a personal God who cannot be compressed into a faceless, heartless culture. Imperial Christianity, Medieval hierarchy and even modern theocracy must necessarily fail to make God equivalent to culture. Too closely associating God with culture forces the divine to abide by human rules. We dilute the potency of the often-radical demands made by religious ethics in failing to recognize how greatly they diverge from the rules of the world. We come too close to merely ratifying our own environmental destructiveness when we begin believing that religious precepts have been adequately incorporated into our cultural institutions. This sort of view only serves to increase our tendency to turn our culture into an idol.

Transforming Culture

> The life of money-making is one undertaken under compulsion, and wealth is evidently not the good we are seeking; for it is merely useful and for the sake of something else. —Aristotle[16]

While Niebuhr goes into great detail in explaining two other types they, to some extent, represent variants of God against Culture and God of

---

[16] Aristotle, *The Nicomachean Ethics* (Minneapolis MN: Filiquarian Publishing, 2007) 10.

Culture.[17] His final category, the one that is of most use in addressing social ethics in an intelligent and responsible way, is God transforming Culture. This type recognizes all the truths embodied in the earlier ones (that the religious message seems to contradict our cultural experiences, that faith in God has been in some senses incorporated into culture, that we use concrete expressions to give our faith life, etc.,). This "conversionist" view, offers a greater degree of possibility for human action than one capable of seeing only sin and shortcoming in the human soul. It recognizes the presence of sin and the possibility of renewal through the creative activity of God as expressed in our efforts to transcend ourselves in love. It holds in tension both the inseparability of culture and religion, and the radical opposition between them. Where someone who remains unable to reconcile God and culture sees only corruption, the conversionist sees misplaced aims for the good and mistaken commitment and effort. In short, this view better recognizes the possibility for genuinely ethical human behavior. Niebuhr writes, "Christ redirects, reinvigorates, and regenerates that life expressed in all human works"[18] In this program, God and the idea of God, enable human beings to make sound judgments of value and ultimately to transform society.

This is not to say that everything will be perfect, or that a complete transformation will result, but that change is possible. Niebuhr states that, "depravity lies under the curse of transiency and death, not because an external punishment has been visited upon it, but because it is intrinsically self-contradictory."[19] This statement is obviously ambiguous when applied to the environment. Will we stop destroying the planet after we have thoroughly eradicated ourselves or because we recognize the error of our ways? How many landscapes, species, rivers, lakes and

---

[17] These types are "God above culture," a view that radically distinguishes between human law and divine law as mutually exclusive (which suggests that although human rules fall short, they are necessary given our circumstances) and "God and culture in paradox," which claims that these two rules coexist but remain entirely distinct.

[18] Niebuhr, *Christ and Culture*, 209.

[19] Ibid.

forests will be ruined before a change in values enables us to stop? Again, the conversionist view recognizes human capacity for sin but at the same time sees beyond these limitations to the possibility for change. It de-emphasizes attempts to describe human nature as possessing concrete and permanent qualities that exist independently of historical and cultural circumstances. Recognizing the potential and the difficulty involved in changing the very symbols that constitute our social networks, the conversionist reminds us that these are relative and the products of human activity.

Initially this program may appear vague. Making quick absolute pronouncements is so much easier when one begins with simplifying assumptions about human nature as easily malleable (the presupposition behind environmental theologies which suggest that people must be merely taught to love nature) or depraved (Thomas Hobbes). What does the "God transforming culture" motif mean for abating environmentally destructive behavior? In short, it permits us to recognize that human beings are neither wholly altruistic nor self-seeking and that our interests are powerfully guided by our sense of God just as they are by our desire for social approval or our feelings of personal responsibility or our hunger for safety and security.

As explained in chapter 2, environmental theologians must search for more convincing approaches and solutions, otherwise they undermine the plausibility of general ethical approaches to the environment (as opposed to those which propose that self-interest can simply be harnessed for environmental good without considering traditional ethical questions). In order to improve the quality of their work, they must address the human capacity for wrongdoing and our tendency both to resist reformation and to act for the sake of our own benefit even when it harms others. Finally, no environmental theology can be complete without addressing the powerful social forces of consumerism. Expecting that a massive change in heart will be effected by a thorough program which convinces people of nature's value cannot work in a world that is subject to human fallibility and under the illusion that simply improving industrial output will make people fundamentally more happy. The powerful social conditioning and the technologies and cultural mechanisms, which radically extend the influence of human beings over their environment, must be considered in any effort to understand the physical deterioration of our world. Any attempt to improve the environment must account for the powerful economic symbols that direct us and the propensity for self-interest that is the focus of economic analysis.

However, this too often has been taken as a certification for excess in the opposite direction. The importance of the economic motive as a means for allocating resources, understood as both a source and the solution to our environmental woes can easily be exaggerated in such a way that makes alternatives entirely invisible. Habit directs our thinking, simplifying our world and drawing our attention away from central features of our experience. The habit of recognizing only actions based on self-interest fostered by the economic approach distracts us from our many experiences of self-sacrifice and prevents us from understanding an element of the human endeavor which represents an important motive for environmental good. The prevailing opinions that environmental degradation is not a moral issue but can be resolved only through market mechanisms operate under an overly simplistic understanding of human nature. By defining societies merely as "sums of their individuals, each acting in rational self-interest" as opposed to the views of "environmentalists" who "have persisted in introducing an element of mysticism and morality into the greenhouse debate" we invest an unmerited degree of faith in the economic approach.[20] In the language we introduced in the last chapter, this dualism makes our economic ideology into an idol. Defining pollution as "only an economic problem" (excluding political, religious, technological and moral dimensions) and arguing that ethics must be replaced entirely by incentives seriously impairs any community's ability to respond to the problem.[21] In excluding ethical consideration from economic debate we

---

[20] Matt Ridley and Bobbi Low, "Can Selfishness Save the Environment?" from *The Atlantic Monthly*, September 1993, 76–86.
[21] Ruff, "The Economic Common Sense of Pollution."

saw off the very branch that the market sits on, we erode the very thing that enables it to actually work. If people were really as individually selfish as some claim, how could we enact any rules that could serve to direct this behavior in a positive direction? How could we decide what these rules would be? Who would abide by them? Communities do not exist merely to keep individuals from killing one another but to work for a positive good that at times requires self-sacrifice for the good of others. Just as it would be hard to imagine a family in which each member sincerely strived to continually get the better of the others, without a willingness to make self-sacrifices, so too would it be impossible to imagine a whole society structured according to this same narrow principle. If everyone simply stole whatever they could, most markets would become tremendously less efficient and collapse under their own weight.

While we must acknowledge the power of self-seeking individualism, making a virtue out of this necessity and proclaiming it as both an absolute and a natural tendency seriously distorts our understanding of the human condition and the nature of effective programs for change. In proposing economics, or any other social scientific method, as a program which replaces morality we fail to recognize that economics makes metaphysical claims (for example, that people necessarily always want more) just as it proposes an extensive, and often covert, ethical program (which states for instance, that those with wealth *should* have greater power to determine what society produces). The values the market promotes and the insights that it provides are useful. However, regarding its presuppositions as absolute and its initial assumptions as descriptions of human nature, and thus impervious to change through history and across culture, necessarily rules out any effort to question the consumerist tendencies that may be what most set apart our age. In implementing plans to alter incentives we must be careful to also consider the extent to which such programs perpetuate a consumer/producer culture. In short, we cannot make science a substitute for morals.

An environmental effort embodying the spirit of the "God transforming culture" motif represents a very different means of understanding our environmental condition than an institutional approach
that adamantly declares that selfishness lies as the guiding principle
behind all human action. On the one hand, it demands a clear
recognition of the deeply felt values which support a culture (in our case,
the centrality of consumer motives and concern), yet on the other hand
it does not acquiesce to a simplistic formulation of human nature or a
resigned acceptance that one system of thought can provide complete
answers to any of our problems. The idea of God, as the source of
legitimate meaning and devotion, can prevent us from too readily
accepting any system of thought or idea about ourselves as necessarily
absolute. It restrains us from evading responsibility and does not allow
us to attribute our faults as a generation to an eternal and unchanging
human condition. The idea of God further reminds us that the object of
our devotion is not an ever-increasing economic output or even the
promotion of short-term human happiness, but must necessarily account
for a broader circle of concern which extends across generations and to
all of creation.

While the 'God transforming culture' motif may permit us to accept
market incentives for pollution control or switching to clean sources of
energy or other economic tools for improving the welfare of the
environment, it thoroughly works against the illusion that this particular
system of solutions can provide all the answers or be sufficient in itself.
It reminds us of our own complexity and the extent to which any
description of ourselves and our society must remain incomplete and
provisional. This motif holds before us the possibility for radical changes
in the devotion of our energies and the source of our fulfillment.
Directing our efforts and our commitments, the idea of God reminds us
that in our short-term solutions we must not stop seeking much more
fundamental change.

The three variations of God and culture described above are not
three different forms of environmental action, or three unique visions of
economic thought, or even three distinct theologies. Instead, these

various means of understanding the ultimate focus of human devotion and its relation to our cultural forms represent strands of thought woven deeply into the languages and grammars that govern the operation of environmentalists, economists and theologians. "God against Culture," "God of Culture," and "God transforming Culture" are themes that describe how many of us understand the world. We hold these divergent views simultaneously and continuously skip between them.

Unfortunately, the modern person too easily understands her experience in "God of Culture" terms, we feel too comfortable regarding our institutional inheritance and all of its presuppositions as God-given, as ordained since the beginning of time, as fundamental elements of the human condition. But even when we react against this tendency and adopt the "God against Culture" motif, when we exalt indigenous cultures as ethically superior in their care for the environment (a modern variant of Rousseau's exploitive "noble savage"), when we begin believing that 'natural' is equivalent to good and anything "civilized" is evil, we similarly see the world in a particularly modern way. We find it easy to worship those cultural forms that are dominant just as we feel comfortable in our devotion to those ideas which oppose them. The "God transforming Culture" outlook, however, is much more rare in our modern consciousness. For us, the expanse within the boundaries of our human freedom has little room for an active God. Although we may recognize that God should be the object of our devotion we regard God as far removed from this world. We have difficulty conceiving of ourselves as partners with God. As we seek to care for the environment we easily believe that we are acting to procure divine favor but cannot imagine God acting.

Discussions between theologians, economists and environmentalists are interfaith dialogues. They are pluralistic conversations using borrowed language and the overlapping ideas that constitute our sense of our selves. Although all three of these groups remain under the influence of the dominant consumer culture, they each offer very different reflections on what this condition actually means. Their use of different symbol systems and methods will invariably make the conclusions that they draw less accessible to one another. The systems of value that have been built into these symbols insulate and isolate them from those who approach them with a different set of interests. As John Dewey (1859–1952) writes, "The very operation of learning, sets a limit to itself, and makes subsequent learning more difficult."[22] Just as our new knowledge opens whole worlds of possibility, so it also closes us to those things which it takes for granted and directs our attention more strongly to the functioning of its dominant symbols at the expense of other ones. When we begin mistaking reality for what the world means to us we drastically reduce the possibility for deriving the sorts of novel solutions that are necessary in this context. Until we realize that the world is not simply equivalent to our particular experience of the world we severely constrain the very imagination that is our most important resource in preventing the degradation of our environment.[23] The "God transforming culture" motif and its powerful use of the idea of God, represents one means of enabling us to step back from those symbols which have become so powerful for us that we have come to regard them as natural.

---

[22] John Dewey, *Experience and Nature* (New York: Dover, 1958) 280.

[23] Daniel Kahneman writes about the psychological tendency to overvalue what we are experiencing or thinking right now. He provides examples of psychological experiments that illustrate this failure. Kahneman, *Thinking, Fast and Slow*.

CONCLUSION

How large is that thing in the mind which we call thought? Is love square or round? Is the surface of hatred rough or smooth? Is joy an inch or a foot in diameter? —Jonathan Edwards[1]

Habits constitute the self, character is the interpenetration of habits; even in the operation of intelligence. —Abraham Edel and Elizabeth Flower[2]

Upon the death of the mathematician, inventor, and theologian Blaise Pascal (1623–1662), observers found sewn into his clothing a written description of a powerful religious experience that he had had eight years earlier. What theological reminders are so important to us that we would carry them with us during our every waking hour? How would we concisely express the most basic desires that constitute the code of meaning that directs our action?

Elsewhere Pascal writes that humans are ludicrously endowed with a longing for happiness that motivates their every action. And yet he also says:

> What people want is not the easy peaceful life that allows us to think of our unhappy condition nor the dangers of war, nor the burdens of office, but the agitation that takes our mind off it and diverts us. That is why we prefer the hunt to the capture. That is why men are so fond of hustle and bustle; that is why prison is such a fearful

---

[1] Jonathan Edwards, *The Philosophy of Jonathan Edwards from his Private Notebooks*, ed. Harvey Gates Townsend (Eugene: University of Oregon, 1955) 27.

[2] This is written to introduce Dewey's observation that "[c]oncrete habits do all the perceiving, recognizing, imagining, recalling, judging, conceiving, and reasoning that is done." Abraham Edel and Elizabeth Flower, "Introduction," in *The Later Works of John Dewey, Volume 7, 1925–1953*, vii–xxxv (Carbondale IL: Southern Illinois University Press, 2008) xxii.

punishment; that is why the pleasures of solitude are so incomprehensible...those who philosophize about it, holding that people are quite unreasonable to spend all day chasing a hare that they would not have wanted to buy, have little knowledge of our nature. The hare itself would not keep us from thinking about death and the miseries distracting us, but hunting it does so. Telling a man to rest is the same as telling him to live happily. It means advising him to enjoy a completely happy state in which he can contemplate at leisure without cause for distress. It means not understanding human nature.[3]

I do not mean to suggest that the activities of trucking and bartering, our trading and selling, act as the steel and concrete barriers that keep us from plunging off life's highway into the abyss of existential despair. Neither am I insinuating that our economic behavior acts as the opiate of the masses, that it merely serves to intoxicate us, distract and pacify us, that the products and services we spend so much effort attaining represent mere toys that keep us from getting into trouble. Although we may not have as dark an understanding of the human condition as Pascal, certainly we must recognize that the question of meaning in our decision to devote ourselves to buying, selling, increasing employment and wages, acquiring goods, and expanding our economy often goes unasked. Our concern for this means of promoting human well-being so often becomes confused as a final goal, or as a good in itself. This tendency may be invisible to us because we have grown unused to questioning the connection between economic value and value.

In our culture, questions of meaning have always been intimately related to our understanding of God. Historically, this has not meant that God is an abstract representation of meaning, nor that only the Divine legitimates and sanctifies all meaningful activity. God and meaning were merely impossible to separate. Before the modern era, our primary motivations, those things to which we would ultimately devote ourselves, were explicitly related to God. Although we still use theological ideas and language in our discussions of human

---

[3] Pascal, *Pensees*, 68.

commitment, our contemporary sensitivity to charges of superstition and our concern that we may offend others who hold different religious beliefs mean that we seldom mention God.

The value of theological language today exceeds its usefulness as a moral and ethical guide to responsible economic and ecological practices. Its importance reaches beyond the power of its influence in directing our cares and attention toward the natural world. Understanding the extent to which theological ideas lie imbedded in our experience of the world and our selves similarly represents only one use of religious language and thinking to our modern problems. The primary value of such language rests in its ability to enable us to discern how we will devote our tremendous energies, talents, and interests. Through it we can better examine the relationship between ourselves, the communities around us, society, objects, and the world. Rather than merely conflating theology with economics, or evaluating the world only in terms of cost/benefit analysis, or on the basis of prices determined in the marketplace, theological thinking serves as an alternative means of conceptualizing ecological problems. It acts as a critical voice, an alternative language, or system of symbolization that enables a broader understanding of the issues involved. In employing theological ideas like idolatry, faith, sin, redemption, etc., we gain important insights into the right relation between humanity and the environment. The idea of God directs our attention to the way our social lives influence the natural world; it opens us to the concerns that extend beyond our lonely and isolated ego.

This book addressed the extent of the environmental damage that we have done around the world. It discussed the importance of beauty and preservation, the strategy and aims of environmentalists and theologians. It provided long explanations of our dependence on economic thought and its limitations. It included a detailed section listing a few of the shortcomings inherent in a worldview that regards objects only as property. The book raised several theological alternatives to the dominant economic approach. In all of these sections, I attempted to avoid making the sort of sentimental plea on behalf of Earth that does not recognize the original legitimacy of economic ideas that evolved to suit a particular context. Throughout all of these words, paragraphs, and pages, I sought to express my own motivations and interest in this project both indirectly and in those brief chapter introductions where the relevance of these thoughts to our lives is most obvious.

Our unconscious actions and those policies pursued most vigorously by our society evolved in a context that no longer characterizes our experience of the world. Our personal and social goals of producing and having more things, although appropriate to a smaller, agrarian population, can no longer be sustained on our limited, overpopulated planet. Before we can make any substantive changes in our society, we must begin to recognize that the institutions we have inherited and our various means of understanding the individual, society, and the world are not universal, not natural, but culturally conditioned, and not necessarily best adapted to our well-being. Although this may not seem like a very lofty goal, at this stage merely recognizing these simple truths represents an important advance in clarifying the issues at stake in these discussions. Even the most environmentally progressive politicians cannot question the value of economic growth, but incessantly argue that ecology is a "growth industry." Ecologists also often rely too heavily on reconfiguring property rights as a means of abating pollution rather than questioning the assumptions upon which this approach relies. Until we begin to see the pervasiveness of this growth ethic, of understanding the world exclusively in terms of price, the necessary and substantive changes will be impossible.

This is not to say that the work above betrays an unreasonable faith in ideas, or that this is an idealist project that presumes change occurs merely through the simple rearrangement of the synapses and connections in our brains as we learn new ideas. John Dewey, in his book *Human Nature and Conduct,* points out the modern belief in the power of rational resolve, our faith in intellectualized judgment as a sufficient instrument to change ourselves and the world. He notes that a forceful superstition holds sway over many "cultivated persons" who believe that if we are told what to do or pointed in the right direction, this is all that is necessary to achieve some goal or change. The myth is untrue because our intentions so often are thwarted by *habit*, or as Dewey writes, "habits intervene between wish and execution."[4] Our social and economic behaviors are not merely the result of impulse or materialistic drives; they are not a simple form of competitiveness or acquisitiveness, but rather a more complicated system of motives influenced and given shape by habit. For Dewey, habits constitute the self. Social customs "are not direct and necessary consequences of specific impulses (but) social institutions and expectations shape impulses into dominant habits."[5] Rationality works in concert with impulse and habit. This means that while ideas like manifest destiny, socialism, democracy, capitalism, and evolution do have an enormous amount of power in our lives, they cannot be brought into actual existence until they have in some manner been converted into a discrete set of habits guiding our actions and our thoughts. In this book, we have begun with ideas and must now seek to employ these through the forces of habit.

Despite the bleakness of our environmental situation, and the difficulty implicit in this challenge to alter our most basic habits, the adaptability of human beings to change does provide a basis for hope. Great thinkers through history have argued that happiness beyond the joys of possession is more fulfilling and sustaining. I hope that this perspective can be communicated in social scientific and theological dialogue and realized through our actions in the world.

---

[4] John Dewey, *Human Nature and Conduct: An Introduction to Social Psychology* (New York: Henry Holt, 1922) 30.
[5] Ibid., 122.

SELECTED WORKS CITED

Akerlof, George A., and Robert J. Shiller. *Animal Spirits: How Human Psychology Drives the Economy, and Why It Matters for Global Capitalism.* Princeton: Princeton University Press, 2009.

Anderson, Bernhard. "Creation in the Noahic Covenant." In *Cry of the Environment: Rebuilding the Christian Creation Tradition*, edited by Philip N. Joranson and Ken Butigan. Santa Fe NM: Bear, 1984.

Appleton, George. *The Oxford Book of Prayer.* New York: Oxford University Press, 1985.

Aristotle. *The Nicomachean Ethics.* Minneapolis MN: Filiquarian Publishing, 2007.

Asimov, Isaac. *I, Robot.* Garden City NY: Doubleday, 1950.

Augustine. *Writings of Saint Augustine.* New York: Cima Pub. Co., 1948.

Austin, Mary Hunter. *California: The Land of the Sun.* London: A. and C. Black, 1914.

Axelrod, Robert M. *The Evolution of Cooperation.* New York: Basic Books, 1984.

Becker, Carl. *The Heavenly City of the Eighteenth-Century Philosophers.* New Haven: Yale University Press, 1932.

Becker, Gary Stanley. *The Economic Approach to Human Behavior.* Chicago: University of Chicago Press, 1976.

———. *A Treatise on the Family.* Cambridge MA: Harvard University Press, 1981.

Bellah, Robert Neelly. *The Good Society.* New York: Vintage Books, 1992.

Bernstein, Richard J. *Beyond Objectivism and Relativism: Science, Hermeneutics, and Praxis.* Philadelphia: University of Pennsylvania Press, 1983.

Berry, Wendell. *The Unforeseen Wilderness: An Essay on Kentucky's Red River Gorge.* Lexington: University Press of Kentucky, 1971.

The Book of Common Prayer. New York: Church Hymnal Corp., 1979.

Brown, Lester R. *Plan B 4.0: Mobilizing to Save Civilization.* New York: W.W. Norton, 2009.

———."A New Era Unfolds. " In *State of the World 1993: A Worldwatch Institute Report on Progress toward a Sustainable Society*, edited by Lester R. Brown, v. New York: Norton, 1993.

Brunner, Emil. *The Divine Imperative.* Translated by Olive Wyon. Philadelphia: The Westminster Press, 1947.

Buber, Martin. *I and Thou*. Translated by Walter Arnold Kaufmann. New York: Scribner, 1970.

Carson, Rachel. *Silent Spring*. New York: Fawcett Crest, 1962.

Carter, Christine. *Raising Happiness: 10 Simple Steps for More Joyful Kids and Happier Parents*. New York: Ballantine Books, 2010.

Cole, K. C. *Something Incredibly Wonderful Happens: Frank Oppenheimer and the World He Made Up*. Boston: Houghton Mifflin Harcourt, 2009.

Coleridge, Samuel Taylor. "The Statesman's Manual." In *Lay Sermons*, edited by Derwent Coleridge, 3–58. London: Edward Moxon, 1852.

Collingwood, R. G. *The Idea of Nature*. Oxford: Clarendon Press, 1945.

Cooper, James Fenimore. *The Deerslayer*. London: Richard Bentley, 1841.

Cotton, John. "John Cotton's Reply to Roger Williams." In *The Complete Writings of Roger Williams*. New York: Russell and Russell, 1963.

Crosby, Alfred W. *Ecological Imperialism: The Biological Expansion of Europe, 900-1900*. New York: Cambridge University Press, 1986.

Daly, Herman E., John B. Cobb, and Clifford W. Cobb. *For the Common Good: Redirecting the Economy toward Community, the Environment, and a Sustainable Future*. Boston: Beacon Press, 1989.

Descartes, Rene. *The Philosophical Writings of Descartes*. Translated by John Cottingham, Robert Stoothoff, and Dugald Murdoch. Volume 2. New York: Cambridge University Press, 1984.

Devall, Bill, and George Sessions. *Deep Ecology: Living as If Nature Mattered*. Salt Lake City: Gibbs Smith, 1985.

Dewey, John. *Experience and Nature*. New York: Dover, 1958.

———. *Human Nature and Conduct: An Introduction to Social Psychology*. New York: Henry Holt, 1922.

Dillard, Annie. *Pilgrim at Tinker Creek*. New York: Bantam Books, 1974.

Dukeminier, Jesse, and James E. Krier. *Property*. 2nd edition. Boston: Little, Brown, 1988.

Durning, Alan. "Asking How Much Is Enough." In *State of the World: A Worldwatch Institute Report on Progress toward a Sustainable Society*, edited by Worldwatch Institute. New York: Norton, 1991.

———. *How Much Is Enough: The Consumer Society and the Future of the Earth*. London: Earthscan, 1992.

Dwight, Sereno Edwards. *The Life of President Edwards*. New York: G. & C. & H. Carvill, 1830.

Edel, Abraham, and Elizabeth Flower. "Introduction." In *The Later Works of John Dewey, Volume 7, 1925–1953*, vii–xxxv. Carbondale IL: Southern Illinois University Press, 2008.

Edgeworth, Francis Ysidro. *Mathematical Psychics: An Essay on the Application of Mathematics to the Moral Sciences*. London: C. K. Paul, 1881.

Edwards, Jonathan. *The Nature of True Virtue*. Ann Arbor: University of Michigan Press, 1960.

———. *The Philosophy of Jonathan Edwards from His Private Notebooks*. Edited by Harvey Gates Townsend. Eugene: University of Oregon, 1955.

———. *The Works of President Edwards*. Edited by Samuel Austin. Worcester MA: Isaiah Thomas, 1808.

Eisler, Riane Tennenhaus. *The Chalice and the Blade: Our History, Our Future*. Cambridge MA: Harper & Row, 1987.

Ekins, Paul, and Manfred A. Max-Neef. *Real Life Economics: Understanding Wealth Creation*. New York: Routledge, 1992.

Eliot, T.S. *The Complete Poems and Plays: 1909–1950*. New York: Harcourt, Brace, and World, 1952.

Emerson, Ralph Waldo. *The Collected Works of Ralph Waldo Emerson: Nature, Addresses, and Lectures*. Edited by R.E. Spiller, A.R. Ferguson, J. Slater, and J.F. Carr. Volume 1. Cambridge MA: Belknap Press, 1971.

———. *Selections from Ralph Waldo Emerson: An Organic Anthology*. Edited by Stephen Emerson Whicher. Boston: Houghton Mifflin, 1957.

Etzioni, Amitai. *The Moral Dimension: Toward a New Economics*. New York: Free Press, 1988.

Faulkner, William. *Requiem for a Nun*. New York: Vintage Books, 1975.

Feuerbach, Ludwig. *The Essence of Christianity*. Translated by George Eliot. New York: Harper, 1957.

Fingarette, Herbert. *Confucius: The Secular as Sacred*. New York: Harper & Row, 1972.

Fox, Warwick. *Toward a Transpersonal Ecology: Developing New Foundations for Environmentalism*. Boston: Shambhala, 1990.

Geertz, Clifford. *The Interpretation of Cultures: Selected Essays*. New York: Basic Books, 1973.

Glare, P. G. W. *Oxford Latin Dictionary*. Oxford: Clarendon Press, 1968.

Gleick, James. *Chaos: Making a New Science*. New York: Penguin, 1988.

Gould, Stephen J. *The Mismeasure of Man*. New York: Norton, 1996.

Green, Robert W. *Protestantism, Capitalism, and Social Science: The Weber Thesis Controversy*. 2nd edition. Lexington MA: Heath, 1973.

Gustafson, James M. *Ethics from a Theocentric Perspective*. Chicago: University of Chicago Press, 1981.

Hall, Douglas John. *The Steward: A Biblical Symbol Come of Age*. Grand Rapids MI: W.B. Eerdmans, 1990.

Hardin, Garrett. "The Tragedy of the Commons." *Science* 162 (1968): 1243–48.

Heifetz, Ronald A. *Leadership without Easy Answers.* Cambridge MA: Belknap Press of Harvard University Press, 1994.

Heilbroner, Robert. "Rhetoric and Ideology." In *The Consequences of Economic Rhetoric*, edited by Arjo Klamer, Deirdre N. McCloskey, and Robert M. Solow. New York: Cambridge University Press, 1988.

Hessel, Dieter T., and Rosemary Radford Ruether. *Christianity and Ecology: Seeking the Well-Being of Earth and Humans.* Cambridge MA: Harvard University Press, 2000.

Hiebert, Theodore. "The Human Vocation: Origins and Transformations in Christian Traditions." In *Christianity and Ecology: Seeking the Well-Being of Earth and Humans*, edited by Dieter T. Hessel and Rosemary Radford Ruether, 135–154. Cambridge MA: Harvard University Center for the Study of World Religions, 2000.

Hirsch, P., S. Michaels, and R. Friedman. "Clean Models vs. Dirty Hands." In *Structures of Capital: The Social Organization of the Economy*, edited by Sharon Zukin and Paul DiMaggio, 39–56. New York: Cambridge University Press, 1990.

Hobbes, Thomas. *Leviathan.* Charleston SC: Forgotten Books, 1976.

Hyde, Lewis. *Common as Air: Revolution, Art, and Ownership.* New York: Farrar, Straus, and Giroux, 2010.

———. *The Gift: Imagination and the Erotic Life of Property.* New York: Random House, 1983.

James, William. *Pragmatism.* Cambridge MA: Harvard University Press, 1975.

Kahneman, Daniel. *Thinking, Fast and Slow.* New York: Farrar, Straus, and Giroux, 2011.

Karlen, Arno. *Biography of a Germ.* New York: Pantheon Books, 2000.

Kasulis, Thomas P. *Zen Action/Zen Person.* Honolulu: University Press of Hawaii, 1981.

Kaufman, Gordon D. "How Is God to Be Understood in a Theocentric Ethics?" In *James M. Gustafson's Theocentric Ethics: Interpretations and Assessments*, edited by Harlan Beckley and Charles Mason Swezey, 13–35. Macon GA: Mercer University Press, 1988.

Keltner, Dacher. *Born to Be Good: The Science of a Meaningful Life.* New York: W.W. Norton & Co., 2009.

Keynes, John Maynard. *The General Theory of Employment, Interest, and Money.* London: Macmillan, 1936.

Kuhn, Thomas S. *The Structure of Scientific Revolutions.* Chicago: University of Chicago Press, 1996.

Lapham, L.H. *Money and Class in America: Notes and Observations on the Civil Religion*. New York: Ballantine Books, 1989.

Lebow, Victor. "Price Competition in 1955." *Journal of Retailing* (Spring 1955): 1–6.

Leiss, William, Sut Jhally, and Stephen Kline. *Social Communication in Advertising: Persons, Products, and Images of Well-Being*. New York: Methuen, 1986.

Leopold, Aldo. "The State of the Profession [1940]." In *The River of the Mother of God: and Other Essays by Aldo Leopold*, edited by S.L. Flader and J.B. Callicott. Madison WI: University of Wisconsin Press, 1992.

Levitt, Steven D., and Stephen J. Dubner. *Freakonomics: A Rogue Economist Explores the Hidden Side of Everything*. Revised and expanded edition. New York: William Morrow, 2006.

Lévy-Garboua, Louis. *Sociological Economics*. London: Sage Publications, 1979.

Liddell, Henry George, and Robert Scott. *A Lexicon Abridged from Liddell and Scott's Greek-English Lexicon*. New York: Oxford University Press, 2002.

Locke, John. *An Essay Concerning Human Understanding*. Edited by Alexander Campbell Fraser. Volume 2. Oxford: Clarendon Press, 1894.

———. *Two Treatises of Government*. Edited by Peter Laslett. 2nd edition. London: Cambridge University Press, 1967.

Lonergan, Bernard J. F. *Method in Theology*. New York: Herder and Herder, 1972.

Lovejoy, Arthur O. *Essays in the History of Ideas*. New York: Putnam, 1960.

Lovelock, James. *The Ages of Gaia: A Biography of Our Living Earth*. New York: Norton, 1988.

———. *Gaia: A New Look at Life on Earth*. New York: Oxford University Press, 1987.

Macpherson, C. B. *Property: Mainstream and Critical Positions*. Toronto: University of Toronto Press, 1978.

Mankiw, N. Gregory. *Principles of Microeconomics*. 5th edition. Mason OH: South-Western Cengage Learning, 2009.

Marcel, Gabriel. *Being and Having*. Translated by Katharine Farrer. London: Dacre Press, 1949.

Margulis, Lynn, and Dorion Sagan. *Microcosmos: Four Billion Years of Evolution from Our Microbial Ancestors*. New York: Summit Books, 1986.

Mauss, Marcel. *The Gift: Forms and Functions of Exchange in Archaic Societies*. Translated by Ian Cunnison. New York: Norton, 1967.

Meeks, M. Douglas. *God the Economist: The Doctrine of God and Political Economy*. Minneapolis: Fortress Press, 1989.

Merton, Thomas. "Rain and the Rhinoceros." In *The Norton Book of Nature Writing*, edited by Robert Finch and John Elder, 921. New York: W.W. Norton, 1990.

Metzger, Bruce Manning. *Lexical Aids for Students of New Testament Greek.* New edition. Princeton NJ: Theological Book Agency, 1969.

Mirowski, Philip. "Shall I Compare Thee to a Minkowski-Ricardo-Leontief-Metlzer- Matrix of the Mosak-Hicks Type?" In *The Consequences of Economic Rhetoric*, edited by Arjo Klamer, Deirdre N. McCloskey, and Robert M. Solow, 117–145. New York: Cambridge University Press, 1988.

Miyamoto, M. *The Book of Five Rings.* Translated by Thomas Cleary. New York: Bantam Books, 1992.

Murray, Robert. *The Cosmic Covenant: Biblical Themes of Justice, Peace, and the Integrity of Creation.* London: Sheed & Ward, 1992.

Nash, Roderick. *The Rights of Nature: A History of Environmental Ethics.* Madison WI: University of Wisconsin Press, 1989.

———. *Wilderness and the American Mind.* New Haven: Yale University Press, 1967.

Nicholson, Walter. *Microeconomic Theory: Basic Principles and Extensions.* 3rd edition. Chicago: Dryden Press, 1985.

Niebuhr, H. Richard. *Christ and Culture.* New York: Harper, 1956.

———. *Radical Monotheism and Western Culture: With Supplementary Essays.* Louisville KY: Westminster/John Knox Press, 1993.

———. *The Responsible Self: An Essay in Christian Moral Philosophy.* New York: Harper & Row, 1963.

Page, Ruth. *God and the Web of Creation.* London: SCM Press, 1996.

Paley, William. *Natural Theology; or Evidences of the Existence and Attributes of the Deity, Collected from the Appearances of Nature.* London: F. C. and J. Rivington, 1822.

Pascal, Blaise. *Pensees.* London: Penguin Books, 1995.

Peirce, Charles Sanders. *Philosophical Writings of Peirce.* Edited by Justus Buchler. New York: Dover Publications, 1955.

———. "Some Consequences of Four Incapacities." In *Peirce on Signs: Writings on Semiotic by Charles Sanders Peirce*, edited by James Hoopes, 54–84. Chapel Hill: University of North Carolina Press, 1991.

Percy, Walker. *Signposts in a Strange Land.* New York: Farrar, Straus, and Giroux, 1991.

Pinker, Steven. *The Language Instinct.* New York: W. Morrow and Co., 1994.

Postel, Sandra. "Facing Water Scarcity." In *State of the World 1993: A Worldwatch Institute Report on Progress toward a Sustainable Society*, edited by Lester R. Brown. New York: Norton, 1993.

Putnam, Hilary. *Meaning and the Moral Sciences.* Boston: Routledge & K. Paul, 1978.

Rahner, Karl. *Foundations of Christian Faith: An Introduction to the Idea of Christianity.* New York: Crossroad, 1982.

Rasmussen, Larry L. *Earth Community Earth Ethics.* Maryknoll NY: Orbis Books, 1996.

Reisner, Marc. *Cadillac Desert: The American West and Its Disappearing Water.* New York: Viking, 1986.

Ricoeur, Paul. *Freud and Philosophy: An Essay on Interpretation.* New Haven: Yale University Press, 1970.

Rieff, Philip. *Freud: The Mind of the Moralist.* New York: Viking Press, 1959.

Robbins, Lionel Robbins Baron. *An Essay on the Nature and Significance of Economic Science.* 3rd edition. London: Macmillan, 1984.

Rozanov, Boris G., Viktor Targulian, and D.S. Orlov. "Soils." In *The Earth as Transformed by Human Action: Global and Regional Changes in the Biosphere over the Past 300 Years,* edited by B. L. Turner. Cambridge: Cambridge University Press, 1990.

Ruether, Rosemary Radford. *Gaia and God: An Ecofeminist Theology of Earth Healing.* San Francisco: HarperSanFrancisco, 1992.

Ruff, Larry E. "The Economic Common Sense of Pollution." In *Economics of the Environment: Selected Readings,* Third Edition edited by Nancy S. Dorfman and Robert Dorfman. New York: Norton, 1972.

Samuelson, Paul A., and William D. Nordhaus. *Economics.* 12th edition. New York: McGraw-Hill, 1985.

Sandel, Michael J. *What Money Can't Buy: The Moral Limits of Markets.* New York: Farrar, Straus, and Giroux, 2012.

Santmire, H. Paul. *The Travail of Nature: The Ambiguous Ecological Promise of Christian Theology.* Philadelphia: Fortress Press, 1985.

Scarry, Elaine. *The Body in Pain: The Making and Unmaking of the World.* New York: Oxford University Press, 1985.

Schleiermacher, Friedrich. *On Religion: Speeches to Its Cultured Despisers.* Translated by John Oman. New York: Harper, 1958.

Schor, Juliet. *The Overworked American: The Unexpected Decline of Leisure.* New York: Basic Books, 1991.

Sen, Amartya. "Adam Smith's Prudence." In *Theory and Reality in Development: Essays in Honour of Paul Streeten,* edited by Sanjaya Lall and Frances Stewart. Basingstoke, Hampshire: Macmillan, 1986.

———. *On Ethics and Economics.* Oxford: B. Blackwell, 1987.

————. "Rational Fools: A Critique of the Behavioral Foundations of Economic Theory." In *Beyond Self-Interest*, edited by Jane J. Mansbridge, 25–43. Chicago: University of Chicago Press, 1990.

Smith, Adam. *An Inquiry into the Nature and Causes of the Wealth of Nations*. Volume 2. Indianapolis: Liberty Classics, 1981.

————. *The Theory of Moral Sentiments: Or, an Essay Towards an Analysis of the Principles by Which Men Naturally Judge Concerning the Conduct and Character, First of Their Neighbors, and Afterwards of Themselves*. London: Strahan, 1774.

Stegner, Wallace E. *The Sound of Mountain Water*. New York: Ballantine Books, 1972.

Swedborg, R., U. Himmelstrand, and G. Brulin. "The Paradigm of Economic Sociology." In *Structures of Capital: The Social Organization of the Economy*, edited by Sharon Zukin and Paul DiMaggio, 57–86. New York: Cambridge University Press, 1990.

Tanner, Kathryn. *Theories of Culture: A New Agenda for Theology*. Minneapolis: Fortress Press, 1997.

Taylor, Bron Raymond. *Dark Green Religion: Nature Spirituality and the Planetary Future*. Berkeley: University of California Press, 2010.

Taylor, Charles. *Philosophy and the Human Sciences*. Volume 2, Philosophical Papers. Cambridge: Cambridge University Press, 1985.

————. *Sources of the Self: The Making of the Modern Identity*. Cambridge MA: Harvard University Press, 1989.

Thomas, Owen C. *Introduction to Theology*. Revised edition. Wilton CT: Morehouse-Barlow, 1983.

Thompson, William Irwin. *Gaia, a Way of Knowing: Political Implications of the New Biology*. Great Barrington MA: Lindisfarne Press, 1987.

Thoreau, Henry David. *The Illustrated Walden*. Edited by J. Lyndon Shanley. Princeton NJ: Princeton University Press, 1973.

————. *The Natural History Essays*. Salt Lake City: Peregrine Smith Books, 1989.

Tillich, Paul. *Systematic Theology*. Volume 1. Chicago: University of Chicago Press, 1973.

Troeltsch, Ernst. *The Social Teaching of the Christian Churches*. Translated by Olive Wyon. Volume 1. New York: Macmillan, 1931.

Weber, Max. *The Protestant Ethic and the Spirit of Capitalism*. Translated by Talcott Parsons. London: Allen & Unwin, 1930.

White, Lynn, Jr. "The Historical Roots of Our Ecologic Crisis." *Science* 155 no. 3767 (1967): 1203–1207.

Whitehead, Alfred North. *Religion in the Making: Lowell Lectures, 1926.* New York: Fordham University Press, 1926.

———. *Symbolism: Its Meaning and Effect.* New York: Macmillan, 1927.

INDEX

population: African countries, 21–22;
availability of land or, 16–17; effects of
increases in world, 14–15; rapid
growth in Western industrial countries,
23*n*20; world, 22
positive economic theories, 85, 110, 123,
124*n*21, 127
positive externalities, 95*n*5
positive judgments, 182
possessions. *See* ownership;
property/possessions
Postel, Sandra, 17*n*13
"Potent New Greenhouse Gas is Found,
But It's Quite Rare" (Revkin), 52*n*29
Pragmatism (James), 113*n*7
predictions: ability of economics to
manage/predict/explain, 68–69;
economic, 109; future doom, 47;
historical predictions of current
economy, 189; problems of making,
111–112; quantitative methods of, 110
preservation of nature, 36–37, 54
prevention, of waste and pollution, 91–92
"Price Competition in 1955" (Lebow),
148*n*22
price discrimination, 166*n*18
price negotiations, 99*n*9
price/pricing. *See also* value: as equivalent to
valued, 69;
interchangeable/commensurable factors
in, 104–105; law of supply and
demand, 76–77, 104; as regulating
factor, 66
Principles of Microeconomics (Mankiw),
72*n*9
prisoner's dilemma game, 149*n*23
private property, 96, 165
private systems, 199*n*24
privatization, 159*n*4, 163
privilege, 161*n*9
problem solving, market-based methods for,
124
procedures, historical significance of, 147
production process, categories of, 83
productive cooperation models, 101
profit motive, 83–84
Property (Dukeminier and Krier), 165*n*16
Property (Macpherson), 165*n*17

property/possessions. *See also* ownership:
alternatives to ownership, 167–170;
assumptions about, 171–172;
common, 165; concept of, 159;
connection to, 216; constructing
arrangements for, 174; historical
configuration/ownership of, 167*n*19;
lawyers' and economists' concepts of,
164; loss of, 171*n*24; ownership ideals,
158; private property, 96, 165;
problems of defining, 165–166; as a
symbol, 160–161; in terms of natural
rights, 174; understanding of nature of,
167–168
property rights, 164–165
*The Protestant Ethic and the Spirit of
Capitalism,* 172*n*25
Protestantism, 172
Psalms 24:1, 45
psychology, 112*n*6
public goods, conversion to private property
of, 96
punishment, divine, 47
Putnam, Hilary, 179*n*6

Radical Monotheism and Western Culture,
193*n*21
Rahner, Karl, 197, 197*n*22
"Rain and the Rhinoceros" (Merton), 89*n*1
rainforest clearing, 19
rainforests, destruction of, 15
Raising Happiness (Carter), 24*n*27
Rasmussen, Larry L, 51, 51*n*27
"Rational Fools" (Sen), 100*n*10
rationality, 102, 126–127
reality: compared to theory, 117; divine, 26;
mistaking world meaning for, 236;
versus societal convention, 123
Real Life Economics (Ekins and Max-Neef),
146*n*19
real-world objects, 147
reasonable person standard, 81
recessions, 175
reforestation, northeastern United States,
51
Reformation, 171–172
regulations, limits on individual use of
resources, 92–93

reification of symbols, 135*n*7
Reisner, Marc, 10*n*2
relationships: allegorical signs and
metaphorical symbols, 140; culture and
God, 227; human beings and physical
environment, 199; of property
ownership, 166
relativity, 186*n*17
Religion in the Making (Whitehead), 211*n*2
religion(s). *See also* Christianity; faith:
American Academy of Religion, 183;
Center for the Study of World
Religions, 39*n*6; *Dark Green Religion*
(Taylor), 40*n*8; discussions about, 183;
meaning of faith in, 210; *On Religion*
(Schleiermacher), 198*n*23; *Religion in
the Making* (Whitehead), 211*n*2;
scriptural religions and societies
founded on legal principles, 47–48;
Western religions, 41
religious formation, 186–187
religious groups, historical, 222–223
religious interpretations, 5
religiousness: caring for natural world as,
211; using religion versus being
religious, 211
religious ritual, 65
religious symbols, invisible hand, 1–2, 74,
76, 154
religious understanding, 187
religious wars, 184
Requiem for a Nun (Faulkner), 160*n*6
resources: allocation of, 232; Americans'
knowledge of origin of, 64–65;
ecosystems as, 54; limited natural, 16;
non-renewable, 16; substituting,
154*n*26
responsibility: debates over, 42; for
environmental problems, 62–63
The Responsible Self (Neibuhr), 136*n*8,
139*n*12
The Responsible Self (Niebuhr), 138–139
revealed preferences, 99–100
Revkin, Andrew L., 52*n*29
"Rhetoric and Ideology" (Heilbroner),
122*n*20
rich and poor populations, 21–25
Richardson, Annie, 24*n*24

Ricoeur, Paul, 103*n*13
Ridley, Matt, 232*n*20
Rieff, Philip, 98*n*7
rights: of humans to reduce diversity of life
on Earth, 55; inalienable, 46, 173; of
natural phenomena, 58–59; property,
161–162, 164–165
The Rights of Nature (Nash), 48*n*20
rituals, religious, 65
Robb, Carol, 63*n*44
Robbins, Baron, 72*n*6
Robbins, Lionel, 72, 72*n*6
Roman law, 168–169, 168*n*21
romantic/expressivist ideal, 29
Romantic Movement, 221
Rorty, Richard, 115*n*11
Rousseau, Jean-Jacques, 46, 235
Rozanov, Boris G., 17*n*13
Ruether, Rosemary Radford, 39*n*6, 40*n*8,
42–45, 42*n*12, 52, 52*n*30
Ruff, Larry E., 187, 187*n*18, 190, 232*n*21
rules: enactment of, 233; of statistics,
121*n*17; understanding foundations of,
135
rules *(nomia)*, 241
Rwanda, 21–22

sacrality, universal, 44
sacrament, 3, 3*n*2
sacred earth worldview, 42–45
Sagan, Dorion, 43*n*13
salvation, 46, 172
Samuelson, Paul A., 68, 68*n*3, 94*n*3
Sandel, Michael, 111*n*5, 124, 124*n*22, 183,
183*n*12
Santmire, H. Paul, 53, 53*n*31, 61, 61*n*40
scarcity, 73
Scarry, Elaine, 214*n*5
Schleiermacher, Friedrich, 178, 178*n*5,
197–198, 198*n*23
Schor, Juliet, 175*n*29, 218*n*8
science. *See also* social sciences: as branch of
theology, 188; history of
environmental, 27; separating theology
and, 181–182; as substitute for morals,
233; theology and, 179–182
science fiction, 107–108
scientific theories, 124*n*21

wastefulness, individual, 61*n*38
watchmaker God theology, 47–48
water resources: in African countries, 21–
    22; contamination of, 22; movement
    of water, 10*n*3; water.org, 22*n*19
"Water Scarcity and Desertification"
    (Thematic Fact Sheet Series No. 2),
    17*n*12
The Wealth of Nations (Smith), 74
Weber, Max, 172, 172*n*25
well-being: measures of a country's, 63;
    mistaking affluence for, 174; and self-
    interested behavior, 100;
    understanding of economic, 175
West as the Wild, 217*n*7
Western civilization, 157
Western religions, 41
What Money Can't Buy (Sandel), 111*n*5,
    124*n*22, 183*n*12
White, Lynn, Jr., 40–41, 40*n*9, 42, 61, 228
Whitehead, Alfred North, 139, 139*n*13,
    153, 153*n*25, 170, 170*n*23, 211,
    211*n*2
Wilde, Oscar, 90
wilderness: hostility of Judaism and
    Christianity toward, 40*n*8; symbolism
    of, 2
Wilderness and the American Mind (Nash),
    40*n*8
Wildness, 217*n*7
The Works of President Edwards (Edwards),
    132*n*2
world: all-sacred, 45; attempts at
    understanding, 138; differences in
    understanding of, 36; economics as
    means of understanding, 134;
    interpretation of/by economics, 128;
    material versus social, 134; nature of,
    125*n*24; orientation in the, 192;
    separation between God and, 212
World Bank, 105
"World Military Spending" (Shah), 23*n*21
World Resources Institute, 14, 23*n*21
"World's Leading Scientists Issue Urgent
    Warning to Humanity" (Union of
    Concerned Scientists), 13*n*7
worldview: sacred earth, 42–45; types of, 29
worth, current notion of, 104

WYSIATI (what you see is all there is), 135

Zedler's Encyclopedia, 146
Zen Action/Zen Person (Kasulis), 142,
    142*n*16
Zen monk parable, 215–216